An SQL Guide
for
dBASE IV

An SQL Guide for dBASE IV

RICK F. van der LANS

Translated by Andrea Gray

ADDISON-WESLEY
PUBLISHING
COMPANY

Wokingham, England • Reading, Massachusetts • Menlo Park, California • New York
Don Mills, Ontario • Amsterdam • Bonn • Sydney • Singapore • Tokyo
Madrid • San Juan • Milan • Paris • Mexico City • Seoul • Taipei

Translated from the Dutch edition *dBASE IV het SQL Leerboek* published by Academic Service BV.

Cover designed by Hybert Design and Type, Maidenhead and printed by
The Riverside Printing Co. (Reading) Ltd.
Printed in Great Britain by T.J. Press (Padstow) Ltd, Cornwall.

First printed 1991.

British Library Cataloguing in Publication Data

Lans, Rick F. van der
 An SQL guide for dBASE IV.
 1. Databases. Management. Software
 I. Title II.dBASE IV het SQL leerboek. English
 005.7565

  ISBN 0-201-54410-5

Library of Congress Cataloging in Publication Data

Lans, Rick F. van der.
 [dBASE IV, het SQL leerboek. English]
 An SQL guide for dBASE IV / Rick F. van der Lans ;
 translated by Andrea Gray.
 p. cm.
 Translation of: dBASE IV, het SQL leerboek.
 Includes bibliographical references and index.
 ISBN 0-201-54410-5
 1. Data base management. 2. dBase IV (Computer program) 3. SQL
 (Computer program language) I. Title.
 QA76.9.D3L36613 1991
 005.75'65–dc20   90-28267
                                                          CIP

Preface

dBASE IV is a database management system from Ashton-Tate. It is the successor to dBASE III which was in its time one of the most popular and widely sold database management systems for microcomputers.

dBASE IV recognizes two database languages: the well known language implemented in dBASE III with such commands as APPEND and DISPLAY, and SQL. SQL (Structured Query Language) is an internationally standardized database language many manufacturers have implemented as a product. SQL consists of a set of statements for the manipulation, management and security of database data.

SQL is not an isolated part of dBASE IV; rather, it is fully integrated with the other functions. In fact, you need not use the other database statements any more; SQL is quite sufficient. As far as function goes, the two database languages are equivalent and can be used side by side.

If the languages are equivalent, why should we learn and use SQL? There are a number of reasons:

- Some SQL statements have the equivalent effect of many conventional dBASE IV statements. You can, therefore, develop applications more quickly and maintain them more easily.

- SQL lends itself more to joining data from different tables. This has the advantage that you are no longer required to duplicate data in different tables – a technique with many drawbacks.

- With SQL, programmers do not need to take the physical storage of the data into consideration. SQL statements require you only to specify *which* data you want to see or use. How, or in which order that data is physically accessed is completely handled by the database management system.

- SQL is an international standard. Many other database management systems support this database language. By using SQL you can develop dBASE IV applications that access data from other SQL systems.

Topics

In this book we are concerned with SQL as implemented in *dBASE IV*. The following aspects of SQL are covered:

- creation of databases and tables
- querying data (joins, functions and subqueries)
- updating and deleting data
- optimization of statements
- view definition
- data security
- the catalog
- application development with embedded SQL
- importing and exporting of data.

For whom is this book intended?

We recommend this book to those who want to use SQL effectively and efficiently in dBASE IV applications. This book, then, is suitable for the following groups of people:

- Microcomputer owners who have purchased dBASE IV and use it at home.
- Students who need to study SQL and use dBASE IV as the medium for this.
- Programmers who write dBASE IV programs.
- Designers, analysts and consultants who use dBASE IV directly or indirectly and want to understand its possibilities and limitations.
- Home students who are interested in dBASE IV.

A practical book

This book should be seen primarily as a *textbook* in the active sense, and not so much as a reference work. To this end there are many examples and exercises (with answers). Don't ignore the exercises. Experience shows that you will learn the language better and more quickly by practising often and doing many exercises.

From Version 1.0 to Version 1.1

This book describes dBASE IV Version 1.1. This version enhances the first version (Version 1.0) of dBASE IV in the following two areas:

- SQL in Version 1.0 contained a number of errors, known as the Franklin errors, named after the person who discovered them. All known errors have now been rectified.

- In Version 1.1, there are fewer restrictions when including SQL statements and dBASE IV commands in the same program. This results in a great improvement in the integration of SQL into the dBASE IV environment.

Prerequisite knowledge

Some knowledge of dBASE III (Plus) or dBASE IV is necessary, as is a basic understanding of OS/2, MS/DOS or PC/DOS. It is assumed that you have already installed dBASE IV.

And finally ...

I should like to use this preface to thank a number of people for their contributions to this book. I am grateful to Ashton-Tate BV for making dBASE IV and all the necessary documentation available. In particular, I appreciate the comments and advice offered by Mark de Visser from Ashton-Tate BV. I am most grateful also to Corine Cools for reading through the manuscript and to Diane Cools for her typing and correction work.

I want to thank Andrea Gray for the way in which she has translated my book. She has succeeded in preserving my writing style in the English version. I am grateful also to Addison-Wesley, and especially Sarah Mallen, for their smooth management of the translation project.

Finally, I would like to ask readers to send comments, opinions, ideas and suggestions concerning the contents of the book to the publisher: Addison-Wesley Publishers Limited, Finchampstead Road, Wokingham, Berkshire RG11 2NZ, England, marked for the attention of Rick F. van der Lans, An SQL Guide for dBASE IV.

Many thanks in anticipation of your cooperation.

Rick F. van der Lans
Sassenheim, January 1991

Contents

1
Introduction

SQL (Structured Query Language) is a database language used for formulating statements that are processed by a database management system (DBMS). In our case the DBMS is dBASE IV.

The paragraph above contains three important concepts: *database, database management system* and *database language*. In Section 1.1 we explain each of these terms.

SQL is based on the theories of the relational model. In order to use SQL some knowledge of this model is invaluable. Therefore in Section 1.2 we describe the relational model. In Section 1.3 SQL is described in brief; what can be done with the language and how it differs from other languages (such as COBOL or Pascal). Section 1.4 outlines the history of SQL. Although SQL is thought of as a very modern language, it has, in fact, a history dating back to 1972.

Because this book deals with dBASE IV's implementation of SQL we describe the history and relevant aspects of dBASE IV in Section 1.5. dBASE IV recognizes two database languages: the language already found in dBASE III and SQL. In Section 1.6 we describe the similarities and differences between these two languages.

The first chapter closes with a description of the structure of the book. Each chapter is summarized in a few sentences.

1.1 Database, database management system and database language

What is a database? C.J. Date defines the concept *database* as follows (Date, 1986):

> *A database is a collection of stored operational data used by the application systems of some particular enterprise.*

Card deck files are not, then, considered to be databases. On the other hand, the large files of a bank and the state transport department *are* considered to be databases. These databases contain data about addresses and account balances or car registration plates, weights of vehicles and so on. Another example of a database would be a computer at your workplace which has information recorded about your salary.

Data in a database only becomes useful if something is done with it. According to the above definition of a database, this data is managed by special software. We generally call this software a *database management system (DBMS)*. A DBMS enables users to process database data. Without a DBMS it is impossible to look at that data, or to update or delete obsolete data in the database. It is the DBMS alone that knows where and how the data is stored. A definition of a DBMS given by R. Elmasri is as follows (Elmasri, 1989):

> *A DBMS is a collection of programs that enables users to create and maintain a database.*

A DBMS will never change or delete the data in a database of its own accord. Someone or something has to give the command for this to happen. This could be you, as a user, but it could also be a program. In the latter case the program is the user. In other words: a user must be in a position to give a DBMS such commands as 'delete all data about the vehicle with the registration plate number DR-12-DP'.

Commands are given to a DBMS with the help of special languages. These types of languages are called *database languages*. Commands, also known as statements, that are formulated according to the rules of the database language, are entered by users and processed by the DBMS. Every DBMS, from whichever manufacturer, possesses a database language. Some DBMSs even have more than one database language. Although differences exist between all of these languages, they can be divided into groups. The *relational database languages* form one of these groups.

It is also helpful to know how a DBMS stores data in a database. A DBMS uses neither a chest of drawers nor a filing cabinet for holding information; computers work instead with storage media such as tapes, floppy disks and hard disks. The manner in which a DBMS stores information on these media is technically very complex, and will not be explained in detail in this book. In fact, it is not necessary to know this since one of the most important tasks of a DBMS is to offer *data independence*. This means that users do not need to know how or where data is stored: to them a database is a large reservoir of information. Storage methods are also completely independent from the database language being used.

Another important task of a DBMS is to maintain the *integrity* of the database data. This means, first, that the database data always satisfies the rules that apply in the real world. Take, for example, the case of an employee who may only work for one department. It should never be possible, in a database managed by a DBMS, for that particular employee to be registered as working for two departments. Second, integrity means that two different pieces of database data do not contradict one another. This is also known as *data consistency*. (As an example, in one place in a database Mr Johnson may be recorded as being born on 4 August 1964, and in another place he may be given a birth date of 14 December 1946.) These two pieces of data are obviously inconsistent. DBMSs are designed to recognize statements that can be used to specify *integrity rules*. Once these rules are entered, the DBMS will take care of their implementation.

1.2　The relational model

In 1970, when E.F. Codd was still employed by IBM, he introduced the *relational model* in the almost legendary article 'A Relational Model of Data for Large Shared Data Banks' (Codd, 1970). This relational model formed a theoretical basis for database languages. The model consists of a small number of simple concepts for recording data in a database, together with a number of operators to manipulate the information. These concepts and operators are borrowed principally from *set theory* and *Boolean logic*. Later, in 1979, he presented his ideas for an improved version of the model (Codd, 1979).

The relational model has served as an example for the development of various database languages. These database languages are based on the concepts and ideas of that relational model. These languages, therefore, are also called relational database languages, and SQL is clearly an example of one. The rest of this section concentrates on the following relational model terms which will appear extensively in this book:

- table
- column
- row
- primary key
- candidate key
- referential key or foreign key.

Please note that this is not a complete list of all the terms used by the relational model. For more extensive descriptions refer to Date (1986).

1.2.1   Table, column and row

There is only one format in which data can be stored in a relational database: in
tables. The official name for table is actually *relation*. The term *relational model*
stems from this name. We have chosen to use table because that is the word used
in SQL. An example of a table, the PLAYERS table is given below. This table
contains data about five players, the members of a sports club.

```
The PLAYERS table:

PLAYERNO  NAME        INITIALS  TOWN
--------  ---------   --------  ---------
       6  Parmenter   R         Stratford
      44  Baker       E         Inglewood
      83  Hope        PK        Stratford
     100  Parmenter   P         Stratford
      27  Collins     DD        Eltham
```

PLAYERNO, NAME, INITIALS and TOWN are the names of the *columns* in
the table. The PLAYERNO column contains the values 6, 44, 83, 100 and 27.
This set of values is also known as the *population* of the PLAYERNO column.
The PLAYERS table has five *rows*, one for each player.

A table has two special properties:

• The intersection of a row and a column can consist of only one value, an
  atomic value. An atomic value is an indivisible unit. The database language
  can deal with such a unit only in its entirety.

• The rows in a table have no specific order. You don't think in terms of the
  first row, the last row or the following row. The contents of a table consist
  of a *set* of rows in the true sense of the word.

1.2.2   Primary key

The *primary key* of a table is a column (or a combination of a number of columns
from this table) that can used for uniquely identifying rows in the table. (This definition and most of the other definitions in this section are borrowed from Date
(1983).) In other words, two different rows in a table may never have the same
value in their primary key, and for every row in the table the primary key must
have a value. The PLAYERNO column in the PLAYERS table is the primary key
for this table. Two players, therefore, may never have the same number and there
may never be a player without a number.

1.2.3   Candidate key

Some tables contain more than one column (or combination of columns) that can
act as a primary key. Those columns, including the primary key, that possess all

the properties of a primary key are called *candidate keys*. Because a table must possess a primary key, it always has a minimum of one candidate key.

If we assume that in the PLAYERS table the NAME and INITIALS of each player is a unique combination, then these columns exist as a candidate key. This combination of two columns could also be designated as the primary key.

1.2.4   Foreign key

A *foreign key* is a column or (combination of columns) in a table in which the population is a subset of the population of a primary key of a table (this does not have to be another table). Foreign keys are sometimes also called referential keys.

Suppose that next to the PLAYERS table we place a TEAMS table. The TEAMNO column is called the primary key of this table. The PLAYERNO column represents the captain of the particular team. The population of this column represents a subset of the population of the PLAYERNO column in the PLAYERS table. PLAYERNO in TEAMS is called a foreign key.

```
The TEAMS table:

TEAMNO   PLAYERNO   DIVISION
------   --------   --------
     1          6   first
     2         27   second
```

You can see how we are now able to combine the two tables. We do it by including the PLAYERNO column in the TEAMS table, thus establishing a link with the PLAYERNO column from the PLAYERS table.

1.3   What is SQL?

SQL (Structured Query Language) is a *relational database language*. Among other things, the language consists of statements to insert, update, delete, query and protect data. We call SQL a relational database language because it is associated with data that has been defined according to the rules of the relational model.

There are a few things to note about SQL as a database language. Because it is a relational database language it is grouped with the non-procedural database languages. By *non-procedural* we mean that users (with the help of the various statements) have only to specify *which* data they want and not *how* this data must be found. Languages such as COBOL, Pascal or BASIC are examples of procedural languages.

SQL can be used in two ways. First, *interactively*: an SQL statement is entered on the microcomputer and processed for an immediate result. Interactive SQL is intended for application developers and end users who want to access databases themselves.

The second way is called *embedded SQL*. Here, the SQL statements are embedded in a dBASE IV program that could consist of SQL statements alongside dBASE IV statements. Results of these statements are not immediately visible to the user but are processed by the *enveloping* program. This indicates that SQL statements and dBASE IV statements can coexist. Embedded SQL appears mainly in programs developed for end users. These end users do not need to learn SQL in order to access the data, but work from simple screens and menus.

The statements and functional possibilities of interactive and embedded SQL are virtually the same. By this we mean that most statements that can be entered and processed interactively can also be included in a dBASE IV program as embedded SQL. To do this, embedded SQL uses a number of extra statements that enable the juxtaposition of SQL statements and non-SQL statements. In this book we are interested mainly in interactive SQL. Embedded SQL is dealt with separately in a later chapter.

1.4   The history of SQL

The history of SQL is tightly interwoven with the history of an IBM project called *System R*. The purpose of this project was to develop an experimental relational database management system , a system which bore the same name as the project. System R was built in the IBM research laboratory in San Jose, California. The project had to demonstrate that the positive usability features of the relational model could be implemented in a system that satisfied the demands of a modern database management system.

A language called *Sequel* was chosen as the database language for System R (Astrahan, 1980). The first article about this language was written by R.F. Boyce and D.D. Chamberlin (1973). During the project the language was renamed SQL (still often pronounced 'sequel').

The knowledge acquired and the technology developed from the System R project was used to build SQL/DS. SQL/DS was IBM's first commercially available relational database management system and came on to the market in 1981. In 1983 IBM announced DB2, a relational database management system for another operating system environment.

IBM has published a great deal about the development of System R. This was happening at a time in which relational database management systems were being widely talked about at conferences and seminars. It was no wonder that other companies also began to build relational systems. Some of them, Oracle for example, implemented SQL as their database language. In the last few years many implementations of SQL have appeared. Existing database management systems have also been extended to include SQL support.

Around 1983 the ANSI (American National Standards Institute) and the ISO (International Standards Organisation) began to develop an SQL standard. In 1986 the SQL was complete and it is described in the document *ISO 9075 Database Language SQL* (1987); see also Van der Lans (1989). In 1987 work began on the follow-on standard *SQL2* (1989). The SQL2 standard is an extension of the SQL standard. Many new statements have been included and new functions added to some existing statements.

1.5 Ashton-Tate and dBASE IV

In 1981 Ashton-Tate Corporation was founded in the United States. Its first product was a database management system called *dBASE II*. It ran on 8-bit microcomputers, such as the Osborne, and under the then popular operating system CP/M. dBASE II quickly became the most popular and widely sold database management system for microcomputers. In 1983 a version of dBASE II which ran under PC/DOS and MS/DOS on the IBM personal computer became available.

Ashton-Tate announced the successor to its popular dBASE II product in 1984: *dBASE III*. This product had many more functions than its predecessor and at the same time made better use of the 16-bit MS/DOS computers. The positioning of dBASE III was in fact the same as that of dBASE II, but the set of commands was more comprehensive.

At the end of 1985 Ashton-Tate brought out *dBASE III Plus*, a product similar to dBASE III but extended with network facilities and other usability features. Along with the possibility of executing commands, users and programmers could also work via menu structures. The most important advantage of this was the removal of the need for users to learn and retain syntax. Both products, dBASE III and dBASE III Plus, were among the ten most widely sold software packages for microcomputers.

In 1988 Ashton-Tate announced *dBASE IV*. Compared with its predecessors dBASE IV has been enhanced on many fronts. Among other things, it contains the following components:

- *Control Center*: All other dBASE IV components can be started from here.

- *Forms Manager*: Here, screens can be developed so that users can process their data easily without having to learn a complicated language.

- *Report Writer*: Here, layouts of reports can be defined. The user, then, has only to give the name of the report and dBASE IV generates it.

- *Query-By-Example (QBE)*: This function enables everyone to query and process database data, and is particularly suited (and intended) for the answering of ad hoc queries.

- *Application Generator*: A programmer can use this to develop applications that use other dBASE IV components.

- *SQL*: SQL can be used to update and query database data. The language is intended for end users as well as programmers.

For more detailed descriptions of these and other dBASE IV functions we refer you to the various manuals supplied with the product. They are noted in the Bibliography.

1.6   Two database languages

dBASE IV is clearly more than just a database management system. It can process commands for generating reports, developing applications, building screens *and* for working with a database. The database language, therefore, is just a *sub-language* of the total dBASE IV language. In other words, you could say that dBASE IV is an application development system and the database management system is one aspect of that.

If we examine dBASE IV's database management system along with the commands used to access the database we see that dBASE IV actually recognizes two database languages. One is similar to that of dBASE III (Plus) and consists of commands such as APPEND, LIST and BROWSE. All these commands work *row by row*. We will refer to them as the *dBASE IV database commands* in order to differentiate them from the other database language statements.

The other database language is, of course, SQL whose statements include INSERT, UPDATE and SELECT. All SQL statements are designed to process whole sets of rows at a time. This is referred to as *set oriented* in the literature.

Another important difference between the two languages is the method of combining data from different tables. We will illustrate this difference with an example using the two tables, PLAYERS and TEAMS, from Section 1.2. Suppose that we want to know the team number, division, player number, player name and initials of team captains. In dBASE IV the database commands are as follows:

```
SELECT A
USE PLAYERS
SET INDEX TO PNO
SELECT B
USE TEAMS
SET RELATION TO PLAYERNO INTO PLAYERS
DISPLAY ALL TEAMNO, DIVISION, PLAYERNO,
          PLAYERS->NAME, PLAYERS->INITIALS
```

Result:

```
TEAMNO  DIVISION  PLAYERNO  NAME       INITIALS
------  --------  --------  ---------  --------
     1  first           6  Parmenter  R
     2  second         27  Collins    DD
```

We need eight commands, whereas with SQL one statement suffices:

```
SELECT    TEAMNO, DIVISION, TEAMS.PLAYERNO,
          PLAYERS.NAME, PLAYERS.INITIALS
FROM      TEAMS, PLAYERS
WHERE     TEAMS.PLAYERNO = PLAYERS.PLAYERNO
```

In principle, then, the same results are achieved with both languages. Both can work with tables created by the other. What happens internally, though the user does not see this, is that each SQL statement is translated to the corresponding dBASE IV database command.

dBASE IV recognizes what is known as a *mode of operation*, which is switched either to SQL or to the dBASE IV database. The mode of operation determines which statements can be used within a program. If it is switched to SQL, all SQL statements and most dBASE IV commands can be used. There are, nevertheless, a number of dBASE IV database commands which are not permitted in this mode. We list these in Chapter 20. Conversely, if the mode of operation is switched to dBASE IV, only dBASE IV commands are permissible and not SQL statements. In a program, or with interactive use, dBASE IV has a command to enable you to switch from one mode of operation to another, and this can be done as often as desired. The SQL statements and dBASE IV database commands cannot be used interchangeably because they behave differently with the tables and rows (the details of which we give in Chapter 21). There are, nevertheless, commands that make it possible to use in one mode of operation the data created in the other. Note that commands that do not belong to either of the two database languages, such as SET, may be used in either mode of operation.

1.7   The structure of the book

In Chapter 2 we cover a number of general dBASE IV topics, such as starting up dBASE IV, entering and correcting statements and invoking the help function.

Chapter 3 contains a detailed description of the database used by most of the examples and exercises. This database is modelled on the competition administration of a sports club.

Chapter 4 gives a general overview of SQL. After reading this chapter you should have a global view of the possibilities of SQL and a good idea of what awaits you in this book.

Chapter 5 is the first chapter to delve more fully into particular SQL statements. It covers all statements for creating databases, tables and indexes.

Chapters 6 to 14 are about querying tables with the SELECT statement. Many examples are used to illustrate the techniques. We devote a great deal of space to the SELECT statement in this book because many other statements are based on it.

Chapter 15 describes how data can be updated and deleted and how new rows can be added to tables.

Chapter 16 covers how indexes can be used to improve the execution time of particular statements. At the same time, we go into the use of the statistical data collected in the catalog tables.

In Chapter 17 we describe views, or virtual tables. With views we define a 'layer' on the table. The user then sees the table in a form which is most appropriate to his or her needs.

Data security is the subject of Chapter 18. It describes which commands are employed to register users for use of the DBMS. At the same time it also describes how users 'known' to the system can be authorized to execute particular statements on particular data.

Chapter 19 is a description of the catalog which fulfils a very important role within SQL. dBASE IV records data about databases in the catalog, such as columns in a table, names and passwords of users and indexes.

We cover embedded SQL in Chapter 20. By this, we mean the development of dBASE IV programs in which SQL statements are included.

The final chapter, Chapter 21, deals with a number of additional dBASE IV functions, including conversion of files to SQL tables and the importing and exporting of data.

The book is rounded off with a number of appendices and an index. The first appendix gives the answers to the exercises from the various chapters. Appendix B contains definitions of all the SQL statements we discuss. Appendix C describes all the dBASE IV scalar functions. Appendix D outlines dBASE IV's limits and boundaries. Appendix E gives the ASCII character set. Finally, Appendix F is a bibliography.

2

Starting dBASE IV
and entering statements

Before we describe which SQL statements can be used in dBASE IV we need to cover the following topics:

- starting and ending SQL
- entering statements
- retrieving previously entered statements
- correcting statements
- saving statements
- compiling statements
- invoking the HELP function

If you are already acquainted with these topics, you can skip this chapter and go directly to Chapter 3.

2.1 Starting dBASE IV and SQL

You can start dBASE IV and SQL from the dBASE IV directory by typing the word DBASE. dBASE IV can also be started from other directories but in that case the PATH specification in the AUTOEXEC.BAT file has to be modified. Example:

```
PATH C:\DUS;C:\DBASE
```

When dBASE IV is started the screen shown in Figure 2.1 appears. This screen is the *control center*, and from here all dBASE IV components can be started. If you want to use SQL you must first leave the control center by pressing the Esc key or the Ctrl-End keys. Another possibility is to press the F10 key and then choose

the Exit option from the control center menu. In each case you are presented
with an almost completely empty screen (see Figure 2.2).

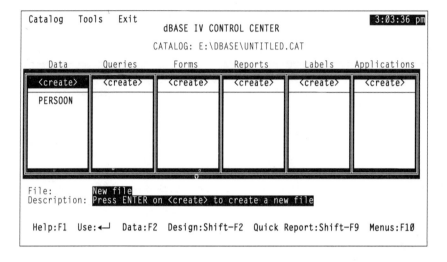

Figure 2.1: The dBASE IV control center

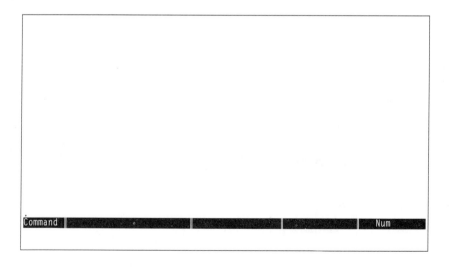

Figure 2.2: The dBASE IV status bar

The white *status bar* is at the bottom of the screen. It shows where you are within dBASE IV and is built up of five sections. The section on the far left tells you which dBASE IV screen you are using. If you are using SQL, then the word SQL is filled in. The next section to the right gives the name of the file you are working with. The next section is not relevant to SQL users. The next section says which database you are using (we come back to that later). And finally, the section on the far right provides information on the status of the keyboard, e.g. whether the Insert key is active or not.

Just above the status bar on the left is the *dBASE IV dot prompt*, which we will refer to as the *prompt* throughout the rest of this book. For dBASE III and dBASE III Plus buffs this is an old concept. You can type a command in after the prompt. If you want to work with SQL, thus switching the *mode of operation*, you have to enter the following command first (followed by the Return key):

```
. SET SQL ON
```

The prompt then changes.

```
SQL.
```

Clearly, SQL statements can now be entered.

You are now, in principle, at a point where interactive SQL statements can be entered. Such statements are covered in Chapter 4.

2.2 The CONFIG.DB file

As soon as it is started dBASE IV checks in the \DBASE directory to see whether there is a *CONFIG.DB* file. If there is, then it is read and executed. In its absence the 'default' start procedure is followed.

You can put various dBASE IV commands into the CONFIG.DB file that the system will execute before the prompt appears. Suppose, for example, that you would like the SQL prompt immediately after start-up, then you can include the following command in the CONFIG.DB file:

```
SQL = ON
```

We are not going to consider which commands are permissible in the CONFIG.DB file at this point; rather, they will crop up in different places in this book in conjunction with other topics.

2.3 Ending SQL

This command enables you to end SQL and leave dBASE IV:

```
SQL. QUIT
```

If you want to end SQL and continue on with other dBASE IVfunctions, this is the command to enter:

```
SQL. SET SQL OFF
```

2.4   Entering SQL statements

You can enter SQL statements in two ways. The most common way is to enter the statement directly after the prompt. In the next table we note the functions of some of the other keys.

Exercise: Type in the following SQL statement practising the use of some of the keys described in the table:

```
SQL. SHOW DATABASE;
```

If you have installed the standard sample supplied with dBASE IV, this is the result of executing that statement:

```
Existing databases are:
  NAME      CREATOR    CREATED  PATH
  SAMPLES              06/12/88 C:\DBASE\SAMPLES
```

The statement above returns a list of all databases (we come back to this in more detail in Chapter 5). At the moment there is only one database, the one provided by Ashton-Tate with the software. Note that below the result table the prompt is there waiting for the following statement.

The second way of entering SQL statements is by pressing the Ctrl-Home keys to get an empty screen into which you can type. If you had already begun an SQL statement, then it appears in the top left of the screen. Now you have many rows available for entering a statement. To process your statement you press the Ctrl-End keys.

Notes:

- **The prompt is always visible when you work with interactive SQL. In the following chapters we will omit the prompt because we are more interested in the formulation of SQL statements than how they are entered.**

- **Each SQL statement should end with a semi-colon. We will also leave these out in the following chapters as they are not part of the statements, but signify the end of them. Nevertheless, don't forget the semi-colon when you do the exercises.**

- **SQL statements do not have to be entered using upper-case letters; lower-case is also permitted.**

function	keystroke
Move the cursor one place to the right	$\rightarrow$
Move the cursor one place to the left	$\leftarrow$
Move the cursor to the previous line	$\uparrow$
Move the cursor to the following line	$\downarrow$
Move the cursor to the beginning of the next word	Control-$\rightarrow$
Move the cursor to the beginning of the previous word	Control-$\leftarrow$
Move the cursor to the beginning of the current line	Home
Move the cursor to the end of the current line	End
Delete the character just left of the cursor	Backspace
Delete the character on which the cursor is placed	Del
Switches modes between insert and overwriting characters (see status bar)	Ins
Turns the numeric mode on or off	Num Lock
Turns capital letters on or off	Caps Lock
Shows help information for the SQL statement currently being entered	F1 Help
Activates the full screen text editor	Control-Home
Ends the full screen text editor	Control-End
Starts the execution of a statement	Return

2.5   Retrieving previously entered statements

dBASE IV saves statements and commands that have already been processed. (In keeping with each language's practice, we refer to the SQL language as statements and to the dBASE IV language as commands; in this chapter, the word statement is sometimes also used to refer to both languages collectively.) The default is to keep the last 20 statements, and these are placed in the so-called *history buffer.*

If you want to execute one of the previous statements again, then you can press the ↑ key. The statement is then placed straight after the prompt and can be executed again (possibly after having been modified) by pressing the Return key. Pressing the ↑ key once gives you the last executed statement; if you press it once more you get the last but one, and so on.

The DISPLAY HISTORY and LIST HISTORY commands enable you to get an overview of everything currently held in the history buffer (don't use a semicolon after these commands as they are not part of SQL). In this context LIST and DISPLAY are equivalent commands.

```
SQL. LIST HISTORY
```

Result:

```
SHOW DATABASE;
LIST HISTORY
```

As we mentioned above, dBASE IV keeps a default of 20 statements. This number can be altered with the following command:

```
SQL. SET HISTORY TO 30
```

The maximum size of the history buffer is determined by the memory available in the computer.

2.6   Correcting statements

Everyone makes the occasional typing error. What does dBASE IV do in this situation? If you type in the following incomplete command and press the Return key:

```
SQL. SET HISTORY TO
```

dBASE IV observes the mistake and presents a framed error message on the screen giving three choices: CANCEL, EDIT and HELP. If you choose CANCEL the statement is erased and you can start again. If you choose EDIT the cursor is positioned after the statement and you can correct it. The third choice speaks for itself.

2.7   Saving statements

The statements in the history buffer remain there only until the end of the particular dBASE IV session. When dBASE IV is restarted the buffer is empty again. If you want to save statements for a longer period you need to store them in a separate file.

There are three steps to saving statements in a file. First, the MODIFY COMMAND command is used to create a file:

```
SQL. MODIFY COMMAND
```

dBASE IV then asks for the name of the file to be created. Note that if the file will contain SQL statements, the file type must be 'PRS'; if not it must be 'PRG'.

Another way is to enter the file name directly after the MODIFY COMMAND command:

```
SQL. MODIFY COMMAND TEST.PRS
```

The MODIFY COMMAND command takes you to the text editor of dBASE IV, where you can begin the second step: entering the statement. As an example, type in the following command:

```
LIST HISTORY
```

The third step is the actual storing of the statement. To do this, press the Ctrl-End keys and choose the `Exit` option from the menu. The LIST command above is now ready for regular use, and is saved until it is explicitly erased.

To execute this command use the DO command:

```
SQL. DO TEST
```

The result is a list of all executed commands:

```
SHOW DATABASE;
LIST HISTORY
SET HISTORY TO 30
MODIFY COMMAND
```

Note: In order to execute this file it is not mandatory to state the file type, but it is not wrong to do so.

2.8   Compiling statements

If we enter a statement interactively for processing or if we use a DO statement to execute a file, then a few things must occur before dBASE IV actually begins the processing. First, it must decide whether the statement is valid for dBASE IV. Second, it must check whether the tables and columns named actually exist. Third, it must ensure that the user has the authority to access the data. Fourth, dBASE IV has to determine the most efficient way to process the statement. Only after all these steps can the actual processing of the statement begin. With some statements this takes less than a second, but with others, for example, complex SQL statements, it can take much longer. This poses no problem if we are only using the statement once, but if it is used repeatedly much time could be wasted.

Statements which we know in advance that we are going to use regularly can be speeded up by *compiling* them. Compilation of a statement involves the execution of all the steps described above. The result of that process is stored in a separate file that then contains a *compiled statement*. When a compiled statement is executed, the controls noted above do not need to be re-processed; the actual processing begins immediately.

Statements can only be compiled if they have been stored in a file. They can be compiled in two ways: *implicitly* or *explicitly*. A statement in a file is automatically compiled when it is executed for the first time with the DO command. The compiled version of the statement is stored in a file with the same file name and a file type of 'DBO'. This is called implicit compilation of statements. If the file is processed a second time and the original file has not been deleted, then dBASE IV goes straight to the compiled version. Otherwise, the statement is compiled again. This means, in fact, that statements in files are *always* compiled before execution.

You can use the COMPILE command to explicitly compile statements in files. Example:

```
SQL. COMPILE TEST
```

The statement in file TEST.PRS is compiled and stored in file TEST.DBO. In fact, the DO command itself processes the COMPILE command behind the scenes.

Note: Compiling statements explicitly only saves time overall when the statements are executed repeatedly and without modification.

2.9   Invoking the HELP function

dBASE IV offers SQL two levels of assistance. General help is available by typing HELP after the prompt (naturally followed by the Return key) or by pressing the F1 key. dBASE IV presents the screen shown in Figure 2.3.

If you need help in formulating a particular command or statement, then you type the beginning of it, for example, SET HISTORY and then press the F1 key. dBASE IV then shows you what you can enter after SET HISTORY.

Figure 2.3: The dBASE IV help screen

3
The sports club sample database

This chapter describes a database that could be used by a sports club to administer its participation in a competition series. Most of the examples and exercises in this book are based on this database so you should study it carefully.

3.1   Description of the sports club

The database consists of four tables:

- PLAYERS
- TEAMS
- GAMES
- PENLTIES

The PLAYERS table contains data about members of the club. Two players cannot have the same combination of name and initials. The PLAYERS table contains no historical data. If a player gives up his or her membership, then he or she disappears from the table. In the case of moving house, the old address is over-written with a new address. In other words, the old address is not retained anywhere.

The sports club has two types of members: *recreational players* and *competition players*. The first group play games only among themselves (that is, no games against players from other clubs). The results of these friendly games are not recorded. Competition players play in teams against other clubs and the results of these games are recorded. Each player, regardless of whether he or she plays competitively, has a unique number assigned by the club. Each competition player must also be registered with the sports league and this organization gives each player a unique league number. If a competition player stops playing in the competition and becomes a recreational player, then his or her league number correspondingly disappears. Therefore, recreational players have no league number, but do have a player number.

The club has a number of teams taking part in the competitions. The captain of each team and the division in which it is currently competing is recorded. Again, no historical data is kept in this table. If a team is promoted or demoted to another division, the record is simply over-written with the new information. The same goes for the captain of the team; when a new captain is appointed, the number of the former captain is over-written.

A team consists of four players. During a game each player plays against one member of the opposing team. A team does not always consist of the same people and reserves are sometimes needed when the regular players are sick or on holiday. A player either wins or loses a match; a draw is not possible. In the GAMES table we show how many matches a particular player for a particular team has won and lost. This table *does* contain historical data. At the beginning of a new season the numbers of won and lost matches are not set to zero, but counted up and brought forward. Thus, a player can appear in the GAMES table more than once, but each time it must be for another team. It is not possible from this table to deduce the composition of a particular team.

If a player is badly behaved (arrives late, behaves aggressively, or does not turn up at all) then the league imposes a penalty in the form of a fine. The club pays these fines and records them in a PENLTIES table. As long as the player continues to play competitively the record of his or her penalties remains in this table.

If a player leaves the club, all his or her data from the four tables is destroyed. If the club withdraws a team, all data for that team is removed from the TEAMS and GAMES tables.

Opposite is a description of the columns in each of the four tables.

PLAYERS	
PLAYERNO	Unique number of the player assigned by the club
NAME	Surname of the player
INITIALS	Initials of the player; no full stops or spaces are used after each separate letter
BIRTH	Year in which the player was born
SEX	Sex of the player: M(ale) or F(emale)
JOINED	Year in which the player joined the club
STREET	Name of the street in which the player lives
HOUSENO	Number of the house
POSTCODE	Postcode
TOWN	Town or city in which the player lives
PHONENO	Area code followed by a hyphen and then sub-scriber's number
LEAGUENO	League number assigned by the league or blank for recreational players

TEAMS	
TEAMNO	Unique number of the team
PLAYERNO	Player number of the player who captains the team
DIVISION	Division in which the league has placed the team

GAMES	
TEAMNO	Number of the team
PLAYERNO	Number of the player
WON	Number of matches that the player has won for this team
LOST	Number of matches that the player has lost for this team

PENLTIES	
PAYMENTNO	Unique number for each penalty the club has re-ceived and paid
PLAYERNO	Number of the player who has incurred the penalty
PEN_DATE	Date on which the penalty has been received and paid
AMOUNT	Amount of the penalty

3.2 The contents of the tables

The contents of the tables are shown below. Except where otherwise mentioned, this data will form the basis of most examples and exercises. Some of the column names in the PLAYERS table have been shortened because of space restraints.

The PLAYERS table:

```
PLAYERNO NAME         INIT BIRTH S JOINED STREET           ...
-------- ----------- ---- ----- - ------ --------------- ---
       6 Parmenter   R    1964  M  1977  Haseltine Lane  ...
      44 Baker       E    1963  M  1980  Lewis Street    ...
      83 Hope        PK   1956  M  1982  Magdalene Road  ...
       2 Everett     R    1948  M  1975  Stoney Road     ...
      27 Collins     DD   1964  F  1983  Long Drive      ...
     104 Moorman     D    1970  F  1984  Stout Street    ...
       7 Wise        GWS  1963  M  1981  Edgecombe Way   ...
      57 Brown       M    1971  M  1985  Edgecombe Way   ...
      39 Bishop      D    1956  M  1980  Eaton Square    ...
     112 Bailey      IP   1963  F  1984  Vixen Road      ...
       8 Newcastle   B    1962  F  1980  Station Road    ...
     100 Parmenter   P    1963  M  1979  Haseltine Lane  ...
      28 Collins     C    1963  F  1983  Old Main Road   ...
      95 Miller      P    1963  M  1972  High Street     ...
```

The PLAYERS table (continued):

```
PLAYERNO ... HOUSENO POSTCODE TOWN       PHONENO     LEAGUENO
-------- --- ------- -------- ---------- ----------- --------
       6 ... 80      1234KK   Stratford  070-476537  8467
      44 ... 23      4444LJ   Inglewood  070-368753  1124
      83 ... 16A     1812UP   Stratford  070-353548  1608
       2 ... 43      3575NH   Stratford  070-237893  2411
      27 ... 804     8457DK   Eltham     079-234857  2513
     104 ... 65      9437AO   Eltham     079-987571  7060
       7 ... 39      9758VB   Stratford  070-347689
      57 ... 16      4377CB   Stratford  070-473458  6409
      39 ... 78      9629CD   Stratford  070-393435
     112 ... 8       6392LK   Plymouth   010-548745  1319
       8 ... 4       6584RO   Inglewood  070-458458  2983
     100 ... 80      1234KK   Stratford  070-494593  6524
      28 ... 10      1294QK   Midhurst   071-659599
      95 ... 33A     57460P   Douglas    070-867564
```

The TEAMS table:

TEAMNO	PLAYERNO	DIVISION
1	6	first
2	27	second

The GAMES table :

TEAMNO	PLAYERNO	WON	LOST
1	6	9	1
1	44	7	5
1	83	3	3
1	2	4	8
1	57	5	0
1	8	0	1
2	27	11	2
2	104	8	4
2	112	4	8
2	8	1	4

The PENLTIES table:

PAYMENTNO	PLAYERNO	PEN_DATE	AMOUNT
1	6	12/08/80	100.00
2	44	05/05/81	75.00
3	27	09/10/83	100.00
4	104	12/08/84	50.00
5	44	12/08/80	25.00
6	8	12/08/80	25.00
7	44	12/30/82	30.00
8	27	11/12/84	75.00

3.3   The structure of the database

Logical relationships exist between the tables; for example, every player number in the PENLTIES table must appear in the GAMES table. Such a relationship is called a *foreign key*. Figure 3.1 is a diagram of all foreign keys (not all columns are shown). An arrow under a column (or combination of columns) represents a *primary key*. An arrow from one table to another represents a foreign key.

The foreign keys are as follows:

- **From TEAMS to PLAYERS:** Each captain of a team is also a player. The set of player numbers from the TEAMS table is a subset of the set of player numbers from the PLAYERS table.

- **From GAMES to PLAYERS:** Each player who competes for a particular team must appear in the PLAYERS table. The set of player numbers from the GAMES table is a subset of the set of players from the PLAYERS table.

- **From GAMES to TEAMS:** Each team that appears in the GAMES table must also be present in the TEAMS table, because a player can only compete for registered teams. The set of team numbers from the GAMES table is a subset of the set of team numbers from the TEAMS table.

- **From PENLTIES to GAMES:** A penalty can only be imposed on players who have participated in the competition. The set of player numbers from the PENLTIES table is a subset of the set of player numbers from the GAMES table.

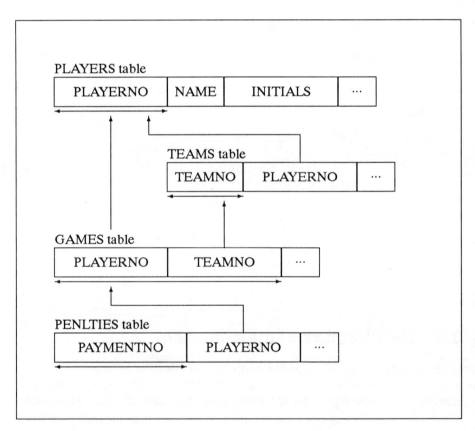

Figure 3.1: Diagram of the relationships between the sports club database tables

4

SQL in a nutshell

In this chapter we use examples to build up a picture of the possibilities of the database language SQL. By the time you have read it you should have an idea of what this book is going to cover. As well as this, we show how you can set up the sample database for yourself. We advise you to actually execute these statements if you have dBASE IV available.

4.1 Creating a database

Before the four tables PLAYERS, TEAMS, GAMES and PENLTIES can be set up, a *database* must first be created. A database in dBASE IV is a delimited environment in which a table can be created. We say delimited because a program cannot access data from different databases simultaneously. It is possible, however, to switch from one database to another in a program.

Below we show how the sports club database can be created. SPORTDB is its name (of course you can use an existing database if you have already set one up):

```
CREATE DATABASE SPORTDB
```

dBASE IV now creates a database called SPORTDB. At the same time the existence of a new database is recorded. In Chapter 5 we describe in greater detail what happens when the CREATE DATABASE statement is executed.

Suppose that you end dBASE IV immediately after entering that statement and decide to continue later on with setting up the SPORTDB database. Each time you start up dBASE IV you need to let it know that you are going to work with that database. The statement to do this is:

25

START DATABASE SPORTDB

4.2   Creating tables

The next step is to create the four tables described in the previous chapter. For this we use the *CREATE TABLE statement*. Shown below are the four CREATE TABLE statements needed.

```
CREATE    TABLE PLAYERS
          (PLAYERNO        SMALLINT,
          NAME            CHAR(15),
          INITIALS        CHAR(3) ,
          BIRTH           SMALLINT,
          SEX             CHAR(1) ,
          JOINED          SMALLINT,
          STREET          CHAR(15),
          HOUSENO         CHAR(4) ,
          POSTCODE        CHAR(6) ,
          TOWN            CHAR(10),
          PHONENO         CHAR(10),
          LEAGUENO        CHAR(4) )

CREATE    TABLE TEAMS
          (TEAMNO          SMALLINT,
          PLAYERNO        SMALLINT,
          DIVISION        CHAR(6) )

CREATE    TABLE GAMES
          (TEAMNO          SMALLINT,
          PLAYERNO        SMALLINT,
          WON             SMALLINT,
          LOST            SMALLINT)

CREATE    TABLE PENLTIES
          (PAYMENTNO       INTEGER ,
          PLAYERNO        SMALLINT,
          PEN_DATE        DATE     ,
          AMOUNT          DECIMAL(7,2))
```

Explanation: In fact, dBASE IV does not require the statements to be entered as precisely as we have done above. In this book we have adopted that type of layout for all SQL statements in order to make them easier to read. But for dBASE IV it doesn't matter whether each line follows on from the last (still separated by spaces or commas of course) or as it is shown above.

For each column a data type is specified (CHAR, INTEGER, SMALLINT, DECIMAL or PEN_DATE). The data type defines which type of value may be entered into the column concerned.

Figure 3.1 shows the primary keys of the tables. In dBASE IV it is not possible to define primary keys in the theoretical sense of the word. But we do advise you to create a unique index on each primary key. The creation of a unique index enables you to *simulate* a primary key.

```
CREATE    UNIQUE INDEX PLA_PRIM ON
          PLAYERS (PLAYERNO)

CREATE    UNIQUE INDEX TEA_PRIM ON
          TEAMS (TEAMNO)

CREATE    UNIQUE INDEX GAM_PRIM ON
          GAMES (TEAMNO, PLAYERNO)

CREATE    UNIQUE INDEX PEN_PRIM ON
          PENLTIES (PAYMENTNO)
```

Users are free to choose any index names. In our four examples we use a particular model: an index name consists of the first three letters of the name of the table on which the index has been defined followed by the word PRIM (standing for primary key). But a name like PLYR_IX2 is also permitted.

If these four CREATE INDEX statements are executed, dBASE IV then checks that the primary key columns contain no duplicate values. Any attempt to update a value or add a row which will lead to duplicate values in the primary key will be rejected. In Section 4.6 we will come back to the use of indexes.

4.3　Populating tables with data

The tables are created and can now be filled with data. For this we use *INSERT statements*. For each table we give two examples. You can deduce what the other INSERT statements will be like by referring to Section 3.1.

```
INSERT INTO PLAYERS VALUES
    (6, 'Parmenter', 'R', 1964, 'M', 1977,
    'Haseltine Lane', '80', '1234KK', 'Stratford',
    '070-476537', '8467')

INSERT INTO PLAYERS VALUES
    (44, 'Baker', 'E', 1963, 'M', 1980,
    'Lewis Street', '23', '4444LJ', 'Inglewood',
    '070-368753', '1124')
```

```
INSERT INTO TEAMS VALUES (1, 6, 'first')

INSERT INTO TEAMS VALUES (2, 27, 'second')

INSERT INTO GAMES VALUES (1, 6, 9, 1)

INSERT INTO GAMES VALUES (1, 44, 7, 5)

INSERT INTO PENLTIES VALUES (1, 6, {12/08/80}, 100)

INSERT INTO PENLTIES VALUES (2, 44, {05/05/81}, 75)
```

Explanation: The result of processing each statement is to add one new row to the table. Each alphanumeric value, such as Parmenter and R, must be enclosed in single quotation marks (see the first INSERT statement). The (column) values are separated by commas. Because dBASE IV still knows the sequence of the columns in the CREATE TABLE statement, it can take the values from the INSERT statement (provided they occur in the same order) and insert them into the correct columns. For the PLAYERS table, therefore, the first value is PLAYERNO, the second NAME, and so on, with the last being LEAGUENO.

4.4   Querying tables

The *SELECT statement* is used to retrieve data from tables. A number of examples will illustrate the diverse possibilities of this statement.

Example 4.1: Get the number, name and year of birth of each player resident in Stratford; sort the result in alphabetical order of name.

```
SELECT    PLAYERNO, NAME, BIRTH
FROM      PLAYERS
WHERE     TOWN = 'Stratford'
ORDER BY NAME
```

Result:

```
PLAYERNO  NAME              BIRTH
--------  ----------------  -----
      39  Bishop            1956
      57  Brown             1971
       2  Everett           1948
      83  Hope              1956
       6  Parmenter         1964
     100  Parmenter         1963
       7  Wise              1963
```

Explanation: Get the number, name and year of birth (SELECT PLAYERNO, NAME, BIRTH) of each player (FROM PLAYERS) resident in Stratford (WHERE TOWN = 'Stratford'); sort the result in alphabetical order of name (ORDER BY NAME). After FROM we specify which table we want to query. The conditions that our requested data must satisfy come after WHERE. SELECT enables us to choose which columns we want to see. And after ORDER BY we specify the column names on which the final result should be sorted.

The table above is the result of the SELECT statement that appears on your screen. dBASE IV does not, in fact, underline the column headings. We have added these for clarity. The layout of the table is determined by dBASE IV and can be altered.

A few words now about the 'default' layout created by dBASE IV. First, the width of a column is determined by the width of the data type of the column. Second, the values in columns with an alphanumeric data type are left-justified, while those in numeric columns are right-justified. Third, there are two spaces between each column of the result table. In Chapter 6 we discuss how the lay-out of the result of a SELECT statement can be adapted.

Example 4.2: Get the number of each player born after 1960 and resident in Stratford; order the result by player number.

```
SELECT    PLAYERNO
FROM      PLAYERS
WHERE     BIRTH > 1960
AND       TOWN = 'Stratford'
ORDER BY PLAYERNO
```

Result:

```
PLAYERNO
--------
       6
       7
      57
     100
```

Example 4.3: Get all the information about each penalty.

```
SELECT    *
FROM      PENLTIES
```

Result:

PAYMENTNO	PLAYERNO	PEN_DATE	AMOUNT
1	6	12/08/80	100.00
2	44	05/05/81	75.00
3	27	09/10/83	100.00
4	104	12/08/84	50.00
5	44	12/08/80	25.00
6	8	12/08/80	25.00
7	44	12/30/82	30.00
8	27	11/12/84	75.00

Explanation: Get for each penalty (FROM PENLTIES) all column values (SELECT *). This statement returns the whole PENLTIES table as a result. The * character is a shorthand notation for 'all columns'.

4.5 Updating and deleting rows

In Section 4.3 we described how to add new rows to a table. This section covers the updating and deleting of existing rows.

Warning: If you actually execute the statements described in this section you will change the contents of the database. In the subsequent sections we assume the original contents of the database.

The *UPDATE statement* is used to change values in rows and the *DELETE statement* to remove complete rows from a table. Let us look at examples of both statements.

Example 4.4: Change the amount of each penalty incurred by player 44 to $200.

```
UPDATE    PENLTIES
SET       AMOUNT = 200
WHERE     PLAYERNO = 44
```

These changes can be seen by issuing an SELECT statement.

```
SELECT    *
FROM      PENLTIES
```

Result:

```
PAYMENTNO  PLAYERNO  PEN_DATE  AMOUNT
---------  --------  --------  ------
        1         6  12/08/80  100.00
        2        44  05/05/81  200.00
        3        27  09/10/83  100.00
        4       104  12/08/84   50.00
        5        44  12/08/80  200.00
        6         8  12/08/80   25.00
        7        44  12/30/82  200.00
        8        27  11/12/84   75.00
```

Example 4.5: Remove each penalty where the amount is greater than $30 (we assume the original contents of the PENLTIES table).

```
DELETE
FROM      PENLTIES
WHERE     AMOUNT > 30
```

Result (seen by issuing a SELECT statement):

```
PAYMENTNO  PLAYERNO  PEN_DATE  AMOUNT
---------  --------  --------  ------
        5        44  12/08/80   25.00
        6         8  12/08/80   25.00
        7        44  12/30/82   30.00
```

4.6   Optimizing query processing

We now look at how SELECT statements are processed, in other words how dBASE IV arrives at the correct answer. We will illustrate this with the following SELECT statement (again, we assume the original contents of the PENLTIES table).

```
SELECT    *
FROM      PENLTIES
WHERE     AMOUNT = 25
```

To process this statement dBASE IV looks row by row through the entire PENL-TIES table. If AMOUNT equals 25, the row is included in the result table. If, like this example, the table contains few rows, dBASE IV can work quickly. But, if a table has thousands of rows and each must be checked, then it could take a great deal of time. In such a case the definition of an *index* can speed up the processing. You could compare an index created with dBASE IV with an index in a book. Later, in Chapter 16, we discuss this more fully.

   An index is defined on a column or combination of columns, for example:

```
CREATE    INDEX AMOUNTIX ON
          PENLTIES (AMOUNT)
```

This statement defines an index called AMOUNTIX on the AMOUNT column in the PENLTIES table. This index ensures that in the above example dBASE IV only needs to look at rows in the database which satisfy the WHERE condition, and is, therefore, quicker to produce an answer. The AMOUNTIX index provides direct access to the rows. It is important to bear in mind the following points:

• Among other reasons, indexes are defined in order to optimize the processing of SELECT statements.

• An index is never explicitly referenced in a SELECT statement.

• During the processing of a statement dBASE IV itself chooses whether an existing index will be used.

• An index may be created or deleted at any time.

• When updating, inserting or deleting rows, dBASE IV also maintains the indexes on the tables concerned. This means that on the one hand the processing time for SELECT statements is reduced, but on the other hand, the processing time for change statements (such as INSERT, UPDATE and DELETE) is increased.

Section 4.2 dealt with a special type of index: the unique index. dBASE IV also uses these for optimizing processing. Unique indexes have another function as well; they guarantee that a particular column or combination of columns contains no duplicate values.

4.7   Views

A table stores rows of actual data. This means that a table occupies a particular amount of storage space; the more rows, the more storage space required. *Views* are tables that are visible to users, but which do not occupy any storage space. A view, therefore, can also be referred to as a *derived* or *virtual* table. A view behaves as though it contains actual rows of data, but in fact it contains none. Instead, the rows are derived from the base table or tables on which the view is defined.

The data in the sports club database is divided into four tables. These tables define the structure of the database. Imagine now that you want a table for registering the player number and age of each player. This data can be retrieved from the database because the PLAYERS table contains a player number and a year of birth for each player. The age can be calculated by subtracting the year of birth from the current year.

The following statement defines a view called AGES that contains the desired data:

```
CREATE   VIEW AGES (PLAYERNO, AGE) AS
SELECT   PLAYERNO, 1990 - BIRTH
FROM     PLAYERS
```

The view AGES has two columns: PLAYERNO and AGE. It is the SELECT statement that determines the contents of the view. By using the SELECT statement shown below you can see the (virtual) contents of the view:

```
SELECT   *
FROM     AGES
```

Result:

```
PLAYERNO  AGE
--------  ---
       6   26
      44   27
      83   34
       2   42
      27   26
     104   20
       7   27
      57   19
      39   34
     112   27
       8   28
     100   27
      28   27
      95   27
```

The contents of the AGES view are *not* stored in the database, but they are derived at the moment a SELECT statement (or another statement) is executed. The use of views, therefore, costs nothing extra in storage space as the contents of a view can only comprise data which is already stored.

Among other things, views can be used to:

- simplify the use of routine or repetitive statements,
- restructure the way in which tables are seen,
- build up SELECT statements in several steps,
- protect data.

Chapter 17 looks at this more closely.

4.8   User and data security

As long as access to a dBASE IV database is not explicitly protected anyone can
see it. That implies that anyone could start up dBASE IV and SQL, look at the
data and possibly change it.

The *PROTECT* command is used to protect data in a database. PROTECT
ensures that every dBASE IV user has to begin by entering a *userid* and *password*. dBASE IV ascertains whether the password appears in the list of authorized userids and passwords. If it is there, the familiar Ashton-Tate logo appears
on the screen. If not, dBASE IV stops and the user's access is refused. The list of
authorized userids and passwords is also secured with PROTECT.

The entitlement to start dBASE IV does not mean that a user may access
all data in every database. Users can create their own tables and access them. To
get at and use tables created by other users requires separate authorization or
privileges. SQL statements are used for this.

Example 4.6: Suppose that two users, DIANE and PETE, have been authorized
with PROTECT to start dBASE IV and SQL. They can create their own tables
but cannot work with tables created by others. The following three statements
give them the required privileges.

```
GRANT    SELECT
ON       PLAYERS
TO       DIANE


GRANT    SELECT, UPDATE
ON       PLAYERS
TO       PETE


GRANT    SELECT, UPDATE
ON       TEAMS
TO       PETE
```

When PETE has started SQL he can, for example, query the TEAMS table:

```
SELECT   *
FROM     TEAMS
```

dBASE IV will give an error message if DIANE enters the same SELECT statement as she has authority only to query the PLAYERS table and not the TEAMS
table.

Introducing users and granting them privileges does have implications for
the security of the database. Not everyone needs access to all the data in the
database. GRANT statements allow users to have access only to that data which
is necessary for them to carry out their work.

4.9   The catalog tables

dBASE IV maintains lists of user names and passwords and the sequence in which columns in the CREATE TABLE statements have been created (see Section 4.2). Where does dBASE IV record all these names, passwords, sequence numbers and so on? dBASE IV manages, for its own use, a number of tables in which this data is stored. These tables are called *catalog tables*. Each catalog table is an ordinary SQL table that may be queried using SELECT statements. Catalog tables, however, *cannot* be accessed using statements like UPDATE and DELETE. In any case, this is not necessary as dBASE IV maintains these tables itself.

Among others, dBASE IV manages the following catalog tables:

SYSDBS   This contains, for each database, the name, the owner and the directory in which the database is stored.

SYSTABLS   This contains for each table, among other things, the number of columns and the owner (this is the user who created the table).

SYSCOLS   This contains for each column, among other things, the data type, the table to which the column belongs and the sequence number of the column in the table.

SYSIDXS   This contains for each index, among other things, the table on which the index is defined, and the manner in which the index is ordered.

SYSAUTH   This contains such information as the name of the table on which each privilege is granted and the user who has been granted the privilege.

SYSVIEWS   This contains for each view, among other things, the view definition (the SELECT statement).

Here are two examples of querying the catalog tables.

Example 4.7: Give the name, data type and sequence number of each column in the PLAYERS table; order the result by sequence number.

```
SELECT    COLNAME, COLTYPE, COLNO
FROM      SYSCOLS
WHERE     TBNAME = 'PLAYERS'
ORDER BY COLNO
```

Result:

```
COLNAME      COLTYPE   COLNO
----------   -------   -----
PLAYERNO     N             1
NAME         C             2
INITIAL      C             3
BIRTH        N             5
SEX          C             6
JOINED       N             7
STREET       C             8
HOUSENO      C             9
POSTCODE     C            10
TOWN         C            11
PHONENO      C            12
LEAGUENO     C            13
```

Explanation: Give the name, data type and sequence number (SELECT COLNAME, COLTYPE, COLNO) of each column (FROM SYSCOLS) in the PLAYERS table (WHERE TBNAME = 'PLAYERS'); order the result by sequence number (ORDER BY COLNO).

Example 4.8: Give the names of the indexes defined on the TEAMS table.

```
SELECT    IXNAME
FROM      SYSIDXS
WHERE     TBNAME = 'TEAMS'
```

Result (for example):

```
IXNAME
--------
TEA_PRIM
TEA_REF
```

Chapter 19 is entirely devoted to the structure of catalog tables. In the other chapters the effect particular statements can have on the contents of the catalog tables is described. In other words, when processing a particular statement leads to a change in the catalog data, this change is explained. Therefore, this book discusses the catalog tables as an integral part of dBASE IV.

5
Creating databases and tables

This chapter describes the statements for creating databases and tables. We are taking the view that the user knows which data must be stored and what the structure of the data is: that is, which tables are to be created and what the appropriate columns are. In other words, the user has, at his or her disposal, a ready-to-use database design.

If you have the dBASE IV software, we advise you to set up the sample database described in Chapter 3 of this book and fill the tables with the same data. Then you can recreate the examples and work through and correct the exercises yourself.

Note that in this and the following chapters a special notation is used to define the statements. A description of this notation is given in Appendix B. That appendix also contains the definitions of all the SQL statements.

5.1 Creating databases

Each table you create belongs to a *database*. You should consider a database, then, to be a collection of related tables. Tables in different databases cannot be accessed simultaneously. There is only ever one accessible database; therefore, just one collection of tables. It *is* possible to move from one database to another, however.

Because each table belongs to a database, we have to create a database before we can create any tables. To do this we use the *CREATE DATABASE statement.*

```
<create database statement> ::=
   CREATE DATABASE [ <directory path> ] <database name>

<directory path> ::= \ { <file> \ }...

<file> ::= <file name> [ . <file type> ]
```

Example 5.1: Create a new database called SPORTDB.

```
CREATE DATABASE SPORTDB
```

What is the effect of this statement? Below is a summary of what dBASE IV creates.

• A subdirectory of the \DBASE directory is defined. This new directory has the same name as the database (in our case SPORTDB).

• All catalog tables are put into this new directory, which means that each database has its own catalog.

• The SYSDBS table records that a new database has been created. (The SYSDBS table is a separate table which is also part of the catalog but unlike the other catalog tables it sits in the \DBASE\SQLHOME directory and there is only one of them. The SYSDBS table is created when dBASE IV is installed.)

If you want to put a new database in a particular directory then you can specify the directory path before the database name.

Example 5.2: Place the new database TESTDB1 in a subdirectory of the root directory.

```
CREATE DATABASE \TESTDB1
```

A new database can also be created as a subdirectory of an existing directory.

Example 5.3: Place the TESTDB2 database in a subdirectory of the \ABC directory.

```
CREATE DATABASE \ABC\TESTDB2
```

Note: The CREATE DATABASE statement can only be used in interactive SQL.
       dBASE IV records in the SYSDBS catalog table that a new table has been created. The structure is given below. The NAME column is the primary key.

column name	description
NAME	Name of the database
CREATOR	Owner of the database
CREATED	Date on which the database was created
PATH	The specification of the directory path in which the database was created

SYSDBS is the only catalog table that keeps data about multiple databases. Therefore, it cannot be queried using the SELECT statement; *SHOW DATA-BASE statement* is used here. This statement is used to find out which databases have been created.

```
<show database statement> ::=
    SHOW DATABASE
```

Example:

```
SHOW DATABASE
```

Result:

```
Existing databases are:
NAME        CREATOR    CREATED  PATH
SPORTDB                07/23/88 C:\DBASE\SPORTDB
TESTDB1                08/12/88 C:\TESTDB1
TESTDB2                08/12/88 C:\ABC\TESTDB2
```

5.2 Naming databases

The database name must satisfy a number of conditions. It can be a maximum of 8 characters long, can contain letters, numerals and the underscore character, and must begin with a letter. At the same time, the name of a new database cannot be the same as the name of an existing database.

Words which are used in SQL statements and have a special meaning, like CREATE or SELECT, may not be used as database names. Such words are called *reserved words* or key words. In Appendix B we give a list of reserved words.

It would pay to also avoid words which have a special meaning within the operating system environment, such as CON and LPT. We also suggest that you avoid using dBASE IV keywords in database names at all times.

5.3   Starting and stopping databases

As soon as the database has been created you can work with it (as long as dBASE IV has not been ended in the meantime). For example, you can create tables, fill them with data and query them. We call a just-created database the *current* database. There can only ever be one current database. Before most SQL statements can be executed there must be a current database. Simply starting dBASE IV and SQL does not establish a current database. This means that when you start SQL, you have to identify which database you want to work with. We use the START DATABASE statement to establish a 'current' database.

```
<start database statement> ::=
   START DATABASE <database name>
```

Example:

```
START DATABASE SPORTDB
```

You can also get dBASE IV to start a database automatically by putting the following command in the CONFIG.DB file (see Chapter 2):

```
SQLDATABASE = SPORTDB
```

You stop the current database with the following statement:

```
STOP DATABASE
```

```
<stop database statement> ::=
   STOP DATABASE
```

It is not possible to start two databases at the same time. A START DATABASE statement stops any current database before it starts the new database. Therefore, it is not necesary to explicitly stop a database if you want to work with tables from another database.

When you leave SQL via the SET SQL OFF command, and later come back to it, dBASE IV still knows which database was current.

5.4   Dropping databases

A database can be deleted using the DROP DATABASE statement.

```
<drop database statement> ::=
    DROP DATABASE <database name>
```

The effect of the DROP DATABASE statement is:

• All tables and other objects belonging to the database, such as views and indexes, are dropped (these are all the files with the file types DBF and MDX).

• All catalog tables are dropped.

• The SYSDBS table is updated (the table itself remains in existence).

The directory is *not* deleted. Therefore, all the other files in the directory remain.

Note: The DROP DATABASE statement can only be used in interactive SQL and when the database concerned is *not* current.

5.5 Creating tables

The *CREATE TABLE statement* is used to set up tables in which rows of data can be stored.

Here is an example of a CREATE TABLE statement, the one used to create the PLAYERS tables in the sports club database.

```
CREATE TABLE PLAYERS (
        PLAYERNO    SMALLINT ,
        NAME        CHAR(15) ,
        INITIALS    CHAR(3)  ,
        BIRTH       SMALLINT ,
        SEX         CHAR(1)  ,
        JOINED      SMALLINT ,
        STREET      CHAR(15) ,
        HOUSENO     CHAR(4)  ,
        POSTCODE    CHAR(6)  ,
        TOWN        CHAR(10) ,
        PHONENO     CHAR(10) ,
        LEAGUENO    CHAR(4)  )
```

When a table is created dBASE IV records the name of the user who entered the CREATE TABLE statement, and this user automatically becomes the *owner* of the table. Table names are unique within a database. Or, in other words, two tables may only have the same name if they belong to different databases.

What is this user name, in fact? If you have protected dBASE IV with the PROTECT command, everyone starting it must enter a userid among other things. If a table is created by this user, dBASE IV automatically records his or her userid as the owner of the table.

```
<create table statement> ::=
    CREATE TABLE <table name>
        ( <table element> [ {,<table element>}... ] )

<table element> ::=
    <column name> <data type>

<data type> ::=
    <numeric data type> |
    <alphanumeric data type> |
    <date data type> |
    <logical data type>

<numeric data type> ::=
    NUMERIC ( <precision> , <scale> ) |
    SMALLINT |
    INTEGER |
    DECIMAL ( <precision> , <scale> ) |
    FLOAT ( <precision> , <scale> )

<alphanumeric data type> ::=
    CHAR ( <length> )

<date data type> ::=
    DATE

<logical data type> ::=
    LOGICAL

<precision> ::= <integer>

<scale> ::= <integer>

<length> ::= <integer>
```

If you work without a security mechanism, users do not have to enter a userid and password, in which case dBASE IV records no owner. (dBASE IV actually fills the column with blanks instead of an owner.)

The creation of a table causes a file to be created with the same name and a file type of 'DBF'. The file type is also referred to as the *suffix*. This file is stored in the directory in which the database belongs. So if we create a table called PLAYERS, dBASE IV builds a file called PLAYERS.DBF.

Each column has a data type, the specification of which is mandatory. SQL recognizes the following data types:

NUMERIC(p,q)   A number of maximum p digits with $p - (q + 1)$ digits before the decimal point and q digits after the point. For example, a column with the data type NUMERIC(12,4) can have a maximum of 7 digits before the point and 4 after (one position is reserved for the decimal point and one for the sign (–)). The p value cannot exceed 20 and must be greater than or equal to $q+2$. The q value must lie between 0 and 18. A column, then, with the data type NUMERIC(6,2) can contain values from 9999.99 to –999.99 inclusive.

SMALLINT   A column with the data type SMALLINT is converted to NUMERIC(6,0).

INTEGER   A column with the data type INTEGER is converted to NUMERIC(20,0).

DECIMAL(p,q)   A column with the data type DECIMAL(p,q) is converted to NUMERIC(p+1,q). This means that the p value may be up to 19.

FLOAT(p,q)   A column with the data type FLOAT(p,q).

CHAR(n)   A word of up to n characters ($1 <= n <= 254$).

DATE   The values in a column of this data type represent dates. A date consists of three parts: a year, a month and a day. We will discuss the specification and the presentation of dates later.

LOGICAL   This data type can have only two values, *true* or *false*. dBASE IV stores T for the value true and F for false.

Note: The MEMO data type that may be used in dBASE IV database statements is not permitted in SQL.

Each table can have up to 255 columns. At the same time, the maximum length of a row is 4000 bytes. (In Appendix D the other limits and boundaries of dBASE IV are noted.) The length of a row is found by adding the respective lengths of all columns and adding 1. The length of a column is, of course, dependent on the data type chosen. The table below gives an overview of this.

data type	length in bytes
SMALLINT	6
INTEGER	20
DECIMAL(p,q)	p+1
NUMERIC(p,q)	p
FLOAT(p,q)	p
CHAR(n)	n
DATE	8
LOGICAL	1

5.6   Naming tables and columns

As with database names, table and column names must satisfy certain conditions.
Table names can be up to 8 characters long, consist only of letters, digits and
the underscore character and must begin with a letter. Two tables in the same
database may not have the same name.

Column names can be up to 10 characters long, consist only of letters, digits
and the underscore character and must begin with a letter. A table may not have
two columns with the same name.

Table and column names may not be reserved words. In Appendix B we
include a list of such words. At the same time, words which have a special meaning
for the operating system should be avoided, such as CON and LPT. This applies
also to reserved words from other dBASE IV commands.

Exercise

5.1   Write a CREATE TABLE statement for a table called DEPTS and with
columns: DEPTNO (5 character code), BUDGET (maximum amount of
500000) and LOCATION (name with a maximum of 30 characters).

5.7   Recording tables in the catalog

dBASE IV uses two tables to record tables and columns in the catalog: SYS-
TABLS and SYSCOLS respectively. A description of these tables is given below.
Some of the columns are explained in other chapters. The TBNAME column is
the primary key of the SYSTABLS table. The primary key of the SYSCOLS table
is formed by the TBNAME and COLNAME columns.

SYSTABLS	
TBNAME	Name of the table or view (depending on the column TYPE)
CREATOR	Name of the owner (or creator) of the table or view
TBTYPE	The type of table: T for actual table, V for view, D for a table created by the SAVE clause of the SELECT statement (without the KEEP option) and K for a table created with the SAVE clause of the SELECT statement, but with the KEEP option
COLCOUNT	Number of columns in the table or view
CLUSTERRID	Not used
INDXCOUNT	Number of indexes defined on the table. In the case of a view this value is set to zero
CREATED	Date on which the table (or view) was created
UPDATED	Date on which the last ALTER TABLE or RUNSTATS statement was executed against the table
CARD	Number of rows in the table; in the case of a view this value is set to zero
NPAGES	Number of physical *pages* that the table uses on disk

SYSCOLS	
COLNAME	Name of the column
TBNAME	Name of the table of which the column is a part
TBCREATOR	Name of the owner (or creator) of the table of which the column is a part
COLNO	Sequence number of the column in the table; this sequence is the same as the sequence of columns in the CREATE TABLE statement
COLTYPE	Data type of the column: C(har), D(ate), F(loat), L(ogical) or N(umeric)
COLLEN	If the COLTYPE is C(har), F(loat) or N(umeric), the length is given here; D(ate) has a fixed length of 8 and L(ogical) of 1.
COLSCALE	If the value of the COLTYPE is F(loat) or N(umeric) the number of digits after the decimal point is given
NULLS	Not used
COLCARD	The number of different values in the column
UPDATES	Set to Y if the column can be updated, otherwise N
HIGH2KEY	The second highest value in the column
LOW2KEY	The second lowest value in the column

Exercise

5.2   Show how the SYSTABLS and SYSCOLS tables would be updated if the
CREATE TABLE statement from the first exercise in this chapter were
executed.

5.8   Dropping tables

The *DROP TABLE statement* is used to delete a table from the database. dBASE
IV removes the descriptions of the tables from the SYSTABLS and SYSCOLS
tables, plus all views, indexes, privileges and synonyms dependent on this table.

```
<drop table statement> ::=
   DROP TABLE <table identifier>

<table identifier> ::= <table name>
```

Example 5.4: Delete the PLAYERS table.

```
DROP TABLE PLAYERS
```

5.9   Altering the table structure

The *ALTER TABLE statement* is used to add new columns to a table after it has
been created and put into use.

```
<alter table statement> ::=
   ALTER TABLE <table identifier>
      ADD ( <table element> [ {,<table element>}... ] )

<table identifier> ::= <table name>

<table element> ::=
   <column name> <data type>
```

Suppose that the TEAMS table has the following structure and contents:

```
TEAMNO  PLAYERNO  DIVISION
------  --------  --------
     1         6  first
     2        27  second
```

The table must be extended to include a new column called TYPE. This column shows whether the team is a men's or women's one. The statement to do this is:

```
ALTER   TABLE TEAMS
ADD     ( TYPE CHAR(1) )
```

The TEAMS table now looks like this:

```
TEAMNO  PLAYERNO  DIVISION  TYPE
------  --------  --------  ----
     1         6  first
     2        27  second
```

The TYPE column is filled with a blank. If the new column has a numeric data type (SMALLINT, INTEGER, DECIMAL, NUMERIC or FLOAT) or the data type DATE, then the column is left empty. If the column has a data type of LOG-ICAL, then an F is placed in it.

5.10   Synonyms for table names

The *CREATE SYNONYM statement* is used to define a synonym for a table name. You can use synonyms in other statements instead of the original name. Note, however, that the definition of a synonym does not mean that a new table has been created.

```
<create synonym statement> ::=
   CREATE SYNONYM <table name>
      FOR <table identifier>

<table identifier> ::= <table name>
```

Example 5.5: The user KAREN wants to use MEMBERS as a synonym for the PLAYERS table.

```
CREATE SYNONYM MEMBERS FOR PLAYERS
```

When this statement has been processed the next two SELECT statements become equivalent:

```
SELECT    *
FROM      PLAYERS
```

and

```
SELECT    *
FROM      MEMBERS
```

Use the DROP SYNONYM statement to delete synonyms.

```
<drop synonym statement> ::=
   DROP SYNONYM <table identifier>

<table identifier> ::= <table name>
```

Example 5.6: Delete the synonym MEMBERS.

```
DROP SYNONYM MEMBERS
```

Synonyms are recorded by dBASE IV in the SYSSYNS table. The SYNAME column is the primary key of the SYSSYNS table.

SYSSYNS	
SYNAME	Synonym for the table name
CREATOR	Name of the user who entered the synonym
TBCREATOR	Name of the owner (or creator) of the table
TBNAME	Name of the table on which this synonym has been defined

Naming rules for synonyms are the same as those for tables. It follows, then, that a synonym may not be created which has the same name as an existing table or synonym.

6
SELECT statement: common elements

The most important and most used SQL statement is the SELECT statement. This statement is used to query data in the tables, the result of this always being a table. A result table like this can be used as the basis of a report.

This book deals with the SELECT statement in nine chapters. This first chapter describes a number of common elements important to many SQL statements and certainly crucial to the SELECT statement. For those of you who are familiar with programming languages and other database languages, most of these concepts will be well known. In this chapter we also discuss how dBASE IV processes a SELECT statement.

We cover the following common elements:

- literal
- memory variable
- system variable
- numeric expression
- alphanumeric expression
- logical expression
- date expression
- scalar function
- statistical function

```
<literal> ::=
   <numeric literal> |
   <alphanumeric literal> |
   <date literal> |
   <logical literal>

<numeric literal> ::=
   <integer literal> |
   <decimal literal> |
   <floating point literal>

<integer literal> ::= [ + | - ] <integer>

<decimal literal> ::=
   [ + | - ] <integer> [ .<integer> ] |
   [ + | - ] <integer>. |
   [ + | - ] .<integer>

<floating point literal> ::= <mantissa> [ E<exponent> ]

<alphanumeric literal> ::=
   ' [ <character>... ] ' |
   """ [ <character>... ] """

<date literal> ::=
   "{" <year> . <month> . <day> "}"

<logical literal> ::=
   .T. | .t. | .Y. | .y. | .F. | .f. | .N. | .n.

<mantissa> ::= <decimal literal>

<exponent> ::= <integer literal>

<character> ::= <non quote character> | ''

<non quote character> ::=
   <digit> | <letter> | <special character>

<year> ::= <integer>

<month> ::= <integer>

<day> ::= <integer>

<integer> ::= <digit>...
```

6.1   Literals

A *literal* is a fixed or unchanging value. Literals are used, for example, in conditions for selecting rows in SELECT statements and in INSERT statements for specifying values in a new row. Each literal has a particular data type, just like a column in a table. SQL recognizes these types of literals (the names are derived from their respective data types):

- integer literal
- decimal literal
- floating point literal
- alphanumeric literal
- date literal
- logical literal

An *integer literal* is a whole number without a decimal point, possibly preceded by a plus or minus sign. Examples are:

```
 38
+12
-3404
 -16
```

The following examples are *not* correct integer literals:

```
342.16
-14E5
 jim
```

A *decimal literal* is a number with or without a decimal point and possibly preceded by a plus or minus sign. Every integer literal is by definition a decimal literal. Examples are:

```
   49
 18.47
-3400
  -16
0.83459
 -349
```

A *floating point literal* is a decimal literal followed by an exponent. Examples are:

Floating point literal	Value
49	49
18.47	18.47
-34E2	-3400
0.16E4	1600
4E-3	0.004

An *alphanumeric literal* is a string of zero or more alphanumeric characters enclosed in quotation marks. The quotation marks are not considered to be part of the literal. Rather, they define the beginning and end of the string. Double quotation marks (") can be used instead of single ones in dBASE IV. The following characters are permitted in an alphanumeric literal:

```
all lower case letters   (a-z)
all upper case letters   (A-Z)
all digits               (0-9)
all remaining characters (such as ' + -  ? = and _)
```

As you will note, an alphanumeric literal can contain quotation marks. For every single quotation mark within an alphnumeric literal you must use two quotation marks instead, separate from the quotation marks already being used to enclose the literal. Some examples of correct alphanumeric literals are:

```
Alphanumeric literal   Value
--------------------   -------
'Collins'              Collins
'''tis'                'tis
'!?-@'                 !?-@
''
''''                   '
'1234'                 1234
"aap"                  aap
```

A few incorrect examples include:

```
'Collins
''tis
'''
```

A *date literal* consists of year, month and day components and therefore represents a date. The three components are separated by colons. Examples include:

```
Date literal   Value
------------   ----------------
{12/08/80}     8 december 1980
{12/08/1980}   8 december 1980
{6/8/80}       8 june 1980
{05/30/2000}   30 may 2000
```

There are only two *logical literals*: *true* and *false*. The value true can be specified in an SQL statement in four equivalent ways:

```
.T.
.t.
.Y.
.y.
```

The same applies for the value false:

```
.F.
.f.
.N.
.n.
```

Exercise

6.1 Say which of the literals below are correct and which are incorrect; give the data type of the literal as well.

1.   `41.58E-8`
2.   `JIM`
3.   `'jam'`
4.   `'A'14`
5.   `'!?'`
6.   `-3400`
7.   `'14E6'`
8.   `',,,,'`
9.   `'.T.'`
10. `.f.`

6.2 Memory variables

A *memory variable* is a variable with a name. dBASE IV recognizes two types of memory variables: the *simple variable* and the *array element*, an array element being part of an array. A specified value can be assigned to a memory variable, so the value of a memory variable can change in time. The *STORE command* or the = sign is used to assign this value. If the memory variable does not yet exist, dBASE IV creates it. Note that these two commands are not part of SQL.

```
<memory variable> ::=
   <simple variable> |
   <array element>

<simple variable> ::= < variable name>

<array element> ::=
   <array name> "[" <numeric expression>
                   [ , <numeric expression> ] "]"
```

Example 6.1: Create the simple variable TNR and give it the value 2.

```
STORE 2 TO TNR
```

or

```
TNR = 2
```

Every memory variable has a data type, for example, numeric or alphanumeric. The data type is derived from the value assigned to it. The command used to create the memory variable TNR does not need to specify the numeric data type. However, the data type can change if another type of value is assigned to the variable.

A simple memory variable name can be up to ten characters long, and can consist of only letters, digits, and the underscore character.

A special type of memory variable in dBASE IV is the *array*. This is a one or two dimensional list of memory variables. The individual elements of an array are accessible via the array name followed by one or two sequence numbers. As opposed to simple memory variables, arrays must be explicitly declared before they can be used in commands (for example in the STORE command). Here is a definition of the command you use to declare arrays.

```
<declare array command> ::=
   DECLARE <array> [ {,<array>}... ]

<array> ::=
   <array name> "[" <numeric expression>
                    [ , <numeric expression> ] "]"
```

Example 6.2: Declare an array called PLNUMBERS in which 20 values could be stored; assign the value 4 to element 1.

```
DECLARE PLNUMBERS[20]

PLNUMBERS[1] = 4
```

Memory variables may be used in SQL statements. Example:

```
STORE 'Collins' to PNAME

SELECT    PLAYERNO, NAME, INITIALS
FROM      PLAYERS
WHERE     NAME = PNAME
```

Result:

```
PLAYERNO  NAME        INITIALS
--------  ----------  --------
      27  Collins     DD
      28  Collins     C
```

Example:

```
DECLARE PLNUMBERS[3]

PLNUMBERS[1] = 27

SELECT    PLAYERNO, NAME, INITIALS
FROM      PLAYERS
WHERE     PLAYERNO = PLNUMBERS[1]
```

Result:

```
PLAYERNO  NAME        INITIALS
--------  ----------  --------
      27  Cools       DD
```

Memory variables are used principally in embedded SQL. Therefore we will cover their use in Chapter 20.

6.3   System variables

A *system variable* is one which gets a value at the moment the statement using the variable is executed. System variables can have different values at different points in time. Every system variable has a data type: for example, integer, decimal or alphanumeric. The most important difference between memory and system variables is that a memory variable can have a value explicitly assigned to it and a system variable cannot. dBASE IV itself gives a system variable its value.

dBASE IV recognizes only one system variable, USER, whose data type is CHAR(8). The value of USER is the name of the user (userid) currently identified to dBASE IV. If dBASE IV is not being used with the PROTECT option, the value of USER is eight blanks.

6.4   Numeric expressions

A *numeric expression* is an arithmetic expression with either integer, decimal or floating point values.

```
<numeric expression> ::=
   <numeric literal> |
   <column identifier> |
   <memory variable> |
   <scalar function> |
   <statistical function> |
   <date expression> - <date expression>
   <numeric expression> <numeric operator>
      <numeric expression> |
   ( <numeric expression> )

<column identifier> ::=
   [ <table identifier> . ] <column name>

<scalar function> ::=
   <function name> ( [ <parameter> [ {,<parameter>}... ] ] )

<parameter> ::= <expression>

<numeric operator> ::=
   * | / | + | - | ** | ^
```

Examples:

```
Numeric expression   Value
------------------   -----
14 * 8                 112
(-16 + 43) / 3           9
5 * 4 + 2 * 10          40
18E3 + 10E4          118E3
12.6 / 6.3             2.0
```

These operators may be used in a numeric expression:

```
Operator  Meaning
--------  -------------------
*         multiply
/         divide
+         add
-         subtract
**        raise to the power
^         raise to the power
```

Numeric literals and columns with a numeric data type can be used alongside these operators. If required, brackets can be used in numeric expressions.

Before we give any examples, you should note the following points:

- The calculation of the value of a numeric expression is performed in keeping with the following priorities: (1) left to right, (2) brackets, (3) multiplication and division, (4) addition and subtraction, (5) raising to the power.

- The data type of a numeric expression is taken from the most precise data type that occurs in the expression. The floating point data type is more precise than the decimal data type which is more precise than the integer data type.)

- Column identifiers that occur in a numeric expression must have a numeric data type.

Examples (the AMOUNT column has value 25 and the memory variable XYZ has the value 4):

```
Numeric expression  Value
------------------  ------
6 + 4 * 25             106
6 + 4 * AMOUNT         106
0.6E1 + 1 * AMOUNT  106.E0
(6 + 4) * 25           250
(50 / 10) * 5           25
50 / (10 * 5)            1
25**2                  625
XYZ^3                   64
```

Incorrect numeric expressions:

```
86 + 'Jim'
((80 + 4)
4/2 (* 3)
```

Example 6.3: Find the players who have lost at least twice as many games as won for at least one team.

To answer this we need to use an expression:

```
SELECT    *
FROM      GAMES
WHERE     WON >= LOST * 2
```

Result:

```
TEAMNO  PLAYERNO  WON  LOST
------  --------  ---  ----
     1         6    9     1
     1        57    5     0
     2        27   11     2
     2       104    8     4
```

Normally, dBASE IV would calculate to 10 decimal places, but you can use the *SET PRECISION command* to alter the degree of precision. Here is an example. The result of the calculation (1/3)*3 is 0.9999999999. After

```
SET PRECISION TO 20
```

is processed, the result is 1.0000000000. By increasing the precision in the SET PRECISION command, you achieve a better result. The precision must lie between 10 and 20 inclusive.

A date expression has as its value a given day. One date expression can be subtracted from another, giving a result which is the number of days between the two dates. This number is, of course, a numeric value.

```
Numeric expression                 Value
------------------------------     -------
{12/31/88} - {12/21/88}             10
{12/31/88} - {01/01/88}             365
({12/31/88} - {01/01/00}) / 10     3250.60
```

Example 6.4: Give the numbers and dates of the penalties incurred within 200 days after 1 December 1980.

```
SELECT    PAYMENTNO, PEN_DATE
FROM      PENLTIES
WHERE     PEN_DATE - {80.12.01} < 200
```

Result:

```
PAYMENTNO  PEN_DATE
---------  --------
        1  12/08/80
        2  05/05/81
        5  12/08/80
        6  12/08/80
```

We will return to date expressions in Section 6.7 and in Section 6.9 we will cover statistical functions.

6.5 Alphanumeric expressions

Just as a numeric expression has a numeric value, an *alphanumeric expression* has an alphanumeric value. dBASE IV recognizes a single alphanumeric data type: CHAR.

```
<alphanumeric expression> ::=
   <alphanumeric literal> |
   <column identifier> |
   USER |
   <memory variable> |
   <scalar function> |
   <statistical function> |
   <alphanumeric expression> + <alphanumeric expression> |
   ( <alphanumeric expression> )

<column identifier> ::=
   [ <table identifier> . ] <column name>

<scalar function> ::=
   <function name> ( [ <parameter> [ {,<parameter>}... ] ] )

<parameter> ::= <expression>
```

Examples:

```
Alphanumeric expression  Value
-----------------------  -----------
'Jim'                    Jim
'Pete and Jim'           Pete and Jim
'1845'                   1845
TOWN                     Stratford   (for example)
USER                     PETE        (for example)
'data'+'base'            database
```

Scalar functions are dealt with in Section 6.8 .

Exercise

6.2 Determine the values of the following numeric and alphanumeric expressions:

1. $400 - (20 * 10)$
2. $(400 - 20) * 10$
3. $400 - 20 * 10$
4. $400 / 20 * 10$
5.   'Jim''s'

6.6   Logical expressions

A *logical expression*, like a logical literal, has two possible values: true or false.

```
<logical expression> ::=
   <logical literal> |
   <column identifier> |
   <memory variable>

<logical literal> ::=
   .T. | .t. | .Y. | .y. | .F. | .f. | .N. | .n.

<column identifier> ::=
   [ <table identifier> . ] <column name>
```

Examples (the CHOSEN column has the value true and the memory variable NO
the value false):

```
Logical expression  Value
------------------  -----
.T.                 true
.f.                 false
CHOSEN              true
NO                  false
```

6.7   Date expressions

The value of a *date expression* identifies a year, a month and a day. The following
applies to the examples below:

- The PEN_DATE column has the value 30 January 1988
- the scalar function DATE has the system date as its value
- the scalar function CTOD converts an alphanumeric literal to a date
- the memory variable YESTERDAY has the value 29 January 1988

```
Date expression   Value
----------------  -----------------
{08/28/88}        28 August 1988
DATE              30 January 1988
CTOD('12/25/77')  25 December 1977
DATE()            5 August 1988
YESTERDAY         29 January 1988
```

```
<date expression> ::=
   <date literal> |
   <column identifier> |
   <memory variable> |
   <scalar function> |
   <statistical function> |
   <date expression> { + | - } <numeric expression> |
   <numeric expression> + <date expression>

<date literal> ::=
   "{" <year> . <month> . <day> "}"

<column identifier> ::=
   [ <table identifier> . ] <column name>

<scalar function> ::=
   <function name> ( [ <parameter> [ {,<parameter>}... ] ] )

<parameter> ::= <expression>
```

A number can be added to or subtracted from a date expression, the result being a new date as many days later (for addition) or earlier (for subtraction) than the original date expression. In doing these calculations dBASE IV takes into consideration the different lengths of months and leap years.

```
Date expression      Value
----------------     ----------------
{08/22/88} + 4       26 August 1988
4 + {08/22/88}       26 August 1988
{12/04/88} - 5       29 November 1988
{11/04/88} - 5       30 October 1988
{11/04/88} - 366     4 November 1987
{11/04/87} - 366     3 November 1986
```

A date literal consists of three components: a year, a month and a day. The sequence in which three components must be specified depends on the SET DATE command. You can use this command to determine the order of the three components and what the separator character is. A code is used in the command to define these choices. In the table below we show the codes that dBASE IV recognizes and what presentation format they represent. In this book, unless otherwise mentioned, we assume the following SET DATE command (which is the default setting):

```
SET DATE TO AMERICAN
```

code	meaning
AMERICAN	\<month> / \<day> / \<year>
ANSI	\<year> . \<month> . \<day>
BRITISH	\<day> / \<month> / \<year>
FRENCH	\<day> / \<month> / \<year>
GERMAN	\<day> . \<month> . \<year>
ITALIAN	\<day> - \<month> - \<year>
JAPAN	\<year> / \<month> / \<day>
USA	\<month> - \<day> - \<year>
MDY	\<month> / \<day> / \<year>
DMY	\<day> / \<month> / \<year>
YMD	\<year> / \<month> / \<day>

The *SET CENTURY command* is used to specify whether the century must be given before the year. After the command

```
SET CENTURY ON
```

has been processed the year 1988 must be entered as 4 digits. You may not omit the number 19. If you *did* just enter 88, then dBASE IV assumes 0088. The SET CENTURY OFF command allows you to omit the century.

The SET DATE and SET CENTURY commands can be specified in the CONFIG.DB file like this:

```
DATE = ANSI
CENTURY = OFF
```

In the next section we discuss which scalar functions are available.

6.8   Scalar functions

Scalar functions are used to perform calculations. A scalar function has zero, one or more *parameters*. The value of a scalar function depends on the values of the parameters. Below we give an example of the SQRT function:

```
SQRT(16)
```

Explanation: SQRT is the name of the scalar function and the number 16 is the parameter. SQRT stands for *square root* so for SQRT(16) the root of the number 16 is calculated.

In Appendix C all the scalar functions are described. In this section we look at just a few examples.

Example 6.5: Give the number, name and length of the name of each player.

```
SELECT    PLAYERNO, NAME, LEN(RTRIM(NAME))
FROM      PLAYERS
```

Result:

PLAYERNO	NAME	LEN(RTRIM(NAME))
6	Parmenter	9
44	Baker	5
83	Hope	4
2	Everett	7
27	Collins	7
:	:	:

Explanation: For each player in the PLAYERS table we find the value of the scalar function LEN(...). The parameter of this function is itself a function: RTRIM. The RTRIM function removes all blanks (trailing blanks) from the end of an alphanumeric value. In this example, then, all the blanks are removed from the names before the length is calculated.

Example 6.6: Get the number and name of each player whose name has exactly seven letters.

```
SELECT    PLAYERNO, NAME
FROM      PLAYERS
WHERE     LEN(RTRIM(NAME)) = 7
```

Result:

PLAYERNO	NAME
2	Everett
27	Collins
104	Moorman
28	Collins

Explanation: From the PLAYERS table dBASE IV finds, using the LEN function, the players whose names have seven letters. Again, trailing blanks are not counted.

Example 6.7: For each penalty incurred, give the payment number, the date and the day on which the penalty was paid.

```
SELECT    PAYMENTNO, DMY(PEN_DATE), CDOW(PEN_DATE)
FROM      PENLTIES
```

Result:

```
PAYMENTNO   DMY(PEN_DATE)      CDOW(PEN_DATE)
---------   ---------------    ---------------
        1   8 December 80      Monday
        2   5 May 81           Tuesday
        3   10 September 83    Saturday
        4   8 December 84      Saturday
        5   8 December 80      Monday
        6   8 December 80      Monday
        7   30 December 82     Thursday
        8   12 November 84     Monday
```

Example 6.8: Give the initials and surname of each player resident in Stratford.

```
SELECT    RTRIM(INITIALS) + '. ' + RTRIM(NAME)
FROM      PLAYERS
WHERE     TOWN = 'Stratford'
```

Result:

```
RTRIM(INITIALS) + '. ' + RTRIM(NAME)
-------------------------------------
R. Parmenter
PK. Hope
R. Everett
GWS. Wise
M. Brown
D. Bishop
P. Parmenter
```

Explanation: First, the initials are printed, followed by a full stop and a space. Finally, the surname is printed.

Example 6.9: For each penalty, get the payment number, the amount and, with the help of a bar chart, the height of the amount. An 'X' in a bar equates with $5.

```
SELECT    PAYMENTNO, AMOUNT, REPLICATE('X', AMOUNT/5)
FROM      PENLTIES
```

Result:

```
PAYMENTNU  AMOUNT  REPLICATE('X', AMOUNT/5)
---------  ------  ------------------------
        1  100.00  XXXXXXXXXXXXXXXXXXXX
        2   75.00  XXXXXXXXXXXXXX
        3  100.00  XXXXXXXXXXXXXXXXXXXX
        4   50.00  XXXXXXXXXX
        5   25.00  XXXXX
        6   25.00  XXXXX
        7   30.00  XXXXXX
        8   75.00  XXXXXXXXXXXXXX
```

6.9   Statistical functions

Statistical functions are used like scalar functions to perform calculations. They also have parameters. The difference between statistical and scalar functions is that all statistical functions always have one parameter and that the value of that parameter consists of a *set of elements*. Scalar functions, on the other hand, can have zero, one or more parameters whose values consist of one element. SQL recognizes the following statistical functions:

function	meaning
COUNT	Counts the number of values in a column or the number of rows in a table
MIN	Determines the smallest value in a column
MAX	Determines the largest value in a column
SUM	Calculates the sum of the values in a column
AVG	Calculates the arithmetic average of the values in a column

We cover statistical functions in Chapter 9.

6.10   The clauses in the SELECT statement

In the previous sections we looked at a number of common elements. In this and the following sections we see how those common elements can be used in SELECT statements. A SELECT statement is composed of a number of clauses, as the definition below shows.

```
<select statement> ::=
   <select clause>
   <from clause>
 [ <where clause> ]
 [ <group by clause>
 [ <having clause> ] ]
 [ <order by clause> |
   <save clause> ]
```

Note: In Chapter 13 we extend this definition of the SELECT statement.
The following rules are important when you formulate SELECT statements:

- Each SELECT statement has a minimum of two clauses: the SELECT and
  the FROM clause. The other clauses, such as WHERE, GROUP BY and
  ORDER BY, are not mandatory.

- The order of the clauses is fixed; a GROUP BY clause, for example, may
  never come before a WHERE or FROM clause, and the ORDER BY
  clause (when used) is always the last.

- A HAVING clause can only be used if there is a GROUP BY clause.

- A SELECT statement may not contain an ORDER BY clause and a SAVE
  clause.

Below we give a few examples of correct SELECT statements. What follows each
different clause is, for the sake of clarity, represented as three dots.

```
SELECT   ...
FROM     ...
ORDER BY ...

SELECT   ...
FROM     ...
GROUP BY ...
HAVING   ...

SELECT   ...
FROM     ...
WHERE    ...
```

In the following two sections, we use two examples to illustrate how dBASE IV
processes SELECT statements; in other words, which steps dBASE IV executes
in order to achieve the desired result.

Exercises

6.3   What is the minimum number of clauses that must be present in a SELECT statement?

6.4   May a SELECT statement have an ORDER BY clause but no WHERE clause?

6.5   May a SELECT statement have a HAVING clause without a GROUP BY clause?

6.6   Decide what in the following SELECT statements is incorrect:

```
1.    SELECT    ...
      WHERE     ...
      ORDER BY ...

2.    SELECT    ...
      FROM      ...
      HAVING    ...
      GROUP BY ...

3.    SELECT    ...
      ORDER BY ...
      FROM      ...
      GROUP BY ...
```

6.11   Processing a SELECT statement: example 1

This section shows the steps involved when dBASE IV processes a SELECT statement. It takes the following statement as its starting point:

```
SELECT    PLAYERNO
FROM      PENLTIES
WHERE     AMOUNT > 25
GROUP BY PLAYERNO
HAVING    COUNT(*) > 1
ORDER BY PLAYERNO
```

This SELECT statement gives the answer to the question: Find the number for each player who has incurred at least one penalty of more than \$25; order the result by player number (the smallest number first).

Figure 6.1 shows the order in which dBASE IV processes the different clauses. What you will immediately notice is that dBASE IV changes the order of clauses from how the statement was entered. Be careful never to confuse the two.

Explanation: Processing each clause gives rise to an *intermediate result table* that consists of *zero or more rows* and *one or more columns*. This means that every

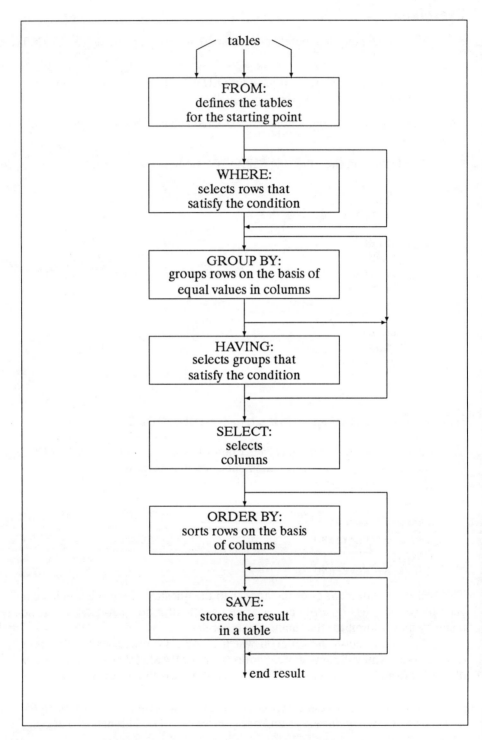

Figure 6.1: The clauses in the SELECT statement

clause, barring the first, has a table of zero or more rows and one or more columns as its input. The first clause, the FROM clause, picks out data from the database, and has as its input *one or more tables* from the database. These tables that still have to be processed by a subsequent clause are called *intermediate result tables*. You do not see these intermediate tables during the execution of a statement.

We now examine the clauses one by one.

6.11.1   The FROM clause

Only the PENLTIES table is named in the FROM clause. For dBASE IV, this means that it will work with this table. The intermediate result from this clause is an exact copy of the PENLTIES table:

Intermediate result:

PAYMENTNO	PLAYERNO	PEN_DATE	AMOUNT
1	6	12/08/80	100.00
2	44	05/05/81	75.00
3	27	09/10/83	100.00
4	104	12/08/84	50.00
5	44	12/08/80	25.00
6	8	12/08/80	25.00
7	44	12/30/82	30.00
8	27	11/12/84	75.00

6.11.2   The WHERE clause

The WHERE clause specifies AMOUNT > 25 as a condition. All rows where the value in the AMOUNT column is more than 25 satisfy the condition. Therefore, the rows with payment numbers of 5 and 6 are discarded, while the remaining rows form the intermediate result table from the WHERE clause:

PAYMENTNO	PLAYERNO	PEN_DATE	AMOUNT
1	6	12/08/80	100.00
2	44	05/05/81	75.00
3	27	09/10/83	100.00
4	104	12/08/84	50.00
7	44	12/30/82	30.00
8	27	11/12/84	75.00

6.11.3   The GROUP BY clause

The GROUP BY clause groups the rows in the intermediate result table. dBASE IV divides the data into groups on the basis of the values in the PLAYERNO column (GROUP BY PLAYERNO). Rows are grouped together if, in the grouping column, they contain the same values. The rows with PAYMENTNOs of 2 and 7, for example, form one group, because the PLAYERNO column has the value of 44 in both rows.

Intermediate result

```
PAYMENTNO   PLAYERNO   PEN_DATE                AMOUNT
---------   --------   --------------------    --------------
1                  6   12/08/80                100.00
2, 7              44   05/05/81, 12/30/82      75.00, 30.00
3, 8              27   09/10/83, 11/12/84      100.00, 75.00
4                104   12/08/84                50.00
```

Explanation: Thus, for all but the PLAYERNO column there can be more than one value in a row. The PAYMENTNO column, for example, contains two values in the second and third rows. This is not as strange as it might seem, because the data is grouped and each row is actually formed from a group of rows. It is only in the PLAYERNO column that a single value for each row of the intermediate table may be found, since this is the column by which the result is grouped.

6.11.4   The HAVING clause

In some ways you could compare this fourth clause with the WHERE clause. The difference is that the WHERE clause acts on the intermediate table from the FROM clause and the HAVING clause on the grouped intermediate result table of the GROUP BY clause. In fact, the effect is the same; when you include a HAVING clause dBASE IV also selects rows by referring to a condition. In this case the condition is:

```
COUNT(*) > 1
```

This condition is satisfied in all rows (groups) where more than one penalty exists. Chapter 10 looks at this condition in detail.

Intermediate result:

```
PAYMENTNO   PLAYERNO   PEN_DATE                AMOUNT
---------   --------   --------------------    --------------
2, 7              44   05/05/81, 12/30/82      75.00, 30.00
3, 8              27   09/10/83, 11/12/84      100.00, 75.00
```

6.11.5   The SELECT clause

The SELECT clause specifies which columns must be presented for the final result table. In other words, the SELECT clause selects columns.

Intermediate result:

```
PLAYERNO
--------
      44
      27
```

6.11.6 The ORDER BY clause

This last clause has no impact on the contents of the intermediate result table, but sorts the final remaining rows. In this example the data is sorted on PLAYERNO.
The end result is:

```
PLAYERNO
--------
      27
      44
```

6.11.7 The SAVE clause

There is no SAVE clause, in this example, so the result is not stored.

Before we continue, there are a few points to note. First, dBASE IV does not show the user any of the intermediate result tables; it is presented as a single, large process, and the only table the end user gets to see is the end result table. Second, dBASE IV does not actually process the statements in the way which is described here. In practice, dBASE IV processes as many clauses as possible simultaneously, in order to speed up the execution of the statement. Chapter 16 examines how dBASE IV actually processes the statements. The method of processing described above, though, is extremely well suited if you want to determine the end result of a SELECT statement 'by hand'.

6.12 Processing a SELECT statement: example 2

Here is another example of SELECT statement processing.

Example 6.10: Get the player number and the league number of each player resident in Stratford; order the result by league number.

```
SELECT     PLAYERNO, LEAGUENO
FROM       PLAYERS
WHERE      TOWN = 'Stratford'
ORDER BY LEAGUENO
SAVE TO  TEMP NEW
```

6.12.1 The FROM clause

Intermediate result:

```
PLAYERNO  NAME              ...  LEAGUENO
--------  ----------------  ---  --------
       6  Parmenter         ...  8467
      44  Baker             ...  1124
      83  Hope              ...  1608
       2  Everett           ...  2411
      27  Collins           ...  2513
     104  Moorman           ...  7060
       7  Wise              ...
      57  Brown             ...  6409
      39  Bishop            ...
     112  Bailey            ...  1319
       8  Newcastle         ...  2983
     100  Parmenter         ...  6524
      28  Collins           ...
      95  Miller            ...
```

6.12.2 The WHERE clause

Intermediate result:

```
PLAYERNO  NAME              ...  LEAGUENO
--------  ----------------  ---  --------
       6  Parmenter         ...  8467
      83  Hope              ...  1608
       2  Everett           ...  2411
       7  Wise              ...
      57  Brown             ...  6409
      39  Bishop            ...
     100  Parmenter         ...  6524
```

6.12.3 The GROUP BY clause

There is no GROUP BY clause, therefore the intermediate result remains unchanged.

6.12.4 The HAVING clause

There is no HAVING clause, therefore the intermediate result remains unchanged.

6.12.5 The SELECT clause

In the SELECT clause the PLAYERNO and LEAGUENO columns are noted and this gives the following intermediate result table:

```
PLAYERNO   LEAGUENO
--------   --------
       6   8467
      83   1608
       2   2411
       7
      57   6409
      39
     100   6524
```

6.12.6 The ORDER BY clause

Intermediate result:

```
PLAYERNO   LEAGUENO
--------   --------
       7
      39
      83   1608
       2   2411
      57   6409
     100   6524
       6   8467
```

6.12.7 The SAVE clause

The result is saved in a table called NEW that is created first by dBASE IV. This table creation process does not appear on the screen, but is implicitly included in the SAVE statement. You can now query the NEW table.

```
SELECT    *
FROM      NEW
```

Result:

```
PLAYERNO   LEAGUENO
--------   --------
       7
      39
      83   1608
       2   2411
      57   6409
     100   6524
       6   8467
```

In the following chapters the different clauses will be discussed in greater depth.

Exercise

6.7 Take the following SELECT statement and calculate the intermediate result table after each clause has been processed. Give the final result as well.

```
SELECT    PLAYERNO
FROM      PENLTIES
WHERE     PEN_DATE > {12/08/80}
GROUP BY  PLAYERNO
HAVING    COUNT(*) > 1
ORDER BY  PLAYERNO
```

6.13   The layout of the result

dBASE IV creates a standard layout for the results of SELECT statements. First,
the column names are printed, followed by the rows. In this way, there is a standard method of presentation for each data type. You can use various SET commands to adapt the layout. This section tells you what these commands are.

```
<set command> ::=
   SET HEADING { ON | OFF } |
   SET PAUSE { ON | OFF } |
   SET POINT TO <character> |
   SET SEPARATOR TO <character> |
   SET DECIMALS TO <integer> |
   SET DATE TO <date code>
```

The *SET HEADING command* enables you to suppress column headings. The
default is to have them printed.

   The *SET PAUSE command* causes dBASE IV to pause temporarily when
presenting the result if the screen display is full. If a random key is pressed,
dBASE IV continues with the presentation on a new screen.

   The *SET POINT command* defines which character is to be used as a decimal point. The dBASE IV default is a full stop. The character may be any character apart from a digit or a blank.

   The *SET SEPARATOR command* defines how thousands are separated,
the default being the comma.

   The *SET DECIMALS command* is used to define the maximum number
of decimal places to be shown. The default is two decimal places. The range of
possibilities lies between 0 and 18 inclusive.

   The *SET DATE command* is used to define how dates should be presented.
We refer you to Section 6.7 for more information about this.

   All these options can also be specified in the CONFIG.DB file.

7

SELECT statement: the FROM clause

In this second chapter about the SELECT statement we describe the FROM clause which is used to specify which table or tables are to be queried.

```
<from clause> ::=
    FROM <table reference> [ {,<table reference> }... ]

<table reference> ::=
    <table identifier> [ <pseudonym> ]

<table identifier> ::= <table name>
```

7.1   Table identifiers in the FROM clause

We have already seen many examples of the FROM clause in the previous chapters. This is the clause where we name the tables from which we want to see data. We refer then to a *table identifier*.

In place of a table name you can also specify a view name or a synonym. In this case we also speak of a table identifier.

7.2   The column identifier

Before a column name (in the SELECT clause, for example) you may also specify the name of the table to which the column belongs. We call that *qualification* of a column. In fact, each reference to a column consists of two parts:

```
<table identifier> . <column name>
```

The second part is, of course, the column name itself, such as PLAYERNO or NAME. This is the only part that must always be used. The first part is the table name, for example, PLAYERS or TEAMS. Together these two components form the *column identifier* You don't have to specify both parts, but it is not wrong to do so.

Example 7.1: Find the number of each team. Here are two possible solutions.

```
SELECT    TEAMNO
FROM      TEAMS

SELECT    TEAMS.TEAMNO
FROM      TEAMS
```

7.3   Multiple table identifiers

Up until now we have used only one table identifier in the FROM clause. If we want to present data in our result table from different tables, then these must all be named in the FROM clause.

Example 7.2: Find the team number and name of the captain of each team.
    The TEAMS table holds information about team numbers and the player numbers of the respective captains. However, the names of the captains are not stored in the TEAMS table, but in the PLAYERS table. In other words, we need both tables. Both must be mentioned in the FROM clause.

```
SELECT   TEAMNO, NAME
FROM     TEAMS, PLAYERS
WHERE    TEAMS.PLAYERNO = PLAYERS.PLAYERNO
```

The intermediate result from the FROM clause:

TEAMNO	PLAYERNO	DIVISION	PLAYERNO	NAME	...
1	6	first	6	Parmenter	...
1	6	first	44	Baker	...
1	6	first	83	Hope	...
1	6	first	2	Everett	...
1	6	first	27	Collins	...
1	6	first	104	Moorman	...
1	6	first	7	Wise	...
1	6	first	57	Brown	...
1	6	first	39	Bishop	...
1	6	first	112	Bailey	...
1	6	first	8	Newcastle	...
1	6	first	100	Parmenter	...
1	6	first	28	Collins	...
1	6	first	95	Miller	...
2	27	second	6	Parmenter	...
2	27	second	44	Baker	...
2	27	second	83	Hope	...
2	27	second	2	Everett	...
2	27	second	27	Collins	...
2	27	second	104	Moorman	...
2	27	second	7	Wise	...
2	27	second	57	Brown	...
2	27	second	39	Bishop	...
2	27	second	112	Bailey	...
2	27	second	8	Newcastle	...
2	27	second	100	Parmenter	...
2	27	second	28	Collins	...
2	27	second	95	Miller	...

Explanation: Each row from the TEAMS table is lined beside each row from the PLAYERS table. This results in a table in which the total number of columns equals the number of columns in one table *plus* the number of columns in the other table, and in which the total number of rows equals the number of rows in one table *multiplied* by the number of rows in the other table. We call this result the *Cartesian product* of the tables concerned.

In the WHERE clause each row is now selected where the values in the TEAMS.PLAYERNO column equal those in the PLAYERS.PLAYERNO column:

TEAMNO	PLAYERNO	DIVISION	PLAYERNO	NAME	...
1	6	first	6	Parmenter	...
2	27	second	27	Collins	...

End result:

```
TEAMNO  NAME
------  ---------
     1  Parmenter
     2  Collins
```

In this example, it is essential to identify the table name before the PLAYERNO column, otherwise it would be unclear to dBASE IV which PLAYERNO column was intended.

Conclusion: If, in the FROM clause, you use a column name that appears in more than one table, it is *mandatory* to include a table identifier with the column identifier.

Example 7.3: For each penalty, find the payment number, the amount of the penalty, the name and initials of the player who incurred the penalty.

The payment numbers, amounts and player numbers are held in the PENLTIES table, while names and initials are found in the PLAYERS table. Both tables must be mentioned in the FROM clause:

```
SELECT   PAYMENTNO, AMOUNT, PENLTIES.PLAYERNO,
         NAME, INITIALS
FROM     PENLTIES, PLAYERS
WHERE    PENLTIES.PLAYERNO = PLAYERS.PLAYERNO
```

Intermediate result from the FROM clause:

```
PAYMENTNO PLAYERNO AMOUNT ... PLAYERNO NAME       INITIALS ...
--------- -------- ------ --- -------- ---------- -------- ---
        1        6 100.00 ...        6 Parmenter  R         ...
        1        6 100.00 ...       44 Baker      E         ...
        1        6 100.00 ...       83 Hope       PK        ...
        1        6 100.00 ...        2 Everett    R         ...
        :        :      :           : :          :
        2       44  75.00 ...        6 Parmenter  R         ...
        2       44  75.00 ...       44 Baker      E         ...
        2       44  75.00 ...       83 Hope       PK        ...
        2       44  75.00 ...        2 Everett    R         ...
        :        :      :           : :          :
        3       27 100.00 ...        6 Parmenter  R         ...
        3       27 100.00 ...       44 Baker      E         ...
        3       27 100.00 ...       83 Hope       PK        ...
        3       27 100.00 ...        2 Everett    R         ...
        :        :      :           : :          :
        :        :      :           : :          :
```

Intermediate result from the WHERE clause:

```
PAYMENTNO PLAYERNO AMOUNT ... PLAYERNO NAME       INITIALS  ...
--------- -------- ------ --- -------- --------- --------   ---
        1        6 100.00 ...        6 Parmenter R          ...
        2       44  75.00 ...       44 Baker     E          ...
        3       27 100.00 ...       27 Collins   DD         ...
        4      104  50.00 ...      104 Moorman   D          ...
        5       44  25.00 ...       44 Baker     E          ...
        6        8  25.00 ...        8 Newcastle B          ...
        7       44  30.00 ...       44 Baker     E          ...
        8       27  75.00 ...       27 Collins   DD         ...
```

End result:

```
    PAYMENTNO  PLAYERNO  AMOUNT  NAME       INITIALS
    ---------  --------  ------  ---------  --------
            1         6  100.00  Parmenter  R
            2        44   75.00  Baker      E
            3        27  100.00  Collins    DD
            4       104   50.00  Moorman    D
            5        44   25.00  Baker      E
            6         8   25.00  Newcastle  B
            7        44   30.00  Baker      E
            8        27   75.00  Collins    DD
```

To avoid ambiguity the table name must be specified before the PLAYERNO column in the SELECT clause.

7.4   The pseudonym

In cases where multiple table identifiers appear in the FROM clause, it is some-times easier to use *pseudonyms*. Another name for a pseudonym is *alias*. Pseud-onyms are temporary, alternative names for table names. In the second example from the previous section we repeated the table name in its entirety. In place of table names we can also use synonyms as this next example shows.

```
SELECT   PAYMENTNO, AMOUNT, PN.PLAYERNO, NAME, INITIALS
FROM     PENLTIES PN, PLAYERS P
WHERE    PN.PLAYERNO = P.PLAYERNO
```

In fact, in this example a pseudonym is not vital, but we will be formulating SE-LECT statements in this book where the table name is repeated many times, and then the value of pseudonyms becomes more obvious. Pseudonyms make for eas-ier formulation of statements and, at the same time, give a more convenient, clear structure to a statement.

A pseudonym can be up to eight characters long, can include only letters, digits and the underscore character and must begin with a letter. Two pseudonyms in the same statement may not, of course, have the same name. If you give a pseudonym a one-letter name, then the letters A to J may not be used.

7.5   Various examples

This section looks at a few examples illustrating various aspects of the FROM clause.

Example 7.4: Get numbers of the captains who have incurred at least one penalty.

```
SELECT    T.PLAYERNO
FROM      TEAMS T, PENLTIES PN
WHERE     T.PLAYERNO = PN.PLAYERNO
```

Explanation: The TEAMS table includes all the players who are captains. By using the player numbers we can look up in the PENLTIES table whether a particular captin has incurred a penalty. For that reason, both tables are included in the FROM clause. The intermediate result from the FROM clause becomes:

TEAMNO	PLAYERNO	DIVISION	PAYMENTNO	PLAYERNO	...
1	6	first	1	6	...
1	6	first	2	44	...
1	6	first	3	27	...
1	6	first	4	104	...
1	6	first	5	44	...
1	6	first	6	8	...
1	6	first	7	44	...
1	6	first	8	27	...
2	27	second	1	6	...
2	27	second	2	44	...
2	27	second	3	27	...
2	27	second	4	104	...
2	27	second	5	44	...
2	27	second	6	8	...
2	27	second	7	44	...
2	27	second	8	27	...

Intermediate result from the WHERE clause:

TEAMNO	PLAYERNO	DIVISION	PAYMENTNO	PLAYERNO	...
1	6	first	1	6	...
2	27	second	3	27	...
2	27	second	8	27	...

End result:

PLAYERNO
6
27
27

Note: dBASE IV does not automatically remove duplicate values from the end result. In our example, then, player 27 appears twice because he incurred two penalties. If you don't want duplicate values in your result, then you need to use the word DISTINCT directly after the SELECT (we go into more detail in Chapter 9).

```
SELECT    DISTINCT T.PLAYERNO
FROM      TEAMS T, PENLTIES PN
WHERE     T.PLAYERNO = PN.PLAYERNO
```

End result:

PLAYERNO
6
27

Example 7.5: Give the names and initials of the players who have played at least one match. Watch out, a competition player does not have to appear in the GAMES table (perhaps if he or she has been injured for the whole season).

```
SELECT    DISTINCT P.NAME, P.INITIALS
FROM      PLAYERS P, GAMES GAM
WHERE     P.PLAYERNO = GAM.PLAYERNO
```

Result:

```
NAME        INITIALS
---------   --------
Parmenter   R
Baker       E
Hope        PK
Everett     R
Collins     DD
Moorman     D
Brown       M
Bailey      IP
Newcastle   B
```

Work out for yourself how this SELECT statement could give rise to duplicate values if DISTINCT were not used.

Example 7.6: For each row in the GAMES table, give the player number, the team number, the name of the player and the division in which the team plays.

```
SELECT   GAM.PLAYERNO, GAM.TEAMNO , P.NAME, T.DIVISION
FROM     GAMES GAM, PLAYERS P, TEAMS T
WHERE    GAM.PLAYERNO = P.PLAYERNO
AND      GAM.TEAMNO   = T.TEAMNO
```

Result:

```
PLAYERNO   TEAMNO   NAME        DIVISION
--------   ------   ---------   --------
       6        1   Parmenter   first
      44        1   Baker       first
      83        1   Hope        first
       2        1   Everett     first
      57        1   Brown       first
       8        1   Newcastle   first
      27        2   Collins     second
     104        2   Moorman     second
     112        2   Bailey      second
       8        2   Newcastle   second
```

The sequence of the table identifiers in a FROM clause naturally has no influence on the result the clause produces or on the end result of the statement. The SELECT clause is the only clause where you can define the order of presentation of the columns. The ORDER BY clause defines the order of the values in the rows. Therefore, the next two statements are equivalent:

```
SELECT   PLAYERS.PLAYERNO
FROM     PLAYERS, TEAMS
WHERE    PLAYERS.PLAYERNO = TEAMS.PLAYERNO
```

and

```
SELECT    PLAYERS.PLAYERNO
FROM      TEAMS, PLAYERS
WHERE     PLAYERS.PLAYERNO = TEAMS.PLAYERNO
```

7.6   Mandatory use of pseudonyms

In some SELECT statements there is no choice about whether a pseudonym is to be used or not. This situation arises when the same table is mentioned more than once in the FROM clause. Consider this example.

Example 7.7: Get the numbers of the players who are older than R. Parmenter.

```
SELECT    Q.PLAYERNO
FROM      PLAYERS Q, PLAYERS P
WHERE     P.NAME = 'Parmenter'
AND       P.INITIALS = 'R'
AND       Q.BIRTH < P.BIRTH
```

The intermediate result from the WHERE clause is a multiplication of the PLAYERS table by itself (for simplicity we have shown only the rows from the P.PLAYERS table in which player 6 is found: R. Parmenter):

PLAYERNO	...	BIRTH	...	PLAYERNO	...	BIRTH	...
6	...	1964	...	6	...	1964	...
44	...	1963	...	6	...	1964	...
83	...	1956	...	6	...	1964	...
2	...	1948	...	6	...	1964	...
27	...	1964	...	6	...	1964	...
104	...	1970	...	6	...	1964	...
7	...	1963	...	6	...	1964	...
57	...	1971	...	6	...	1964	...
39	...	1956	...	6	...	1964	...
112	...	1963	...	6	...	1964	...
8	...	1962	...	6	...	1964	...
100	...	1963	...	6	...	1964	...
28	...	1963	...	6	...	1964	...
95	...	1934	...	6	...	1964	...
:	:	:	:	:	:	:	:
:	:	:	:	:	:	:	:

The intermediate result from the WHERE clause is:

```
PLAYERNO   ...   BIRTH   ...   PLAYERNO   ...   BIRTH   ...
--------   ---   -----   ---   --------   ---   -----   ---
      44   ...   1963    ...          6   ...   1964    ...
      83   ...   1956    ...          6   ...   1964    ...
       2   ...   1948    ...          6   ...   1964    ...
       7   ...   1963    ...          6   ...   1964    ...
      39   ...   1956    ...          6   ...   1964    ...
     112   ...   1963    ...          6   ...   1964    ...
       8   ...   1962    ...          6   ...   1964    ...
     100   ...   1963    ...          6   ...   1964    ...
      28   ...   1963    ...          6   ...   1964    ...
      95   ...   1934    ...          6   ...   1964    ...
```

The end result is:

```
PLAYERNO
--------
      44
      83
       2
       7
      39
     112
       8
     100
      28
      95
```

In the previous examples the table name was specified before the column name in order to uniquely identify the column. In the example immediately above, this does not help because both tables have the same name. In other words, if a FROM clause refers to two tables with the same name, pseudonyms must be used.

Note: It would have been sufficient to give only one of the tables a pseudonym in that example.

```
SELECT    P.PLAYERNO
FROM      PLAYERS P, PLAYERS
WHERE     PLAYERS.NAME = 'Parmenter'
AND       PLAYERS.INITIALS = 'R'
AND       P.BIRTH < PLAYERS.BIRTH
```

Exercises

7.1   Say why the SELECT statements below are not correctly formulated.

```
1.    SELECT   PLAYERNO
      FROM     PLAYERS, TEAMS

2.    SELECT   PLAYERS.PLAYERNO
      FROM     TEAMS
```

7.2   For each clause of the following statement, determine the intermediate result and the end result. Also give a description of the question which underlies the statement.

```
SELECT   PLAYERS.NAME
FROM     TEAMS, PLAYERS
WHERE    PLAYERS.PLAYERNO = TEAMS.PLAYERNO
```

7.3   For each penalty, find the payment number, the amount, and the number and name of the player who incurred it.

7.4   For each penalty incurred by a team captain, find the payment number and the captain's name.

7.5   Give the numbers and names of the players who live in the same town as player 27.

7.6   Give the number and name of every competition player, as well as the number and name of the captain of each team for whom that player has competed; the result may *not* contain competition players who are themselves captains. Desired result:

PLAYERNO	NAME (PLAYERS)	PLAYERNO	NAME (CAPTAIN)
44	Baker	6	Parmenter
8	Newcastle	6	Parmenter
8	Newcastle	27	Collins
:	:	:	:
:	:	:	:

8

SELECT statement: the WHERE clause

In the WHERE clause, the rows which must be provided for the final result are defined by a condition or series of conditions.

How, then, is a WHERE clause processed? dBASE IV looks at all the rows individually which appear in the intermediate result table of a FROM clause. If, for a particular row, the condition is true, the row concerned is passed to the intermediate result table for the WHERE clause. This process can be formally described in the following way:

```
WHERE-RESULT := [] ;
FOR EACH R IN FROM-RESULT DO
    IF CONDITION = TRUE THEN
        WHERE-RESULT :+ R;
OD;
```

Explanation: The WHERE-RESULT and the FROM-RESULT represent two sets in which rows of data can be temporarily stored. R represents a row from a set. The symbol [] represents the empty set. A row is added to the set with the operator :+. This notation method is also used later in the book.

In the previous chapters you have seen many examples of possible conditions in the WHERE clause. In this chapter the following forms of it are described:

- the simple comparison
- logical expression
- conditions coupled with AND, OR and NOT
- the BETWEEN operator
- the IN operator

```
<condition> ::=
   <boolean term> |
   <condition> OR <boolean term>

<boolean term> ::=
   <boolean factor> |
   <boolean term> AND <boolean factor>

<boolean factor> ::=
   <predicate> |
   ( <condition> )

<predicate> ::=
   NOT <predicate>                                        |
   <expression> <comparison operator> <expression>       |
   <expression> <comparison operator> <subquery>         |
   <logical expression>                                  |
   <expression> [ NOT ] BETWEEN <expression>
      AND <expression>                                   |
   <expression> [ NOT ] IN ( <expression>
      [ {,<expression>}... ] )                           |
   <expression> [ NOT ] IN <subquery>                    |
   <column identifier> [ NOT ] LIKE
      { <mask> | <memory variable> }                     |
   <expression> <comparison operator> ALL <subquery>  |
   <expression> <comparison operator> ANY <subquery>  |
   <expression> <comparison operator> SOME <subquery> |
   EXISTS <subquery>

<expression> ::=
   <numeric expression> |
   <alphanumeric expression> |
   <logical expression> |
   <date expression>

<comparison operator> ::=
   = | < | > | <= | >= | <> | !< | !> | != | #
```

- the LIKE operator
- the IN operator with subquery
- the comparison operator with subquery
- the ANY and ALL operators
- the EXISTS operator

General rule: Statistical functions are not permitted in the condition of a WHERE clause!

8.1 The simple comparison

A simple comparison is formed by an expression (for example 83 or 15 * 100), followed by a *comparison operator* (for example < or =) and then another expression. The value on the left of the operator is compared with the expression on the right. The true or false condition is dependent on the operator. dBASE IV recognizes the following comparison operators:

comparison operator	meaning
=	equal to
<	less than
>	greater than
!<	not less than
!>	not greater than
<=	less than or equal to
>=	greater than or equal to
<> or != or #	not equal to

Example 8.1: Get the player numbers which have a league number of 7060

```
SELECT    PLAYERNO
FROM      PLAYERS
WHERE     LEAGUENO = '7060'
```
Result:

```
PLAYERNO
--------
     104
```

Explanation: The PLAYERNO is not printed for any row where the LEAGUENO does not equal 7060; in other words, where the condition LEAGUENO = '7060' is not true.

Example 8.2: Give the number, the year of birth and the year of joining the club for each player who joined precisely 17 years after he or she was born.

```
SELECT    PLAYERNO, BIRTH, JOINED
FROM      PLAYERS
WHERE     BIRTH + 17 = JOINED
```
Result:

```
PLAYERNO  BIRTH  JOINED
--------  -----  ------
      44   1963    1980
```

The condition in this statement could be expressed in other ways:

```
WHERE BIRTH = JOINED - 17
WHERE BIRTH - JOINED + 17 = 0
```

Both expressions in a comparison must have the same data type; a numeric value may not be compared with an alphanumeric value. Therefore, the following SELECT statement is not acceptable:

```
SELECT    *
FROM      PLAYERS
WHERE     NAME = 24
```

When comparing alphanumeric values, one expression is less than another if it comes first in alphabetical order. Examples:

```
Condition              Value
------------------     -----
'Jim' < 'Pete'         TRUE
'Truck' >= 'Trees'     TRUE
'Jim' = 'JIM'          FALSE
```

Whether two alphanumeric values equal one another is, in part, dependent on the SET EXACT command. When the SET EXACT command is set to ON, two alphanumeric values are equal if they are the same length and if all individual characters in equal ordinal positions are the same. Examples:

```
Condition              Value
------------------     -----
'Jan' = 'Jan'          TRUE
'Ja'  = 'Jan'          FALSE
'Jan' = 'Ja'           FALSE
```

When EXACT is set to OFF, the two alphanumeric values are equal when all characters in the alphanumeric value to the right of the equals sign are the same as characters from the left hand alphanumeric value whose ordinal position is the same.

```
Condition              Value
------------------     -----
'Jan' = 'Jan'          TRUE
'Ja'  = 'Jan'          FALSE
'Jan' = 'Ja'           TRUE
```

You can define the status of the EXACT switch in the CONFIG.DB file with the following command:

```
EXACT = ON
```

One date is less than another if it comes before the other in time. Examples:

```
Condition                 Value
-----------------------   -----
{85.12.08} < {85.12.09}   TRUE
{80.05.02} > {79.12.31}   TRUE
```

Note: In cases where the expressions left and right of the comparison operator have a LOGICAL data type, only the = and <> operators can be used.

Exercises

8.1 Find the number of each player born after 1960 (give at least two possible SELECT statements).

8.2 Get the number of each team whose captain is someone other than player 27.

8.3 Get the number of each player who has won more games than lost in at least one team.

8.4 Find the number of each player who has played a total of ten matches for at least one team

8.2 The logical expression as a condition

The simplest form of a condition is the *logical expression*. Suppose that the PLAYERS table has a column called CHOSEN. This column is defined with a data type of LOGICAL and says whether a player is medically fit or not. The following statement allows us to find out which players are already fit to play. Notice the condition in the WHERE clause.

```
SELECT    *
FROM      PLAYERS
WHERE     CHOSEN
```

If the value of the CHOSEN column equals *true*, that row is included in the result. The following condition, though more complex, is correct as well:

```
SELECT    *
FROM      PLAYERS
WHERE     CHOSEN = .T.
```

The condition NOT CHOSEN is used to find all players who are still *not* fit.

8.3 Multiple conditions with AND, OR and NOT

A WHERE clause may contain multiple conditions if the *AND, OR* and *NOT* operators are used.

Example 8.3: Get the number, name, sex and year of birth of each male player born after 1970.

```
SELECT    PLAYERNO, NAME, SEX, BIRTH
FROM      PLAYERS
WHERE     SEX = 'M'
AND       BIRTH > 1970
```

Result:

```
PLAYERNO  NAME   SEX  BIRTH
--------  -----  ---  -----
      57  Brown  M     1971
```

Explanation: For every person in the PLAYERS table where the value in the SEX column equals M and the value in the BIRTH column is greater than 1970, dBASE IV returns three columns to the result table.

Example 8.4: Get the numbers, names and places of residence of all players who live in Plymouth or Eltham.

```
SELECT    PLAYERNO, NAME, TOWN
FROM      PLAYERS
WHERE     PLACE = 'Plymouth'
OR        PLACE = 'Eltham'
```

Result:

```
PLAYERNO  NAME     TOWN
--------  -------  --------
      27  Collins  Eltham
     104  Moorman  Eltham
     112  Bailey   Plymouth
```

Note: This SELECT statement would return an *empty result table* if OR were replaced by AND. The reason is obvious. When a WHERE clause contains more than one AND or OR operator, the evaluation of the condition takes place from left to right. So in the WHERE clause (assume C1 to C4 represent conditions):

```
WHERE C1 AND C2 OR C3 AND C4
```

C1 AND C2 are evaluated first. Suppose that the result of this is A1; at this point A1 OR C3 is evaluated, giving a result of A2. The final result is the value of A2 AND C4. The process can also be represented in this way:

```
C1 AND C2 --> A1
A1 OR  C3 --> A2
A2 AND C4 --> result
```

By using brackets you can influence the order in which the conditions are evaluated. Consider the following WHERE clause:

```
WHERE (C1 AND C2) OR (C3 AND C4)
```

The processing sequence now becomes:

```
C1 AND C2 --> A1
C3 AND C4 --> A2
A1 OR  A2 --> result
```

With any given value for C1, C2, C3 and C4 the results of the first and second examples are unlikely to be the same. Suppose, for example, that C1, C2 and C3 are true and that C4 is false. The result of the first example is false and of the second true.

A NOT operator can be specified before each condition. The NOT operator changes the value of a condition to true if it is false and false if it is true.

Example 8.5: Find the numbers, names and towns of players who *do not* live in Stratford.

```
SELECT    PLAYERNO, NAME, TOWN
FROM      PLAYERS
WHERE     TOWN <> 'Stratford'
```

Result:

```
PLAYERNO  NAME        TOWN
--------  ---------   ----------
      44  Baker       Inglewood
      27  Collins     Eltham
     104  Moorman     Eltham
     112  Bailey      Plymouth
       8  Newcastle   Inglewood
      28  Collins     Midhurst
      95  Miller      Douglas
```

This query can be formulated in another way:

```
SELECT    PLAYERNO, NAME, TOWN
FROM      PLAYERS
WHERE     NOT TOWN = 'Stratford'
```

Explanation: The rows where the condition TOWN = 'Stratford' is true are not returned. The reason is that the NOT operator has switched the truth of the condition.

Example 8.6: Give the number, town and year of birth of each player who lives in Stratford, or was born in 1963, but do not include those who were born in Stratford and born in 1963.

```
SELECT    PLAYERNO, TOWN, BIRTH
FROM      PLAYERS
WHERE     (TOWN = 'Stratford'
OR        BIRTH = 1963)
AND NOT (TOWN = 'Stratford'
AND       BIRTH = 1963)
```

Result:

```
PLAYERNO  TOWN        BIRTH
--------  ----------  --------
       6  Stratford      1964
      44  Inglewood      1963
      83  Stratford      1956
       2  Stratford      1948
      57  Stratford      1971
      39  Stratford      1956
     112  Plymouth       1963
      28  Midhurst       1963
```

The *truth table* below contains all possible values with AND, OR and NOT for two conditions A and B

A	B	A AND B	A OR B	NOT A
TRUE	TRUE	TRUE	TRUE	FALSE
TRUE	FALSE	FALSE	TRUE	FALSE
FALSE	TRUE	FALSE	TRUE	TRUE
FALSE	FALSE	FALSE	FALSE	TRUE

Exercises

8.5 Give the name and town of each female player who is *not* a resident of Stratford.

8.6 Find the player numbers of those who joined the club between 1970 and 1980.

8.7 Find the numbers, names and years of birth of players born in a leap year. Just in case you need a reminder, a leap year is one in which the year figure is divisible by four, except with centuries the year figure must be divisible by 400. Therefore, 1900 was not a leap year, while 2000 will be.

8.8 For each competition player born after 1965 who has won at least one match, give his or her name and initials, and the divisions of the teams in which the player has ever played.

8.4   The BETWEEN operator

SQL recognizes a special operator which allows you to determine whether a value occurs within a given range of values.

Example 8.7: Find the number and year of birth of each player born between 1962 and 1964.

```
SELECT    PLAYERNO, BIRTH
FROM      PLAYERS
WHERE     BIRTH >= 1962
AND       BIRTH <= 1964
```

Result:

```
PLAYERNO  BIRTH
--------  -----
       6   1964
      44   1963
      27   1964
       7   1963
     112   1963
       8   1962
     100   1963
      28   1963
      95   1963
```

This statement can also be written using the *BETWEEN operator* and the result stays the same:

```
SELECT    PLAYERNO, BIRTH
FROM      PLAYERS
WHERE     BIRTH BETWEEN 1962 AND 1964
```

If E2 and E3 are expressions, then:

```
E1 BETWEEN E2 AND E3
```

is equivalent to:

```
(E1 >= E2) AND (E1 <= E3)
```

At the same time it follows that:

```
E1 NOT BETWEEN E2 AND E3
```

is equivalent to:

```
NOT (E1 BETWEEN E2 AND E3)
```

and equivalent to:

```
(E1 < E2) OR (E1 > E3)
```

Note: BETWEEN can be used with all data types, except LOGICAL.

Exercises

8.9 Get the payment number of each penalty between $50 and $100.

8.10 Get the payment number of each penalty which is *not* between $50 and $100.

8.5   The IN operator

Conditions can sometimes become rather cumbersome if you have to determine whether a value in a column appears in a given set of values which could be very large. Here is an illustration of this.

Example 8.8: Find the number, name and town of each player who lives in Inglewood, Plymouth, Midhurst or Douglas.

```
SELECT    PLAYERNO, NAME, TOWN
FROM      PLAYERS
WHERE     TOWN = 'Inglewood'
OR        TOWN = 'Plymouth'
OR        TOWN = 'Midhurst'
OR        TOWN = 'Douglas'
```

Result:

```
PLAYERNO  NAME        TOWN
--------  ---------   ---------
      44  Baker       Inglewood
     112  Bailey      Plymouth
       8  Newcastle   Inglewood
      28  Collins     Midhurst
      95  Miller      Douglas
```

The statement and the result are correct, of course, but the statement is rather long-winded. The *IN operator* can be used to simplify the statement:

```
SELECT    PLAYERNO, NAME, TOWN
FROM      PLAYERS
WHERE     TOWN IN ('Inglewood', 'Plymouth', 'Midhurst',
          'Douglas')
```

This condition is read as follows: Each row whose TOWN value occurs in the set of four place names satisfies the condition.

Example 8.9: Get the numbers and years of birth of the players born in 1962, 1963 or 1970.

```
SELECT    PLAYERNO, BIRTH
FROM      PLAYERS
WHERE     BIRTH IN (1962, 1963, 1970)
```

Result:

```
PLAYERNO  BIRTH
--------  -----
      44   1963
     104   1970
       7   1963
     112   1963
       8   1962
     100   1963
      28   1963
      95   1963
```

The following rules apply to the set of values after the IN operator:

- All literals in a set must have the same data type. The set (12, 24, '36'), for example, is not permitted.

- Statistical functions are not allowed as expressions in the WHERE clause.

Suppose that E1, E2, E3 and E4 are expressions, then the condition:

```
E1 IN (E2, E3, E4)
```

is equivalent to the condition:

```
(E1 = E2) OR (E1 = E3) OR (E1 = E4)
```

At the same time it follows that the condition:

```
E1 NOT IN (E2, E3, E4)
```

is equivalent to:

```
NOT (E1 IN (E2, E3, E4))
```

and equivalent to:

```
(E1 <> E2) AND (E1 <> E3) AND (E1 <> E4)
```

In Section 8.7 we discuss other forms of the IN operator.

Exercises

8.11 Find the payment number for each penalty of $50, $75, or $100.

8.12 Give the numbers of the players who do not live in Stratford or Douglas.

8.6   The LIKE operator

The LIKE operator is used to select rows which contain an alphanumeric value with a particular pattern or mask.

Example 8.10: Find the name and number of each player whose name begins with a capital B.

```
SELECT   NAME, PLAYERNO
FROM     PLAYERS
WHERE    NAME LIKE 'B%'
```

Result:

```
NAME     PLAYERNO
------   --------
Baker          44
Brown          57
Bishop         39
Bailey        112
```

After the *LIKE operator* you find an alphanumeric literal: 'B%'. Because this literal comes after a LIKE operator and not after a comparison operator, the percent sign and another literal, the underscore, have a special meaning. Such a literal is called a *pattern* or a *mask*. In a mask, the percent sign stands for zero, one or more random characters, while the underscore stands for exactly one character.

In the SELECT statement above, then, we asked for the players whose name begins with the capital B followed by zero, one or more characters.

Note: You can also use an asterisk (∗) instead of a percent sign, and a question mark instead of an underscore to achieve the same effect.

Example 8.11: Get the name and number of each player whose name ends with the small letter *r*.

```
SELECT   NAME, PLAYERNO
FROM     PLAYERS
WHERE    NAME LIKE '%r'
```

Result:

```
NAME       PLAYERNO
---------  --------
Parmenter         6
Baker            44
Parmenter       100
Miller           95
```

Example 8.12: Get the name and number of each player whose name has the letter *e* as the penultimate letter.

```
SELECT    NAME, PLAYERNO
FROM      PLAYERS
WHERE     NAME LIKE '%e_'
```

Result:

NAME	PLAYERNO
Parmenter	6
Baker	44
Bailey	112
Parmenter	100
Miller	95

If neither an underscore nor a percent sign is needed to specify the condition, you can use the = operator. The condition

```
NAME LIKE 'Baker'
```

is equivalent to

```
NAME = 'Baker'
```

Suppose that A is an alphanumeric column and M a mask, then:

```
A NOT LIKE M
```

is equivalent to:

```
NOT (A LIKE M)
```

Exercises

8.13 Find the number and name of each player whose name contains the combination of letters *is*.

8.14 Find the number and name of each player whose name is six characters long.

8.15 Find the number and name of each player whose name is at least six characters long.

8.16 Find the number and name of each player whose name has an *l* as the third and penultimate letter.

8.7   The IN operator with subquery

Section 8.5 discussed the IN operator. If the value of a particular column occurs in a set of expressions, the row concerned satisfies the condition made using the IN operator. The expressions in such a set are written into the statement one by one by a user. The IN operator can also take another form whereby it is not necessary to explicitly list the individual expressions. Instead, dBASE IV determines the value of the literals at the point when the statement is processed. This process is the subject of this section.

Example 8.13: Get the number, name and initials of each player who has played at least one match.

      This question actually consists of two parts. First, we need to work out which players have played at least one match, and then we need to look for the numbers and names of these players. The GAMES table contains data to answer the first part, so with the following simple statement we can find out the player numbers:

```
SELECT    PLAYERNO
FROM      GAMES
```

Result:

```
PLAYERNO
--------
       6
      44
      83
       2
      57
       8
      27
     104
     112
       8
```

But how do we use those numbers to look up the relevant names and initials of the players from the PLAYERS table? In terms of what we have covered so far in this book, there is only one way to do it. We note down the numbers on a piece of paper and type in the next statement:

```
SELECT    PLAYERNO, NAME, INITIALS
FROM      PLAYERS
WHERE     PLAYERNO IN (6, 44, 83, 2, 57, 8, 27, 104, 112)
```

Result:

```
PLAYERNO   NAME        INITIALS
--------   ---------   --------
       6   Parmenter   R
      44   Baker       E
      83   Hope        PK
       2   Everett     R
      27   Collins     DD
     104   Moorman     D
      57   Brown       M
     112   Bailey      IP
       8   Newcastle   B
```

This way works, of course, but it is very clumsy, and would be impractical if the GAMES table had many different player numbers. Because this type of statement is very common, SQL offers the possibility of including SELECT statements *within* other statements. The statement for the example above now looks like this:

```
SELECT    PLAYERNO, NAME, INITIALS
FROM      PLAYERS
WHERE     PLAYERNO IN
          (SELECT   PLAYERNO
           FROM     GAMES)
```

We now have no set of expressions after the IN operator as we did in the example in Section 8.5. Instead there is another SELECT statement. This SELECT statement is called a *subquery*. A subquery has a result, of course, just like a 'normal' SELECT statement. In this example the result looks like this (remember that it is an intermediate result that is not actually seen during processing):

```
(6, 44, 83, 2, 57, 8, 27, 104, 112)
```

When dBASE IV processes the SELECT statement it replaces the subquery with the intermediate result of the subquery:

```
SELECT    PLAYERNO, NAME, INITIALS
FROM      PLAYERS
WHERE     PLAYERNO IN (6, 44, 83, 2, 57, 8, 27, 104, 112)
```

This now looks like a familiar statement. The result of this statement is the same as the end result that we have already shown.

The most important difference between the use of the IN operator with a set of expressions as opposed to with a subquery is that in the first instance the set of values is fixed in advance by the user, and in the second instance the values are not known until they are determined by dBASE IV.

Example 8.14: Get the number and name of each player who has played at least one match for the first team.

```
SELECT    PLAYERNO, NAME
FROM      PLAYERS
WHERE     PLAYERNO IN
          (SELECT   PLAYERNO
          FROM      GAMES
          WHERE     TEAMNO = 1)
```

The intermediate result of the subquery:

```
(6, 44, 83, 2, 57, 8)
```

The result of the entire statement:

```
PLAYERNO  NAME
--------  ---------
       6  Parmenter
      44  Baker
      83  Hope
       2  Everett
      57  Brown
       8  Newcastle
```

As you can see, a subquery itself may contain conditions; even other subqueries are allowed.

Example 8.15: Give the number and name of each player who has played at least one game for the team which is *not* captained by player 6.

```
SELECT    PLAYERNO, NAME
FROM      PLAYERS
WHERE     PLAYERNO IN
          (SELECT   PLAYERNO
          FROM      GAMES
          WHERE     TEAMNO NOT IN
                    (SELECT   TEAMNO
                    FROM      TEAMS
                    WHERE     PLAYERNO = 6))
```

The intermediate result of the *subsubquery* is:

```
(1)
```

In the subquery, now, dBASE IV searches for all players who do *not* appear in the set of teams captained by player 6.
    Intermediate result:

```
(27, 104, 112, 8)
```

Result of the statement:

```
PLAYERNO  NAME
--------  ---------
      27  Collins
     104  Moorman
     112  Bailey
       8  Newcastle
```

As usual, users do not see any of the intermediate results.

When is a condition with an IN operator and a subquery true, and when is it false? Suppose that C is a column and that $v_1, v_2, \ldots, v_n$ are values from which the intermediate result of subquery S are formed. It follows that:

```
C IN (S)
```

is equivalent to:

```
(C = v1) OR (C = v2) OR ... OR (C = vn) OR false
```

Note that at the end of this 'long-hand' condition the word *false* occurs. This means that the entire condition is *false* if the subquery returns no result.

We can apply the same reasoning to NOT IN. The following condition:

```
C NOT IN (S)
```

is equivalent to:

```
(C <> v1) AND (C <> v2) AND ... AND (C <> vn) AND true
```

This condition says that if the subquery returns no rows the condition is *true*.

In Section 8.11 we deal more extensively with the possibilities and limitations of subqueries.

Exercises

8.17 Get the number and name of each player who has incurred at least one penalty.

8.18 Get the number and name of each player who has incurred at least one penalty of more than $50.

8.19 Find the team numbers and player numbers of the team captains from the first division who live in Stratford.

8.20 Get the the number and name of each player for whom at least one penalty has been received and who is not a captain of a team which plays in the first division.

8.8   The comparison operator with subquery

Subqueries can be placed not only after the IN operator, but also after the comparison operators, such as = or >.

Example 8.16: Find the number and name of the player who captains team 1.

```
SELECT    PLAYERNO, NAME
FROM      PLAYERS
WHERE     PLAYERNO =
          (SELECT    PLAYERNO
           FROM      TEAMS
           WHERE     TEAMNO = 1)
```

The intermediate result of the subquery is player number 6. These values can now replace the subquery

```
SELECT    PLAYERNO, NAME
FROM      PLAYERS
WHERE     PLAYERNO = 6
```

Result:

```
PLAYERNO  NAME
--------  ---------
       6  Parmenter
```

The = operator is only valid if the subquery returns one value at that precise point in time. The statement above could also have been formulated with an IN operator. There are, however, two reasons why the = operator must be chosen over the IN operator when a subquery returns one value.

- By using the = operator you signal that the subquery always has one value. If the subquery returns multiple values, then, either the contents of the database are not correct or the database structure is not as you expected. In both cases the = operator is functioning as a means of control.

- By using = operator you give the optimizer information about the expected number of values to be returned by the subquery, namely one. On the basis of this information the optimizer can decide on the most appropriate processing strategy.

Example 8.17: Find the number and name of each player who is older than R. Parmenter.

```
SELECT    PLAYERNO, NAME
FROM      PLAYERS
WHERE     BIRTH <
          (SELECT    BIRTH
           FROM      PLAYERS
           WHERE     NAME = 'Parmenter'
           AND       INITIALS = 'R')
```

The intermediate result of the subquery is the year 1964. The result the user sees is:

```
PLAYERNO  NAME
--------  ---------
      44  Baker
      83  Hope
       2  Everett
       7  Wise
      39  Bishop
     112  Bailey
       8  Newcastle
     100  Parmenter
      28  Collins
      95  Miller
```

As we have already mentioned, we return in more detail to subqueries in the last section of this chapter. What we want to point out here is that a subquery in a condition with a comparison operator should always return *only one value*. The statement below, then, is incorrect and would not be processed by dBASE IV.

```
SELECT    *
FROM      PLAYERS
WHERE     BIRTH <
          (SELECT   BIRTH
           FROM     PLAYERS)
```

Exercises

8.21 Get the number and name of each player who is the same age as R. Parmenter, but R. Parmenter's number may not appear in the result.

8.22 Find the number of each player who has won as many games for team 2 as player 8 has won for that team. Exclude player 8 from the result.

8.9   The ALL and ANY operators

The ALL and ANY operators look rather like the IN operator with a subquery. The SOME operator has the same meaning as the ANY operator.

Example 8.18: Give the numbers, names and years of birth of the oldest players. The oldest players are those whose year of birth is less than or equal to that of each other player.

```
SELECT    PLAYERNO, NAME, BIRTH
FROM      PLAYERS
WHERE     BIRTH <= ALL
          (SELECT   BIRTH
           FROM     PLAYERS)
```

Result:

```
PLAYERNO  NAME     BIRTH
--------  -------  -----
       2  Everett  1948
```

Explanation: The intermediate result of the subquery consists of the year of birth of all players. In the SELECT statement dBASE IV looks to see if the year of birth of each player is less than or equal to each year of birth recorded in the intermediate result.

With the IN operator we signal precisely when such a condition is true or false. We do the same for the ALL operator. If $y_1, y_2, \ldots, y_n$ are the years of birth of all players returned by the subquery (S), it follows that:

```
BIRTH <= ALL (S)
```

is equivalent to:

```
(BIRTH <= y1) AND
(BIRTH <= y2) AND ... AND
(BIRTH <= yn) AND true
```

This means that if the subquery returns no result the condition is *true*.

Example 8.19: Get the numbers, names and years of birth of players who are not amongst the oldest.

```
SELECT    PLAYERNO, NAME, BIRTH
FROM      PLAYERS
WHERE     BIRTH > ANY
          (SELECT   BIRTH
           FROM     PLAYERS)
```

The intermediate result of the subquery again consists of all the years of birth. But this time dBASE IV looks for all the players whose year of birth is greater than that of at least one other player. When such a year of birth is found dBASE IV knows that this player is not the oldest. The end result of this statement is the group of all players except the oldest one. The previous example showed that Everett is is the oldest player.

If $y_1, y_2, \ldots, y_n$ are all the years of birth returned by the subquery S, it follows that:

```
BIRTH > ANY (S)
```

is equivalent to:

```
(BIRTH > y1) OR
(BIRTH > y2) OR ... OR
(BIRTH > yn) OR false
```

From this we can deduce that if the subquery returns no values the condition is *false*.

Instead of the greater than operator and the less than or equal to operator that we used in these two examples, each comparison operator may be used.

Try to deduce for yourself that the condition C = ANY (S) is equivalent to C IN (S). And try to prove that the condition C <> ALL (S) is equivalent to C NOT IN (S) and also equivalent to NOT (C IN (S)).

The condition C = ALL (S) is, by definition, false if the subquery returns multiple values, because the value in a column can never be equal to two or more different values at the same time. We can illustrate this proposition with a simple example. Suppose that v_1 and v_2 are two different values from the intermediate result of subquery S, then it follows that: C = ALL (S) is equal to: (C = v1) AND (C = v2). By definition, this is false.

The converse applies for the condition: C <> ANY (S). If the subquery returns multiple values, the condition is, by definition, true. Because, again, if the result of subquery S consists of the values v_1 and v_2, then: C <> ANY (S) is equivalent to: (C <> v1) OR (C <> v2). And this is, by definition, true.

Exercises

8.23 Get the player numbers of the oldest players from Stratford.

8.24 Get the player number of each player who has incurred at least one penalty (do not use the IN operator).

8.10 The EXISTS operator

We have already seen that a subquery can be coupled to a main query with the IN, ANY, ALL and comparison operators. Still, there is another operator: the *EXISTS operator*.

Example 8.20: Find the names and initials of players who have incurred at least one penalty.

This question can be answered using an IN operator:

```
SELECT    NAME, INITIALS
FROM      PLAYERS
WHERE     PLAYERNO IN
          (SELECT  PLAYERNO
           FROM     PENLTIES)
```

Result:

```
NAME        INITIALS
---------   --------
Parmenter   R
Baker       E
Collins     DD
Moorman     D
Newcastle   B
```

It can also, however, be answered using the EXISTS operator.

```
SELECT   NAME, INITIALS
FROM     PLAYERS
WHERE    EXISTS
         (SELECT  *
         FROM     PENLTIES
         WHERE    PLAYERNO = PLAYERS.PLAYERNO)
```

We now come to something new in the subquery. The column identifier PLAY-ERS.PLAYERNO refers to a table that has been mentioned in the main part of the statement. We call such a subquery a *correlated subquery*. By using the named column identifier we establish a relationship between the subquery and the main statement.

But what does this statement mean exactly? For every player in the PLAY-ERS table dBASE IV looks separately to see whether the subquery returns a row or not. In other words, it checks to see whether there is a result (WHERE EX-ISTS). If the PENLTIES table contains at least one player number the same as that of the player concerned, then that row satisfies the condition. We will give an example. For the first row in the PLAYERS table, which is player 6, dBASE IV executes the following subquery (behind the screen):

```
SELECT   *
FROM     PENLTIES
WHERE    PLAYERNO = 6
```

The (intermediate) result consists of one row, so in the end result we see the name of the player whose number is 6.

Similarly, dBASE IV executes the subquery for the second, third and subsequent rows of the PLAYERS table. The only thing that changes each time is the value for PLAYERS.PLAYERNO in the condition of the WHERE clause. Therefore, the subquery can have a different intermediate result for each player in the PLAYERS table.

Example 8.21: Get the names and initials of the players who are not team captains.

```
SELECT   NAME, INITIALS
FROM     PLAYERS
WHERE    NOT EXISTS
         (SELECT  *
         FROM     TEAMS
         WHERE    PLAYERNO = PLAYERS.PLAYERNO)
```

Result:

```
NAME        INITIALS
---------   --------
Baker       E
Hope        PK
Everett     R
Moorman     D
Wise        GWS
Brown       M
Bishop      D
Bailey      IP
Newcastle   B
Parmenter   P
Collins     C
Miller      P
```

In Chapter 14 we return to the EXISTS operator and correlated subqueries.

Exercises

8.25 Give the name and initial(s) of each player who is captain of at least one team.

8.26 Give the name and initial(s) of each player who is not a captain of a team in which player 112 has played.

8.11   The subquery

As we have seen, subqueries may be used in conjunction with the IN, ANY, ALL and EXISTS operators. A *subquery* is a SELECT statement within a SELECT statement. Another word for subquery is *subselect* or *innerselect*. The definition of a subquery SELECT statement is somewhat different from that of a 'normal' SELECT statement:

```
<subquery> ::=
   SELECT { <expression> | * }
   <from clause>
   [ <where clause> ]
   [ <group by clause>
   [ <having clause> ] ]
```

There are three differences to note:

1. The SELECT clause may contain only one expression or the asterisk.
    In a SELECT clause only one column expression may be specified, other-
    wise the subquery returns a table consisting of a number of columns. Each
    row, then, contains multiple values. For conditions whose form is a sub-
    query, dBASE IV compares the result of the subquery with a single value
    like 'Jim', 18 or 280.14. Such a value is completely different from a set of
    values like <'Jim', 14>, <'Pete', 25> or <'Regina', 83>. The asterisk can
    only be used with EXISTS.

2. The SELECT clause cannot contain the DISTINCT operator.
    The meaning of a set of values does not change if duplicate values are omit-
    ted or if the values are rearranged. As far as being interpreted by a subquery
    goes, the sets below are equivalent:

        (1, 4, 8)
        (8, 1, 4)
        (4, 4, 1, 8)
        (8, 1, 4, 8, 1, 4)

3. An ORDER BY clause is not permitted (for the same reason as DISTINCT
    is inappropriate).

An important aspect of the subquery is the *range* of the columns. In order to
explain this concept well, we need first to understand another concept: the *query
block*. This next SELECT statement is constructed from five query blocks.

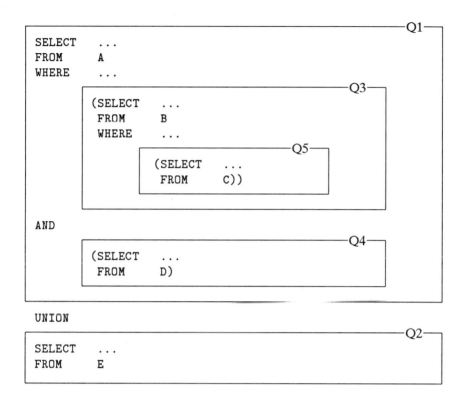

A SELECT clause marks the beginning of a query block. A subquery belongs to the query block formed by the main statement of which it is a subquery. The columns of a table may be used in any place in the query block in which the table is specified. Therefore, in the example, columns from table A may be used in query blocks Q1, Q3, Q4 and Q5, but not in Q2. We can say, then, that Q1, Q3, Q4 and Q5 is the range of the columns from table A. Columns from table B may only be used in query blocks Q3 and Q5, making Q3 and Q5 the range of the table B columns.

Example 8.22: Give the number and name of each player who has incurred at least one penalty.

```
                                                          ┌─Q1─┐
SELECT    PLAYERNO, NAME
FROM      PLAYERS
WHERE     EXISTS
                                              ┌─────────Q2─┐
          (SELECT    *
           FROM      PENLTIES
           WHERE     PLAYERS.PLAYERNO = PLAYERNO)
```

The columns from the PLAYERS table may be used in the query blocks Q1 and Q2, while columns from the PENLTIES table may only be used in query block Q2.

In this example we take the PLAYERNO column from the PLAYERS table to use in Q2. What would happen if, instead of PLAYERS.PLAYERNO, we specified only PLAYERNO? In this case, dBASE IV would interpret the column as being PLAYERNO from the PENLTIES table and this would produce another result. To be precise, the NAME for *each* player would be presented because PLAYERNO = PLAYERNO is valid for every row in the PENLTIES table.

Query block Q2 is called a *correlated subquery* because it contains a column belonging to a table that is specified in another query block.

If there is no table name specified before a column name in a subquery, dBASE IV looks first to see whether the column belongs to one of the tables named in the subquery's FROM clause. If so, then dBASE IV assumes that the column belongs to that table. If not, then dBASE IV looks to see if the the column belongs to a table named in the FROM clause of the query block of which the subquery forms a part. In fact, you will write much clearer statements by explicitly mentioning table names before the column names in these situations.

How does dBASE IV process the statement above? We will illustrate it by using intermediate results from the various clauses. The intermediate result of the FROM clause in query block Q1 is a copy of the PLAYERS table:

```
PLAYERNO  NAME         ...
--------  ----------   ---
       6  Parmenter    ...
      44  Baker        ...
      83  Hope         ...
       2  Everett      ...
      27  Collins      ...
       :  :
       :  :
```

To process the WHERE clause dBASE IV executes the subquery against each row in the intermediate result. The intermediate result of the subquery for the first row, where the PLAYERNO equals 6, looks like this:

```
PAYMENTNO   PLAYERNO   PEN_DATE   AMOUNT
---------   --------   --------   ------
        1          6   12/08/80   100.00
```

There is only one row in the PENLTIES table in which the player number equals the player number from the row in the PLAYERS table. The condition of query block Q1 is true, since the intermediate result of the query block consists of at least one row.

The intermediate result of the subquery for the second row from query block Q1 consists of three rows:

```
PAYMENTNO   PLAYERNO   PEN_DATE   AMOUNT
---------   --------   --------   ------
        2         44   05/05/81   75.00
        5         44   12/08/80   25.00
        7         44   12/30/82   30.00
```

We see, then, that player 44 will appear in the end result. The following player, number 83, will not be included in the end result as no row in the PENLTIES table records a player number of 83.

The final result of the statement is:

```
PLAYERNO   NAME
--------   ---------
       6   Parmenter
      44   Baker
      27   Collins
     104   Moorman
       8   Newcastle
```

In processing a correlated subquery, dBASE IV considers a column from the outer or enveloping query block to be a literal for the subquery.

As mentioned in Chapter 6, dBASE IV tries, in reality, to find the most efficient processing method. Irrespective of the processing method the result is always the same.

Here are a couple of variants on the above example.

```
SELECT    PLAYERNO, NAME
FROM      PLAYERS
WHERE     EXISTS
          (SELECT    *
          FROM       PENLTIES
          WHERE      PLAYERS.PLAYERNO = PLAYERS.PLAYERNO)
```

The subquery is executed separately for each player. The WHERE clause in the subquery contains a condition which is always true, so the subquery always returns one row. Conclusion: this statement returns the names of all players.

This next statement has the same effect as the first example in this section.

```
SELECT    PLAYERNO, NAME
FROM      PLAYERS S
WHERE     EXISTS
          (SELECT   *
          FROM      PENLTIES PN
          WHERE     S.PLAYERNO = PN.PLAYERNO)
```

Note: The pseudonym for the PENLTIES table can be left out without affecting the result.

Exercises

8.27 Which of these SELECT statements are correct and which incorrect? Give reasons.

```
1.    SELECT   ...
      FROM     ...
      WHERE    ... IN
               (SELECT   ...
               FROM      ...
               GROUP BY ...
               HAVING    ... >
                         (SELECT   ...
                         FROM      ...))
      ORDER BY ...

2.    SELECT   ...
      FROM     ...
      WHERE    ... IN
               (SELECT   ...
               FROM      ...
               UNION
               SELECT   ...
               FROM      ...)
```

8.28 Say, for each of the columns below, in which query blocks of the SELECT statement they may be used (refer to the next figure).

1.   A.C1
2.   B.C1
3.   C.C1
4.   D.C1
5.   E.C1

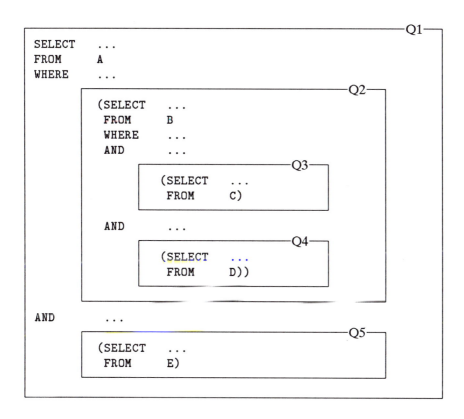

8.29 Give the name and initials of each first division competition player who has won more matches than lost and who has not incurred a single penalty.

8.30 Give the number and name of each player who has played for both the first and second teams.

9
SELECT statement: SELECT clause and functions

The WHERE clause is used to select rows and the intermediate result from this clause forms a *horizontal subset* of a table. In contrast, the SELECT clause selects only columns and not rows, the result forming a *vertical subset* of a table.

The possibilities, limitations and use of the SELECT clause depend on the presence or absence of a GROUP BY clause. This chapter discusses SELECT statements *without* a GROUP BY clause. In Chapter 10, which concentrates on the GROUP BY clause (among other things), we discuss the SELECT clause when the statement *does* contain a GROUP BY clause.

Much of this chapter is devoted to *statistical functions*. In Chapter 6 we referred to these functions, but did not delve into them.

```
<select clause> ::=
    SELECT [ DISTINCT | ALL ] <select list>

<select list> ::=
    [ <table identifier>. ] * |
    <expression> [ {,<expression>}... ]

<table identifier> ::= <table name>
```

117

9.1   Selecting all columns (∗)

An asterisk (∗) is a short form notation for all columns from each table mentioned in the FROM clause. The following two SELECT statements are equivalent:

```
SELECT    *
FROM      PENLTIES
```

and

```
SELECT    PAYMENTNO, PLAYERNO, PEN_DATE, AMOUNT
FROM      PENLTIES
```

(The ∗ symbol, then, does not have the meaning of the multiplication sign in this context.) When a FROM clause refers to more than one table, it is sometimes necessary to use a table identifier in front of the asterisk in order to clarify which columns should be presented.The following three statements are equivalent, for example:

```
SELECT    PENLTIES.*
FROM      PENLTIES, PLAYERS
WHERE     PENLTIES.PLAYERNO = PLAYERS.PLAYERNO
```

and

```
SELECT    PENLTIES.PAYMENTNO, PENLTIES.PLAYERNO,
          PENLTIES.PEN_DATE, PENLTIES.AMOUNT
FROM      PENLTIES, PLAYERS
WHERE     PENLTIES.PLAYERNO = PLAYERS.PLAYERNO
```

and

```
SELECT    PEN.*
FROM      PENLTIES PEN, PLAYERS
WHERE     PEN.PLAYERNO = PLAYERS.PLAYERNO
```

9.2   Expressions in the SELECT clause

In processing the SELECT clause dBASE IV evaluates the intermediate result row by row. Each column expression gives rise to a value in the result row. Most of the examples of the SELECT clause that we have described so far specify only column names, but an expression may take the form of a literal, a calculation or a scalar function.

Example 9.1: Give for each row in the GAMES table the player number, the word 'Tally', the difference between the columns WON and LOST and the value of the WON column multiplied by 10.

```
SELECT    PLAYERNO, 'Tally', WON - LOST,
          WON * 10
FROM      GAMES
```

Result:

```
PLAYERNO           WON - LOST  WON * 10
--------   -----   ----------  --------
       6   Tally            8        90
      44   Tally            2        70
      83   Tally            0        30
       2   Tally           -4        40
      57   Tally            5        50
       8   Tally           -1         0
      27   Tally            9       110
     104   Tally            4        80
     112   Tally           -4        40
       8   Tally            0        40
```

9.3   Removing duplicate rows with DISTINCT

A SELECT clause can be written with one or more column expressions preceded by the word DISTINCT (see the definition at the beginning of this chapter). If you specify DISTINCT, dBASE IV removes duplicate rows from the intermediate result.

Example 9.2: Find all the different place names from the PLAYERS table.

```
SELECT    TOWN
FROM      PLAYERS
```

Result:

```
TOWN
---------
Stratford
Inglewood
Stratford
Stratford
Eltham
Eltham
Stratford
Stratford
Stratford
Plymouth
Inglewood
```

```
Stratford
Midhurst
Douglas
```

In this result table, the towns Stratford, Inglewood and Eltham appear seven, two and two times respectively. If the statement is expanded to include DISTINCT:

```
SELECT   DISTINCT TOWN
FROM     PLAYERS
```

it produces the following result in which all but one of each group of duplicate rows is removed.

```
TOWN
----------
Stratford
Midhurst
Inglewood
Plymouth
Douglas
Eltham
```

A second example is:

```
SELECT   STREET, TOWN
FROM     PLAYERS
```

Result:

```
STREET             TOWN
----------------   ----------
Haseltine Lane     Stratford
Lewis Street       Inglewood
Magdalene Road     Stratford
Stoney Road        Stratford
Long Drive         Eltham
Stout Street       Eltham
Edgecombe Way      Stratford
Edgecombe Way      Stratford
Eaton Square       Stratford
Vixen Road         Plymouth
Station Road       Inglewood
Haseltine Lane     Stratford
Old Main Road      Midhurst
High Street        Douglas
```

This result also contains duplicate rows; for example, Edgecombe Way and Haseltine Lane in Stratford are each mentioned twice. When DISTINCT is added:

```
SELECT    DISTINCT STREET, TOWN
FROM      PLAYERS
```

the result is:

```
STREET              TOWN
---------------     ----------
Edgecombe Way       Stratford
Eaton Square        Stratford
Haseltine Lane      Stratford
High Street         Douglas
Lewis Street        Inglewood
Long Drive          Eltham
Magdalene Road      Stratford
Old Main Road       Midhurst
Station Road        Inglewood
Stoney Road         Stratford
Stout Street        Eltham
Vixen Road          Plymouth
```

DISTINCT, then, is concerned with the *whole row* and not only with the column expression that directly follows the word DISTINCT in the statement. Below we give two constructions in which the use of DISTINCT is superfluous (but not forbidden).

• When the SELECT clause includes the primary keys of all tables specified in the FROM clause, DISTINCT is superfluous. The most important property of a primary key is that the column that forms the primary key never allows duplicate values. A table that has a primary key, therefore, never has duplicate rows. The inclusion of primary key in the end result of a SELECT statement offers a guarantee that no duplicate rows will appear in the end result.

• When the SELECT clause includes all columns that are specified in the GROUP BY clause, DISTINCT is superfluous. The GROUP BY clause groups the rows in such a way that the column(s) on which they are grouped no longer contain duplicate values.

Finally, the user can specify ALL in the same position in the statement as DISTINCT appears. Note that it actually has the opposite effect to DISTINCT, and does not alter the result of a 'normal' SELECT statement. In other words, these two statements are equivalent:

```
SELECT    TOWN
FROM      PLAYERS
```

and

```
SELECT    ALL TOWN
FROM      PLAYERS
```

9.4   An introduction to statistical functions

Expressions in the SELECT clause may contain *statistical functions*. If a SELECT statement has *no* GROUP BY clause, any function in a SELECT clause operates on all rows. SQL recognizes the following statistical functions:

function	meaning
COUNT	Counts the number of values in a column or the number of rows in a table
MIN	Determines the smallest value in a column
MAX	Determines the largest value in a column
SUM	Determines the sum of the values in a column
AVG	Determines the weighted arithmetic mean of the values in a column

If a SELECT clause contains a statistical function, then the entire SELECT statement yields only one row as an end result (we are assuming here that the SELECT statement has *no* GROUP BY clause).

```
<statistical function> ::=
    <count function> |
    <min function> |
    <max function> |
    <sum function> |
    <avg function>
```

Example 9.3: How many players are registered in the PLAYERS table?

```
SELECT   COUNT(*)
FROM     PLAYERS
```

Result:

```
COUNT(*)
--------
      14
```

Explanation: The function COUNT(*) adds up the number of rows remaining from the FROM clause. In this case, the number equals the number of rows in the PLAYERS table.

Example 9.4: How many players live in Stratford?

```
SELECT    COUNT(*)
FROM      PLAYERS
WHERE     TOWN = 'Stratford'
```

Result:

```
COUNT(*)
--------
       7
```

Explanation: Because the SELECT clause is here processed after the WHERE clause, the number of rows where the TOWN column has the value Stratford are counted.

We look at various statistical functions in more detail in the following sections.

9.5 COUNT function

With the COUNT function an asterisk (*) or a column name can be specified between brackets. Both give the same result, so COUNT(*) on the PLAYERS table is, for example, the same as COUNT(PLAYERNO).

```
<count function> ::=
    COUNT ( { * | [ DISTINCT ] <column name> } )
```

Example 9.5: How many league numbers are there?

```
SELECT    COUNT(LEAGUENO)
FROM      PLAYERS
```

Result:

```
COUNT(LEAGUENO)
---------------
             10
```

You can also calculate the number of *different* values in a column.

Example 9.6: How many different place names are there in the TOWN column?

```
SELECT    COUNT(DISTINCT TOWN)
FROM      PLAYERS
```

Result:

```
COUNT(DISTINCT TOWN)
--------------------
                   6
```

Explanation: When DISTINCT is specified before the column name all the duplicate values are removed and then the addition carried out.

A SELECT clause can use multiple functions at the same time.

Example 9.7: Give the number of different place names and the number of different sexes represented.

```
SELECT   COUNT(DISTINCT TOWN), COUNT(DISTINCT SEX)
FROM     PLAYERS
```

Result:

```
COUNT(DISTINCT TOWN)  COUNT(DISTINCT SEX)
--------------------  --------------------
                   6                     2
```

9.6   MAX and MIN functions

With the MAX and MIN functions dBASE IV determines the largest and smallest values respectively in a column.

```
<max function> ::=
   MAX ( <function object> )

<min function> ::=
   MIN ( <function object> )

<function object> ::=
   [ ALL ] <column expression> |
   [ ALL | DISTINCT ] <column name>
```

Example 9.8: What is the highest penalty?

```
SELECT   MAX(AMOUNT)
FROM     PENLTIES
```

Result:

```
MAX(AMOUNT)
-----------
     100.00
```

We can specify the word ALL before the column name without changing the result. By adding ALL you ensure that *all* values are considered. Duplicate values are then included twice in the calculation. In fact, in examples using the MAX and MIN functions, the addition of ALL is superfluous (as is DISTINCT), though it is not wrong. The following statement is equivalent to the one above.

```
SELECT    MAX(ALL AMOUNT)
FROM      PENLTIES
```

Example 9.9: What is the lowest penalty incurred by a player resident in Stratford?

```
SELECT    MIN(AMOUNT)
FROM      PENLTIES
WHERE     PLAYERNO IN
          (SELECT   PLAYERNO
          FROM      PLAYERS
          WHERE     TOWN = 'Stratford')
```

Result:

```
MIN(AMOUNT)
-----------
     100.00
```

Example 9.10: How many penalties are equal to the lowest one?

```
SELECT    COUNT(*)
FROM      PENLTIES
WHERE     AMOUNT =
          (SELECT   MIN(AMOUNT)
          FROM      PENLTIES)
```

Result:

```
COUNT(AMOUNT)
-------------
            2
```

Explanation: The subquery calculates the lowest penalty which is $25. The SELECT statement calculates the number of penalties equal to this amount.

Example 9.11: For each team, give the team number followed by the player number of the player who has won the most matches for that team.

```
SELECT    TEAMNO, PLAYERNO
FROM      GAMES G1
WHERE     WON =
          (SELECT   MAX(WON)
          FROM      GAMES G2
          WHERE     G1.TEAMNO = G2.TEAMNO)
```

Result:

```
TEAMNO  PLAYERNO
------  --------
     1         6
     2        27
```

Statistical functions can occur in calculations. Here are two examples.

Example 9.12: What is the difference between the highest and lowest penalty in cents?

```
SELECT   (MAX(AMOUNT) - MIN(AMOUNT)) * 100
FROM     PENLTIES
```

Result:

```
(MAX(AMOUNT) - MIN(AMOUNT)) * 100
---------------------------------
                             7500
```

Example 9.13: Give the first letter of the name which appears last in alphabetical order in the PLAYERS table.

```
SELECT   SUBSTR(MAX(NAME), 1, 1)
FROM     PLAYERS
```

Result:

```
SUBSTR(MAX(NAME), 1, 1)
-----------------------
W
```

Explanation: First, the MAX function finds the last name in alphabetical order, and then the scalar function SUBSTR picks out the first letter from this name. See Appendix C for a description of the SUBSTR function.

In principle, DISTINCT can be used with the MAX and MIN functions, but this, of course, doesn't change the end result (work out why not for yourself).

When the two functions are applied against an empty table (or an empty intermediate result) they have no value.

9.7   SUM function

The SUM function calculates the sum of all values in a particular column.

```
<sum function> ::=
   SUM ( <function object> )

<function object> ::=
   [ ALL ] <column expression> |
   [ ALL | DISTINCT ] <column name>
```

Example 9.14: What is the total amount of penalties incurred by Inglewood players?

```
SELECT    SUM(AMOUNT)
FROM      PENLTIES
WHERE     PLAYERNO IN
          (SELECT    PLAYERNO
          FROM      PLAYERS
          WHERE     TOWN = 'Inglewood')
```

Result:

```
SUM(AMOUNT)
-----------
     155.00
```

We can specify the word ALL before the column name without affecting the result. By adding ALL you explicitly demand that *all* values are considered. In contrast, the use of DISTINCT within the SUM function *can* alter the end result. If we extend the SUM function in the SELECT statement above with DISTINCT, we get the following result:

```
SELECT    SUM(DISTINCT AMOUNT)
FROM      PENLTIES
WHERE     PLAYERNO IN
          (SELECT    PLAYERNO
          FROM      PLAYERS
          WHERE     TOWN = 'Inglewood')
```

Result:

```
SUM(AMOUNT)
-----------
     130.00
```

Note: As opposed to the COUNT, MIN and MAX functions, the SUM function is only applicable to columns with a numeric data type. The other three functions can be applied to columns of both numeric and alphanumeric data types.

If the SUM function is executed against an empty table (or an empty intermediate result) it has no value.

9.8   AVG function

The AVG function calculates the arithmetic average of the values in a particular column. This function is only permitted with numeric columns.

```
<avg function> ::=
   AVG ( <function object> )

<function object> ::=
   [ ALL ] <column expression> |
   [ ALL | DISTINCT ] <column name>
```

Example 9.15: Give the average amount of penalties incurred by player 44.

```
SELECT    AVG(AMOUNT)
FROM      PENLTIES
WHERE     PLAYERNO = 44
```

Result:

```
AVG(AMOUNT)
-----------
      43.33
```

Explanation: $43.33 is the average of the amounts $75, $25, and $30.

Example 9.16: Which players have incurred a penalty greater than the average penalty?

```
SELECT    DISTINCT PLAYERNO
FROM      PENLTIES
WHERE     AMOUNT >
          (SELECT    AVG(AMOUNT)
          FROM      PENLTIES)
```

Result:

```
PLAYERNO
---------
       6
      27
      44
```

Explanation: The average penalty equals $60 and these players have incurred penalties higher than $60.

Adding the word ALL doesn't affect the result, as it simply reinforces the idea that *all* values are included in the calculation. On the other hand adding DISTINCT within the AVG function does influence the result.

Example 9.17: What is the *unweighted* arithmetic mean of the penalty amounts. By unweighted we mean that each different value is considered only once in the calculation.

```
SELECT    AVG(DISTINCT AMOUNT)
FROM      PENLTIES
```

Result:

```
AVG(DISTINCT AMOUNT)
--------------------
              56.00
```

Explanation: The amount $56 is equal to $100 + $75 + $50 + $30 + $25 divided by 5.

Example 9.18: What is the average length of a name and what is the longest name?

```
SELECT    AVG(LEN(RTRIM(NAME))),
          MAX(LEN(RTRIM(NAME)))
FROM      PLAYERS
```

Result:

```
AVG(LEN(RTRIM(NAME)))   MAX(LEN(RTRIM(NAME)))
---------------------   ---------------------
                 7.29                      10
```

If the AVG function is executed against an empty table (or an empty intermediate result) then it has no result.

9.9 General rule for using statistical functions

In this chapter we have shown that statistical functions may be used in SELECT clauses. We must, however, stress the following important rule:

> *If a SELECT statement has no GROUP BY clause, and if the SELECT clause has one or more statistical functions, any column name specified in that SELECT clause must occur within a statistical function.*

Therefore, the statement below is not correct because the SELECT clause contains a statistical function as an expression, while the PLAYERNO column name appears outside that statistical function.

```
SELECT    COUNT(*), PLAYERNO
FROM      PLAYERS
```

The reason for this restriction is that the result of a statistical function always consists of one value, whereas the result stemming from a column identifier consists of a set of values. SQL cannot present these results together.

Note, however, that this rule is valid only for column identifiers and not, for example, for literals or memory variables. This next statement *is* correct:

```
SELECT    'The number of players is', COUNT(*)
FROM      PLAYERS
```

Result:

```
                                    COUNT(*)
------------------------       --------
The number of players is            14
```

In Chapter 10 we will elaborate on this rule for the SELECT clause where SELECT statements *do* contain a GROUP BY clause.

Exercises

9.1 Determine the value of the functions below for the following set of values in the NUMBER column: { 1, 2, 3, 4, 1, 4, 4, 5 }.

1. COUNT(*)
2. COUNT(NUMBER)
3. MIN(NUMBER)
4. MAX(NUMBER)
5. SUM(NUMBER)
6. AVG(NUMBER)
7. COUNT(DISTINCT NUMBER)
8. MIN(DISTINCT NUMBER)
9. MAX(DISTINCT NUMBER)
10. SUM(DISTINCT NUMBER)
11. AVG(DISTINCT NUMBER)

9.2 What is the average penalty amount?

9.3 What is the average penalty for players who have competed for team 1?

9.4 Give the name and initials of the players who have, for at least one team, won more games than player 27 has won in total.

9.5 How many matches have been won in total, lost in total and what is the tally?

9.6   Give the number and year of birth of each player born in the same year as the youngest player who has played for team 1.

9.7   Give the numbers and names of players whose name is longer than the average length of a name.

10

SELECT statement: GROUP BY and the HAVING clause

The GROUP BY clause groups rows on the basis of similarities between these rows. We could, for example, group players from the PLAYERS table on the basis of the same places of residence, the result of which would be the creation of one group of players per town. From there we could then query how many players were in each group, for example. The question which could be asked is then: 'How many players are there in each town?'

The HAVING clause has a function comparable to the WHERE clause and enables conditions to be applied to groups. Because the HAVING clause can only be used in conjunction with the GROUP BY clause, we discuss them together in this chapter.

```
<group by clause> ::=
    GROUP BY <column identifier> [ {,<column identifier>}... ]

<having clause> ::=
    HAVING <condition>

<column identifier> ::=
    [ <table identifier>. ] <column name>

<table identifier> ::= <table name>
```

10.1 Grouping on one column

The simplest form of the GROUP BY clause is where only one column is grouped. Here is an example.

Example 10.1: Give all the different place names from the PLAYERS table.

```
SELECT   TOWN
FROM     PLAYERS
GROUP BY TOWN
```

You could imagine the intermediate result from the GROUP BY clause to look like this:

```
TOWN        PLAYERNO                     NAME
---------   -------------------------    --------------------
Stratford   6, 83, 2, 7, 57, 39, 100     Parmenter, Hope, ...
Midhurst    28                           Collins
Inglewood   44, 8                        Baker, Newcastle
Plymouth    112                          Bailey
Douglas     95                           Miller
Eltham      27, 104                      Collins, Moorman
```

Explanation: All rows with the same TOWN form a group. Each row in the intermediate result has one value in the TOWN column, while all other columns can contain multiple values. We are showing the columns in this way for illustrative purposes only; dBASE IV would solve this differently internally. Also, in any dBASE IV table columns *cannot* be presented as the PLAYERNO and NAME columns have been. In fact, a column which is not grouped is completely omitted from the end result, but we will return to this later in the chapter.

End result of the statement:

```
TOWN
---------
Stratford
Midhurst
Inglewood
Plymouth
Douglas
Eltham
```

If an intermediate result is grouped, the SELECT clause can include statistical functions.

Example 10.2: For each town, find the number of players.

```
SELECT   TOWN, COUNT(*)
FROM     PLAYERS
GROUP BY TOWN
```

Result:

```
TOWN        COUNT(*)
---------   --------
Stratford       7
Midhurst        1
Inglewood       2
Plymouth        1
Douglas         1
Eltham          2
```

Explanation: The COUNT(*) function is now executed against each grouped row instead of against all rows separately. In other words, the function COUNT(*) is calculated for each grouped row (for each town).

In principle, any statistical function can be used in a SELECT clause as long as that function operates on a column which is *not* grouped.

Example 10.3: For each team, give the team number, the number of players who have played for the team and the total number of matches won.

```
SELECT    TEAMNO, COUNT(*), SUM(WON)
FROM      GAMES
GROUP BY TEAMNO
```

Result:

```
TEAMNO  COUNT(*)  SUM(WON)
------  --------  --------
     1         6        28
     2         4        27
```

10.2   Grouping on two or more columns

A GROUP BY clause may also contain two or more column identifiers. To illustrate this, let's abandon our sample database and use the SUPPLIES table below. This table contains data about the number of articles supplied by manufacturers. The primary key of this table consists of all three columns.

The SUPPLIES table:

ARTNO	SUPNO	NUMBER
1	2	100
1	2	25
1	3	75
2	2	100
2	4	100
2	4	75
1	4	25

Example 10.4: Give all the different combinations of article numbers with sup-
plier numbers.

```
SELECT    ARTNO, SUPNO
FROM      SUPPLIES
GROUP BY ARTNO, SUPNO
```

The result is not grouped by one column, but by two. All rows with the same
ARTNO and the same SUPNO form a group.
The intermediate result from the GROUP BY clause:

ARTNO	SUPNO	NUMBER
1	2	100, 25
1	3	75
1	4	25
2	2	100
2	4	100, 75

The end result:

ARTNO	SUPNO
1	2
1	3
1	4
2	2
2	4

The sequence of the column identifiers in the GROUP BY clause has no effect on
the end result of a statement. The following statement, therefore, is equivalent
to the previous one:

```
SELECT    ARTNO, SUPNO
FROM      SUPPLIES
GROUP BY SUPNO, ARTNO
```

As an example, let us add some functions to the SELECT statement above:

```
SELECT    ARTNO, SUPNO, SUM(NUMBER), COUNT(*), MIN(NUMBER)
FROM      SUPPLIES
GROUP BY SUPNO, ARTNO
```

Result:

ARTNO	SUPNO	SUM(NUMBER)	COUNT(*)	MIN(NUMBER)
1	2	125	2	25
1	3	75	1	75
1	4	25	1	25
2	2	100	1	100
2	4	175	2	75

Example 10.5: For each player who has incurred a penalty, give the number, the name and the total amount in penalties incurred.

```
SELECT    P.PLAYERNO, NAME, SUM(AMOUNT)
FROM      PLAYERS P, PENLTIES PEN
WHERE     P.PLAYERNO = PEN.PLAYERNO
GROUP BY P.PLAYERNO, NAME
```

Result:

P.PLAYERNO	NAME	SUM(AMOUNT)
6	Parmenter	100.00
8	Newcastle	25.00
27	Collins	175.00
44	Baker	130.00
104	Moorman	50.00

Note: A column whose data type is LOGICAL *cannot* be grouped.

10.3   General rule for using statistical functions

In the previous chapter we gave the following rule for the use of statistical functions in the SELECT clause.

If a SELECT statement has no GROUP BY clause, and if the SELECT clause has one or more statistical functions, any column name specified in that SELECT clause must occur within a statistical function.

We now add the following rule:

If a SELECT statement does have a GROUP BY clause, any column name specified in that SELECT clause must occur within a statistical function or in the list of columns given in the GROUP BY clause.

Therefore, the statement below is not correct because the TOWN column appears in the SELECT clause, but does *not* occur within a statistical function or in the list of columns by which the result is grouped.

```
SELECT    TOWN, COUNT(*)
FROM      PLAYERS
GROUP BY PLAYERNO
```

The reason for this restriction is the same as that for the first rule. The result of a statistical function always consists of one value for each group. The result of a column identifier on which grouping is performed also always consists of one value per group. In contrast, the result of a column identifier on which *no* grouping is performed is a set of values. As you know, a result table cannot combine the two types of results arising from a grouped and an ungrouped column identifier.

Exercises

10.1 Show the different years of birth from the PLAYERS table.

10.2 For each year of birth, show the number of players born in that year.

10.3 For each player who has incurred at least one penalty, give the player number, the average penalty and the number of penalties.

10.4 For each team that has played in the first division, give the number of players and the total number of matches won.

10.5 For each player who lives in Douglas, give the name, initials and the number of penalties incurred by him or her.

10.6 For each team, give the team number, the division and the total number of matches won.

10.4   Introduction to the HAVING clause

The GROUP BY clause groups the rows of the result from the FROM clause. The HAVING clause enables you to select groups on the basis of their particular group properties. A condition in a HAVING clause looks a lot like a 'normal' condition in a WHERE clause. There is, nevertheless, one difference: expressions in a HAVING clause condition may contain statistical functions, whereas this is not possible for expressions in a WHERE clause condition.

Example 10.6: Get the number of each player who has incurred more than one penalty.

```
SELECT    PLAYERNO
FROM      PENLTIES
GROUP BY  PLAYERNO
HAVING    COUNT(*) > 1
```

The intermediate result of the GROUP BY clause looks like this (though some column names have been shortened because of lack of space):

PAYMENT	PNO	PEN_DATE	AMOUNT
1	6	12/08/80	100.00
6	8	12/08/80	25.00
3, 8	27	09/10/83, 11/12/84	100.00, 75.00
2, 5, 7	44	05/05/81, 12/08/80, 12/30/82	75.00, 25.00, 30.00
4	104	12/08/84	50.00

In the HAVING condition we specified the selection of groups where the number of rows exceeds one. The intermediate result of the HAVING clause is:

PAYMENT	PNO	PEN_DATE	AMOUNT
3, 8	27	09/10/83, 11/12/84	100.00, 75.00
2, 5, 7	44	05/05/81, 12/08/80, 12/30/82	75.00, 25.00, 30.00

And finally, the end result:

```
PLAYERNO
--------
      27
      44
```

Explanation: Just as with the SELECT clause, the value of a statistical function in a HAVING clause is calculated for each group separately. In this example the number of rows for each group in the intermediate result of the GROUP BY is counted. In the next sections we will discuss examples of the HAVING clause with statistical functions.

10.5   Examples of the HAVING clause

This section contains examples of applications of statistical functions in the HAVING clause.

Example 10.7: Give the number of each player whose last penalty was incurred in 1984.

```
SELECT    PLAYERNO
FROM      PENLTIES
GROUP BY  PLAYERNO
HAVING    MAX(YEAR(PEN_DATE)) = 1984
```

Intermediate result of the GROUP BY clause:

```
PAYMENT  PNO  PEN_DATE                            AMOUNT
-------  ---  ------------------------------      --------------------
1          6  12/08/80                            100.00
6          8  12/08/80                            25.00
3, 8      27  09/10/83, 11/12/84                  100.00, 75.00
2, 5, 7   44  05/05/81, 12/08/80, 12/30/82        75.00, 25.00, 30.00
4        104  12/08/84                            50.00
```

The scalar function YEAR pulls out the year figure from each date, so dBASE IV searches in the PEN_DATE column for the highest year figures for each row. They are 12/08/80, 12/08/80, 11/12/84, 12/30/82 and 12/08/84 respectively.

Result:

```
PLAYERNO
--------
      27
     104
```

Example 10.8: For each player who has incurred more than $150 worth of penalties in total, find the player number, and the total amount of penalties.

```
SELECT    PLAYERNO, SUM(AMOUNT)
FROM      PENLTIES
GROUP BY  PLAYERNO
HAVING    SUM(AMOUNT) > 150
```

Intermediate result from GROUP BY:

```
PAYMENT  PNO  PEN_DATE                            AMOUNT
-------  ---  ------------------------------      --------------------
1          6  12/08/80                            100.00
6          8  12/08/80                            25.00
3, 8      27  09/10/83, 11/12/84                  100.00, 75.00
2, 5, 7   44  05/05/81, 12/08/80, 12/30/82        75.00, 25.00, 30.00
4        104  12/08/84                            50.00
```

Result:

```
PLAYERNO  SUM(AMOUNT)
--------  -----------
      27       175.00
```

Example 10.9: Give the number and the total amount of penalties for each player with the highest penalty total.

```
SELECT    PLAYERNO, SUM(AMOUNT)
FROM      PENLTIES
GROUP BY  PLAYERNO
HAVING    SUM(AMOUNT) >= ALL
          (SELECT   SUM(AMOUNT)
          FROM      PENLTIES
          GROUP BY  AMOUNT)
```

The intermediate result from the GROUP BY clause looks like this:

PAYMENT	PNO	PEN_DATE	AMOUNT
1	6	12/08/80	100.00
6	8	12/08/80	25.00
3, 8	27	09/10/83, 11/12/84	100.00, 75.00
2, 5, 7	44	05/05/81, 12/08/80, 12/30/82	75.00, 25.00, 30.00
4	104	12/08/84	50.00

The result of the subquery is:

```
AMOUNT
------
100.00
 25.00
175.00
130.00
 50.00
```

For each group (read player) dBASE IV determines whether the result of the function SUM(AMOUNT) is greater than or equal to all values in the result of the subquery. The final result then becomes:

```
PLAYERNO   SUM(AMOUNT)
--------   -----------
      27        175.00
```

10.6   General rule for the HAVING clause

In Section 10.3 we outlined rules for the use of columns and statistical functions in SELECT clauses. The HAVING clause requires a similar type of rule, as follows:

Each column name specified in the HAVING clause must occur within a statistical function or must occur in the list of columns named in the GROUP BY clause.

Therefore, the statement below is not correct, because the BIRTH column appears in the HAVING clause, but does *not* appear within a statistical function or in a list of columns by which grouping is performed.

```
SELECT    TOWN, COUNT(*)
FROM      PLAYERS
GROUP BY TOWN
HAVING    BIRTH > 1970
```

The reason for this limitation is the same as that for the SELECT clause rules outlined in Section 10.3.

Exercises

10.7 In which towns are there more than four players?

10.8 Get the number of each player who has incurred more than $150 in penalties.

10.9 Give the name, initials and number of penalties of each player who has incurred more than one penalty.

10.10 Give the number of the team for which the most players have played; at the same time give this number of players.

10.11 Give the team number and the division of each team for which more than four players have competed.

10.12 Give the name and initials of each player who has incurred more than two penalties of more than $40.

10.13 Give the name and initials of each player whose total penalties amount is the highest.

10.14 Get the number of each player whose total amount of penalties equals that of the player whose number is 6.

10.15 Give the numbers of the players who have incurred as many penalties as player 6.

10.16 For each team captained by a player who lives in Stratford, give the team number and the number of players who have won more matches than lost for that team.

11
SELECT statement: the ORDER BY clause

Just what is the sequence in which the rows of a SELECT statement are presented? If the SELECT statement has no ORDER BY clause the sequence is unpredictable. The addition of an ORDER BY clause at the end of a SELECT statement is the only guarantee that the rows in the end result will be sorted in a particular way.

```
<order by clause> ::=
    ORDER BY <sort specification>
            [ {,<sort specification>}... ]

<sort specification> ::=
    <column identifier> [ ASC | DESC ] |
    <sequence number> [ ASC | DESC ]

<column identifier> ::=
    [ <table identifier>. ] <column name>

<table identifier> ::= <table name>
```

11.1   Sorting on one column

The simplest manner of sorting is on one column.

Example 11.1: Find the player number and the date of each penalty; sort the result by player number.

```
SELECT   PLAYERNO, PEN_DATE
FROM     PENLTIES
ORDER BY PLAYERNO
```

Result:

```
PLAYERNO  PEN_DATE
--------  --------
       6  12/08/80
       8  12/08/80
      27  09/10/83
      27  11/12/84
      44  05/05/81
      44  12/08/80
      44  12/30/82
     104  12/08/84
```

Explanation: The eight rows are sorted on the basis of the values in the PLAYERNO column; the lowest value first and the highest value last.

11.2   Sorting with sequence numbers

In the ORDER BY clause we may replace column identifiers with *sequence numbers*. A sequence number assigns a number to each expression in the SELECT clause by which sorting must occur. This next statement is equivalent, then, to the one in the previous section:

```
SELECT   PLAYERNO, PEN_DATE
FROM     PENLTIES
ORDER BY 1
```

The sequence number 1 stands for the first expression in the SELECT clause. In the example above sequence numbers *may* be used in place of column identifiers. It is essential to use sequence numbers when a column expression consists of a function, a literal or a numeric expression.

Example 11.2: For each player who has incurred at least one penalty, give the total penalty amount and sort the result on this total.

```
SELECT    PLAYERNO, SUM(AMOUNT)
FROM      PENLTIES
GROUP BY  PLAYERNO
ORDER BY  2
```

Result:

```
PLAYERNO  SUM(AMOUNT)
--------  -----------
       8        25.00
     104        50.00
       6       100.00
      44       130.00
      27       175.00
```

Sorting on the total is only possible if a sequence number is used, because it is not permitted to say ORDER BY SUM(AMOUNT).

11.3 Ascending and descending sorting

If you don't specify anything after a column identifier or sequence number, dBASE IV sorts the result in *ascending* order. The same result can be achieved by explicitly specifying ASC after the column identifier. If you specify DESC the rows are presented in *descending* order. For each data type we will clarify what ascending order entails. The sorting of values in descending order always gives the reverse presentation of the sorting in ascending order, irrespective of the data type. Ascending order for numeric values means the lowest value is presented first, and the highest last. Ascending order for alphanumeric columns is the same as alphabetical order of words (such as in a dictionary): first, the words beginning with the letter A, then those with the letter B, and so on. Alphanumeric sorting is, nevertheless, not as simple as it seems. For example, does the lower case letter a come before or after the upper case A, and do digits come before or after letters? dBASE IV uses the internal ASCII values of the characters for its sorting. In Appendix E we give the ASCII representations for each character. From this appendix you will deduce that capital letters come before small letters and that digits come before capital letters.

Suppose that the following PEOPLE table is sorted by CODE.

```
NAME      CODE
--------  --------
Bowie     abc
Picasso   ABC
Warhol    ?abc
McLuhan   a bc
Strauss   ////
Chaplin   9abc
```

The SELECT statement:

```
SELECT     *
FROM       PEOPLE
ORDER BY CODE
```

Result:

```
NAME      CODE
-------   ----
Strauss   ////
Chaplin   9abc
Warhol    ?abc
Picasso   ABC
McLuhan   a bc
Bowie     abc
```

Ascending order of dates means that the date which comes in time before another date is presented first.

11.4   Sorting on more than one column

Multiple columns may be specified in an ORDER BY clause. In the first example in this chapter we ordered the result by the PLAYERNO column. Some player numbers appear more than once in the PENLTIES table though and we can't then predict how rows with the same player numbers are going to be sorted. By adding a second column identifier to the ORDER BY clause we eliminate the uncertainty.

Example 11.3: Give the player number and date of each penalty and sort the result by player number and within that by date.

```
SELECT     PLAYERNO, PEN_DATE
FROM       PENLTIES
ORDER BY PLAYERNO, PEN_DATE
```

Result:

```
PLAYERNO   PEN_DATE
--------   --------
       6   12/08/80
       8   12/08/80
      27   09/10/83
      27   11/12/84
      44   12/08/80
      44   05/05/81
      44   12/30/82
     104   12/08/84
```

Explanation: Rows with the same player number are sorted in ascending order on the PEN_DATE column.

If we proceed from this SELECT statement:

```
SELECT   NAME, TOWN
FROM     PLAYERS
```

we can then formulate these ORDER BY clauses (work out the results for yourself):

```
ORDER BY NAME DESC
ORDER BY TOWN ASC, NAME DESC
ORDER BY NAME, TOWN
ORDER BY PLAYERS.NAME
ORDER BY PLAYERS.TOWN DESC, NAME
```

11.5   General rules for sorting

The following rule apply for the ORDER BY clause:

- Sorting on logical values is not permitted.

- You cannot sort by a column or set of columns whose total length exceeds 100 characters. For example, you cannot sort on a column with a data type of CHAR(110).

Exercises

11.1   Give at least three different ORDER BY clauses for sorting the PLAYERS table in ascending order of player number.

11.2   Say which SELECT statements are incorrect:

1.
```
   SELECT   *
   FROM     PLAYERS
   ORDER BY 2
```

2.
```
   SELECT   *
   FROM     PLAYERS
   ORDER BY 20 DESC
```

3.
```
   SELECT   PLAYERNO, NAME, INITIALS
   FROM     PLAYERS
   ORDER BY 2, INITIALS DESC, 3 ASC
```

4.
```
   SELECT   *
   FROM     PLAYERS
   ORDER BY 1, PLAYERNO DESC
```

11.3 Give, separately, for each competition player in each team, the tally of the number of matches won minus the number lost; sort the result in ascending order by the tally.

12

SELECT statement:
the SAVE clause

The final clause in the SELECT statement is the SAVE clause. The SAVE clause added to the end of a SELECT statement enables you to save the result of the statement in a specially created table, rather than showing it on the screen.

```
<save clause> ::=
    SAVE TO TEMP <table identifier>
        [ <column list> ] [ KEEP ]

<table identifier> ::= <table name>

<column list> ::=
    ( <column name> [ {,<column name>}... ] )
```

12.1 Saving the result

If you add the SAVE clause to a SELECT statement and execute it, a new table is created. Here is an example.

Example 12.1: Create a separate table for all penalties incurred in 1984.

```
SELECT    *
FROM      PENLTIES
WHERE     YEAR(PEN_DATE) = 1984
SAVE TO   TEMP PEN84
```

Now no result table appears on the screen. Behind the scenes, dBASE IV creates a new table called PEN84. This table predictably has four columns, PAYMENTNO, PLAYERNO, PEN_DATE and AMOUNT, and these are the columns as the result of the SELECT statement.

A table created in this way behaves as though it is a 'normal' table, that is, it can be accessed via other SQL statements. New rows can be added to the table with INSERT statements, and synonyms and indexes can be defined for the table. The only difference between a table created with the SAVE clause and one created with the CREATE TABLE statement is that if the database is stopped, or SQL ended the former is automatically deleted, while the latter remains stored. Therefore, we call this type of table created by the SAVE clause a *temporary table*.

Example 12.2: Find the player number and the amount of each penalty in the PEN84 table.

```
SELECT    PLAYERNO, AMOUNT
FROM      PEN84
```

Result:

```
PLAYERNO  AMOUNT
--------  ------
     104   50.00
      27   75.00
```

Notes: The new table derives its column name and data types from the PENLTIES table. The data types are the same as those of the expressions in the SELECT clause.

The description of the table is also recorded in the catalog tables, namely the SYSTABLS and SYSCOLS tables.

12.2   Renaming columns

In the SAVE clause you can specify a list of column names. The effect of this is to explicitly name the columns in the new table. In this case, then, the column names are not derived from those of the original table.

Example 12.3: Create a separate table for all names, initials and addresses of players.

```
SELECT    NAME, INITIALS, HOUSENO, STREET, TOWN, POSTCODE
FROM      PLAYERS
SAVE TO   TEMP NAM (NM, IN, HN, ST, TN, PC)
```

The new NAM table has six columns called NM, IN, HN, ST, TN and PC respectively.

```
SELECT   DISTINCT TN
FROM     NAM
```

Result:

```
TN
---------
Stratford
Midhurst
Inglewood
Plymouth
Douglas
Eltham
```

If the SELECT clause contains expressions which are not just column identifiers, but also calculations, literals and functions, then you must include a list of column names in the SAVE clause.

12.3   Keeping created tables

As we mentioned before, a table created by the SAVE clause is automatically dropped when SQL ends or when the database is stopped. By extending the SAVE clause with the KEEP option, the table remains in the database. Note, that after SQL has ended or the database has been stopped this table is no longer accessible via SQL statements. It becomes a dBASE IV file and can be accessed with other dBASE IV commands. SQL recognizes another statement, the DBDEFINE statement, which enables a dBASE IV file to be converted to an SQL table and this can also be applied to a table created by SAVE. We describe the DBDEFINE statement in Chapter 21.

Example 12.4: Create the PEN84 table again so that it can be kept.

```
SELECT   *
FROM     PENLTIES
WHERE    YEAR(PEN_DATE) = 1984
SAVE TO  TEMP PEN84 KEEP
```

12.4   Deleting columns from tables

SQL has no statement for deleting columns. Using the SAVE clause is a simple method of deleting a column. Here is an example to illustrate this.

Example 12.5: Delete the DIVISION column from the TEAMS table.

1. Using a SELECT statement with a SAVE clause, create a table with the same columns as the TEAMS table, but without the DIVISION column. Fill this new table with all the rows from the TEAMS table.

    ```
    SELECT    TEAMNO, PLAYERNO
    FROM      TEAMS
    SAVE TO   TEMP HELP
    ```

2. Use SELECT statements on the catalog tables to determine which views, indexes, synonyms and so on are dependent on the TEAMS table.

3. Drop the old TEAMS table.

    ```
    DROP TABLE TEAMS
    ```

4. Create a table called TEAMS table, but with the structure of the HELP table. Fill this new TEAMS table with all the rows from the HELP table.

    ```
    SELECT    *
    FROM      HELP
    SAVE TO   TEMP TEAMS KEEP
    ```

5. Restore all views, indexes and so on which were deleted automatically by dBASE IV when the original TEAMS table was dropped. These were the objects listed from step 2 of this process.

13
Combining SELECT statements

We can use the UNION operator to combine the results of individual SELECT statements. An individual SELECT statement like this is referred to as a *select block*. The UNION is an extension of the possibilities of the SELECT statement that we have already discussed. In Chapter 6 we gave a definition of the SELECT statement which did not include the UNION, so now we complete the definition with this operator.

```
<select statement> ::=
    <select block>
    [ { UNION <select block> }... ]
    [ <order by clause> |
      <save clause> ]

<select block> ::=
    <select clause>
    <from clause>
    [ <where clause> ]
    [ <group by clause>
    [ <having clause> ] ]
```

13.1   Linking SELECT statements with UNION

If two select blocks are combined with the UNION operator, the end result consists of the resulting rows from either or both of the select blocks. UNION is the equivalent of the *union* operator from set theory.

Example 13.1: Give the number and place of residence of each player from Inglewood and Plymouth.

```
SELECT    PLAYERNO, TOWN
FROM      PLAYERS
WHERE     TOWN = 'Inglewood'
UNION
SELECT    PLAYERNO, TOWN
FROM      PLAYERS
WHERE     TOWN = 'Plymouth'
```

Result:

```
PLAYERNO  TOWN
--------  ---------
      44  Inglewood
       8  Inglewood
     112  Plymouth
```

Explanation: Each of the two select blocks returns a table with two columns and zero or more rows. The UNION operator places the two tables *under* one another, with the end result of the entire statement being one table.

Note: The statement above could also have been formulated using the OR operator, of course:

```
SELECT    PLAYERS, TOWN
FROM      PLAYERS
WHERE     TOWN = 'Inglewood'
OR        TOWN = 'Plymouth'
```

However, it is not always possible to substitute the OR operator for the UNION operator. Here is an example. Suppose that we have the following two tables. The RECPLAY table contains data about recreational players, while the COMP-PLAY table has the data about competition players.

```
The RECPLAY table:

PLAYERNO  NAME
--------  ------
       7  Wise
      39  Bishop
```

The COMPPLAY table:

```
PLAYERNO  NAME
--------  ---------
       6  Parmenter
      44  Baker
      83  Hope
```

Example 13.2: Give the numbers and names of all players.

```
SELECT    PLAYERNO, NAME
FROM      RECPLAY
UNION
SELECT    PLAYERNO, NAME
FROM      COMPPLAY
```

Result:

```
PLAYERNO  NAME
--------  ---------
       7  Wise
      39  Bishop
       6  Parmenter
      44  Baker
      83  Hope
```

When the UNION operator is used, dBASE IV automatically removes all duplicate rows from the end result. Therefore, you may not specify DISTINCT in the SELECT clause of a select block if the UNION operator is also used.

Example 13.3: Give the number of each player who has incurred at least one penalty, or who is a captain or for whom both conditions apply.

```
SELECT    PLAYERNO
FROM      PENLTIES
UNION
SELECT    PLAYERNO
FROM      TEAMS
```

Result:

```
PLAYERNO
--------
       6
       8
      27
      44
     104
```

Explanation: It is clear from the result that all the duplicate rows have been deleted.

You can join more than two select blocks in a SELECT statement. Here is an example.

Example 13.4: Give the number of each player who has incurred at least one penalty, who is a captain, who lives in Stratford or for whom two or three of these conditions apply.

```
SELECT    PLAYERNO
FROM      PENLTIES
UNION
SELECT    PLAYERNO
FROM      TEAMS
UNION
SELECT    PLAYERNO
FROM      PLAYERS
WHERE     TOWN = 'Stratford'
```

Result:

```
PLAYERNO
--------
       2
       6
       7
       8
      27
      39
      44
      57
      83
     100
     104
```

13.2   Rules for using UNION

The following rules for using the UNION operator must be observed:

- The SELECT clauses of all relevant select blocks must have the same number of expressions.

- Expressions which will be combined (or placed under one another) in the end result must have the same data type.

- An ORDER BY clause may only be specified after the last select block. The ordering is performed on the entire end result, only after all intermediate results have been combined.

- The SELECT clauses may not contain DISTINCT, as dBASE IV automatically deletes duplicate rows when a UNION is performed.

The following SELECT statements are not written according to these rules (work through them for yourself):

- ```
  SELECT    *
  FROM      PLAYERS
  UNION
  SELECT    *
  FROM      PENLTIES
  ```

- ```
  SELECT    PLAYERNO, TOWN
  FROM      PLAYERS
  UNION
  SELECT    PLAYERNO, AMOUNT
  FROM      PENLTIES
  ```

- ```
  SELECT    PLAYERNO
  FROM      PLAYERS
  WHERE     TOWN = 'Stratford'
  ORDER BY 1
  UNION
  SELECT    PLAYERNO
  FROM      TEAMS
  ORDER BY 1
  ```

- ```
  SELECT    DISTINCT PLAYERNO
  FROM      PENLTIES
  UNION
  SELECT    PLAYERNO
  FROM      PLAYERS
  ```

Exercises

13.1 Say which of the following statements are correct and which are incorrect and give reasons:

1.
```
SELECT    ...
FROM      ...
GROUP BY  ...
HAVING    ...
UNION
SELECT    ...
FROM      ...
ORDER BY  ...
```

2.
```
SELECT    PLAYERNO, NAME
FROM      PLAYERS
UNION
SELECT    PLAYERNO, POSTCODE
FROM      PLAYERS
```

3.
```
SELECT    TEAMNO
FROM      TEAMS
UNION
SELECT    PLAYERNO
FROM      PLAYERS
ORDER BY 1
```

4.
```
SELECT    DISTINCT PLAYERNO
FROM      PLAYERS
UNION
SELECT    PLAYERNO
FROM      PENLTIES
ORDER BY 1
```

5.
```
SELECT    ...
FROM      ...
GROUP BY  ...
ORDER BY  ...
UNION
SELECT    ...
FROM      ...
```

13.2 If we assume the original contents of the four tables, how many rows are there in the end results of each of the following statements?

```
1.    SELECT    TOWN
      FROM      PLAYERS
      UNION
      SELECT    TOWN
      FROM      PLAYERS

2.    SELECT    PLAYERNO
      FROM      PENLTIES
      UNION
      SELECT    PLAYERNO
      FROM      PLAYERS

3.    SELECT    BIRTH
      FROM      PLAYERS
      UNION
      SELECT    JOINED
      FROM      PLAYERS
```

14
The SELECT statement (continued)

In the previous chapters we have used relatively simple examples to demonstrate and discuss the possibilities of the SELECT statement. We have generally limited ourselves to one particular aspect of SQL in each example. In this chapter we are including examples that demonstrate the combination of a number of aspects of the SELECT statement. The chapter comprises five topics. The first two sections discuss examples of SELECT statements focusing on statistical and administrative applications. And in the following three sections we explore more fully three special forms of the SELECT statement: the *join*, the *negative condition* and the *correlated subquery*.

14.1 Statistical measures

We looked at the statistical functions COUNT, MIN, MAX, AVG and SUM in Chapter 9. These functions can be used to perform statistical analysis, but the whole field of statistics encompasses a much wider range of measures. In this section we discuss how the following statistical measures can be calculated:

- unweighted arithmetic mean
- weighted arithmetic mean
- frequency table
- mode
- median
- range
- average absolute deviation
- variance
- index figures

161

We are not going to use our sample database; instead we will adopt the SALARIES table below, whose NAME column is the primary key.

```
The SALARIES table:

NAME    AMOUNT
-----   ------
Jan       100
Pete      200
Thea      150
Keith     200
Karen     400
```

In the definitions used in this section the term 'set of values' is used, and this is comparable with the population of a column.

Example 14.1: The *unweighted arithmetic mean* of a set of values is equal to the sum of the different values, divided by the number of different values. The unweighted arithmetic mean of the set of AMOUNTs is:

```
SELECT    AVG(DISTINCT AMOUNT)
FROM      SALARIES

          100 + 200 + 150 + 400
Result:   ---------------------  = 212.5
                    4
```

The following statement returns the same result:

```
SELECT    SUM(DISTINCT AMOUNT) / COUNT(DISTINCT AMOUNT)
FROM      SALARIES
```

Example 14.2: The *weighted arithmetic mean* of a set of values is equal to the sum of all values, divided by the number of values. The difference between this and the unweighted arithmetic mean is that, here, values that occur more than once are also included more than once in the calculation. The weighted arithmetic mean of the set of AMOUNTs is:

```
SELECT    AVG(AMOUNT)
FROM      SALARIES

          100 + 200 + 150 + 200 + 400
Result:   ---------------------------  = 210
                       5
```

Example 14.3: A *frequency table* contains, for each value in a set, the frequency with which the value in the set occurs. The frequency table for the set of AMOUNTs is:

```
SELECT    AMOUNT, COUNT(*)
FROM      SALARIES
GROUP BY AMOUNT
```

Result:

```
AMOUNT   COUNT(*)
------   --------
100         1
150         1
200         2
400         1
```

Example 14.4: The *mode* of a set of values is the value with the highest frequency. The mode of the set of AMOUNTs is:

```
SELECT    DISTINCT AMOUNT
FROM      SALARIES
GROUP BY AMOUNT
HAVING    COUNT(*) >= ALL
          (SELECT   COUNT(*)
          FROM      SALARIES
          GROUP BY AMOUNT)
```

The subquery returns a set of frequencies; in our case, the frequencies 1 and 2. dBASE IV automatically removes duplicate values. The whole statement returns each AMOUNT for which the frequency is greater than or equal to all values in the intermediate result from the subquery.

Result:

```
AMOUNT
------
  200
```

Example 14.5: The *median* of a set of values is the middle value when the values are sorted in either ascending or descending order. If the set consists of an even number of values, there is no 'middle' value, so the median then equals the arithmetic mean of the two values between which the middle value should lie.

Determining the median of a column with duplicate values is not possible with interactive SQL. Therefore, our examples will not have duplicate values in the relevant column. In the first example, the following COSTS table is our starting point:

```
The COSTS table:

AMOUNT
-------
    100
    200
    300
    400
    500
```

The median of the AMOUNT column is that value whose sequence number is equal to the total number of values divided by two, plus a half, or rounded up. A value's sequence number can be found by counting the number of values which are less than or equal to the value in question:

```
SELECT    C1.AMOUNT
FROM      COSTS C1, COSTS C2
WHERE     C1.AMOUNT >= C2.AMOUNT
GROUP BY C1.AMOUNT
HAVING    COUNT(*) =
          (SELECT   ROUND(COUNT(*) / 2)
           FROM     COSTS)
```

The intermediate result from the WHERE clause:

```
C1.AMOUNT   C2.AMOUNT
----------  ----------
       100         100
       200         100
       200         200
       300         100
       300         200
       300         300
       400         100
       400         200
       400         300
       400         400
       500         100
       500         200
       500         300
       500         400
       500         500
```

The intermediate result from the GROUP BY clause:

```
C1.AMOUNT  C2.AMOUNT
---------  ----------------------
      100  100
      200  100, 200
      300  100, 200, 300
      400  100, 200, 300, 400
      500  100, 200, 300, 400, 500
```

The result of the subquery is $ROUND(5/2)$ and that equals 3. The intermediate result from the HAVING clause is now easy to calculate:

```
C1.AMOUNT  C2.AMOUNT
---------  -------------
      300  100, 200, 300
```

The end result:

```
C1.AMOUNT
---------
      300
```

If the COSTS table had contained an even number of values, this statement would have returned a wrong answer (or, to be precise, no answer). In this situation, another SELECT statement is needed.

Suppose that the COSTS table has the following contents and that you must find the median.

```
The COSTS table:

AMOUNT
------
   100
   200
   300
   400
```

The median of the AMOUNT column now equals the average of the two middle values. The middle values have sequence numbers that equal the total number of values divided by two, and the total number of values divided by two, plus one, respectively.

The median of the AMOUNT column cannot now be calculated simply using a SELECT statement. An intermediate result has to be stored in a table.

The next statement determines what the two middle values are. The result is saved in a HELP table created especially.

```
SELECT    C1.AMOUNT
FROM      COSTS C1, COSTS C2
WHERE     C1.AMOUNT >= C2.AMOUNT
GROUP BY C1.AMOUNT
HAVING    COUNT(*) =
          (SELECT   COUNT(*) / 2
           FROM     COSTS)
OR        COUNT(*) =
          (SELECT   (COUNT(*) / 2) + 1
           FROM     COSTS)
SAVE TO   TEMP HELP (AMOUNT)
```

The contents of the HELP table are now:

```
AMOUNT
------
   200
   300
```

Calculating the median is now simple:

```
SELECT    AVG(AMOUNT)
FROM      HELP
```

Result:

```
AVG(AMOUNT)
-----------
        250
```

Example 14.6: The *range* (also known as the *spread*) of a set of values is equal to the difference between the highest and lowest values in the set. For the AMOUNT column in the SALARIES table this is:

```
SELECT   MAX(AMOUNT) - MIN(AMOUNT)
FROM     SALARIES
```

Result:

```
MAX(AMOUNT) - MIN(AMOUNT)
-------------------------
                      300
```

Example 14.7: The *average absolute deviation* of a set of values is equal to the weighted arithmetic mean of the absolute deviations of the values with respect to their weighted arithmetic mean.

The average absolute deviation of the AMOUNT column cannot be calculated with a single SELECT statement. Again, an intermediate result must be stored in a table.

The SELECT statement below creates a table and populates it with the absolute deviations:

```
SELECT    ABS(S1.AMOUNT - AVG(S2.AMOUNT))
FROM      SALARIES S1, SALARIES S2
GROUP BY S1.AMOUNT, S1.NAME
SAVE TO  TEMP ABSOLUTE (DEVIATION)
```

The contents of the ABSOLUTE table:

```
DEVIATION
---------
      110
       10
       60
       10
      190
```

You can now calculate the average of these absolute deviations like this:

```
SELECT    AVG(DEVIATION)
FROM      ABSOLUTE
```

Result:

```
AVG(DEVIATION)
--------------
            76
```

Example 14.8: The *variance* of a set of values is equal to the weighted arithmetic mean of the squared deviations of the values with respect to their arithmetic mean.

Just as with the average absolute deviation, a single SELECT statement is not sufficient to perform this calculation. Instead, the process must be split into several statements.

In the statement below, we subtract the weighted arithmetic mean of all amounts from each amount. To get the squared deviation, this result is multiplied by itself:

```
SELECT    (S1.AMOUNT - AVG(S2.AMOUNT)) ** 2
FROM      SALARIES S1, SALARIES S2
GROUP BY S1.AMOUNT, S1.NAME
SAVE TO  TEMP SQUARE (DEVIATION)
```

The contents of the SQUARE table:

```
DEVIATION
----------
    12100
      100
     3600
      100
    36100
```

The variance can now be calculated by taking the weighted arithmetic mean of these squared deviations:

```
SELECT    AVG(DEVIATION)
FROM      SQUARE
```

Result:

```
AVG(DEVIATION)
--------------
         10400
```

Example 14.9: *Index figures* show how particular values in a set are positioned in relation to another value in the same set. This value is called the base value, and is set at 100.

Example: In the SALARIES table, set Thea's AMOUNT as the base value to reduce to 100. In reality, this AMOUNT currently equals 150 and therefore must be multiplied by 100/150. The following statement calculates the index figures for the remaining values, so that all values are scaled by the same amount:

```
SELECT    NAME, AMOUNT, AMOUNT * (100 / 150)
FROM      SALARIES
```

Result:

```
NAME    AMOUNT  AMOUNT * (100 / 150)
-----   ------  --------------------
Jan       100                  66.66
Pete      200                 133.33
Thea      150                 100.00
Keith     200                 133.33
Karen     400                 266.66
```

We were able to write the SELECT statement in this way because it was known that the AMOUNT for Thea was 150. With the following statement, Thea's AMOUNT can be set as the base value, without knowing what the actual AMOUNT is, and index figures (with respect to that AMOUNT) calculated.

```
SELECT    S1.NAME, S1.AMOUNT, S1.AMOUNT * (100 / S2.AMOUNT)
FROM      SALARIES S1, SALARIES S2
WHERE     S2.NAME = 'Thea'
```

Exercise

14.1 The harmonic mean of a set of values is equal to the inverse of the weighted arithmetic mean of the inverse values. The inverse of value A is equal to 1 divided by A. Calculate the harmonic mean for the AMOUNT column in the SALARIES table.

14.2   Administrative applications

This section describes a number of administrative applications. The starting point is a new COSTS table:

```
The COSTS table:

ROWNO   AMOUNT
-----   ------
    1      100
    2      200
    3      150
```

The ROWNO column is the primary key of the COSTS table. A (very) small table has been chosen so that the intermediate results do not become unwieldy.

Example 14.10: Give, for each ROWNO, the AMOUNT plus the sum of that AMOUNT and the AMOUNTs of all the rows with a lower row number (that is, get the cumulative values).

```
SELECT    C1.ROWNO, C1.AMOUNT, SUM(C2.AMOUNT)
FROM      COSTS C1, COSTS C2
WHERE     C1.ROWNO >= C2.ROWNO
GROUP BY C1.ROWNO, C1.AMOUNT
ORDER BY C1.ROWNO
```

The desired result is:

```
ROWNO   AMOUNT   SUM(C2.AMOUNT)
-----   ------   --------------
    1      100              100
    2      200              300
    3      150              450
```

The intermediate result from the FROM clause:

```
C1.ROWNO   C1.AMOUNT   C2.ROWNO   C2.AMOUNT
--------   ---------   --------   ---------
       1         100          1         100
       1         100          2         200
       1         100          3         150
       2         200          1         100
       2         200          2         200
       2         200          3         150
       3         150          1         100
       3         150          2         200
       3         150          3         150
```

The intermediate result from the WHERE clause:

```
C1.ROWNO   C1.AMOUNT   C2.ROWNO   C2.AMOUNT
--------   ---------   --------   ---------
       1         100          1         100
       2         200          1         100
       2         200          2         200
       3         150          1         100
       3         150          2         200
       3         150          3         150
```

The intermediate result from the GROUP BY clause:

```
C1.ROWNO   C1.AMOUNT   C2.ROWNO   C2.AMOUNT
--------   ---------   --------   --------------
       1         100   1          100
       2         200   1, 2       100, 200
       3         150   1, 2, 3    100, 200, 150
```

The intermediate result from the SELECT clause:

```
C1.ROWNO   C1.AMOUNT   SUM(C2.AMOUNT)
--------   ---------   --------------
       1         100              100
       2         200              300
       3         150              450
```

The end result is the same as the table above.

Example 14.11: For each ROWNO, give the AMOUNT and the percentage that the AMOUNT represents of the sum of all AMOUNTs.

```
SELECT    C1.ROWNO, C1.AMOUNT,
          (C1.AMOUNT * 100) / SUM(C2.AMOUNT)
FROM      COSTS C1, COSTS C2
GROUP BY  C1.ROWNO, C1.AMOUNT
ORDER BY  C1.ROWNO
```

The intermediate result from the FROM clause is the same as that of the previous example. However, the intermediate result from the GROUP BY clause is quite different:

```
C1.ROWNO   C1.AMOUNT   C2.ROWNO   C2.AMOUNT
--------   ---------   --------   -------------
       1         100   1, 2, 3    100, 200, 150
       2         200   1, 2, 3    100, 200, 150
       3         150   1, 2, 3    100, 200, 150
```

The intermediate result of the SELECT clause:

```
C1.ROWNO   C1.AMOUNT   (C1.AMOUNT * 100) / SUM(C2.AMOUNT)
--------   ---------   ----------------------------------
       1         100                                22.22
       2         200                                44.44
       3         150                                33.33
```

Work out for yourself what the end result is.

The next question uses the SALARIES table described in the previous section.

Example 14.12: Group the names in the SALARIES table on the basis of the following criteria:

group 1   people whose salary is less than 151

group 2   people whose salary is more than 150 and less than 201

group 3   people whose salary is higher than 200

One possible solution is:

```
SELECT   1, NAME, AMOUNT
FROM     SALARIES
WHERE    AMOUNT BETWEEN 0 AND 150
UNION
SELECT   2, NAME, AMOUNT
FROM     SALARIES
WHERE    AMOUNT BETWEEN 151 AND 200
UNION
SELECT   3, NAME, AMOUNT
FROM     SALARIES
WHERE    AMOUNT > 200
```

Result:

```
              NAME    AMOUNT
----------    -----   ------
1             Jan        100
1             Thea       150
2             Pete       200
2             Keith      200
3             Karen      400
```

Another way of tackling this question is to store the criteria in a separate table (see below). The lowest and highest possible values for each group are recorded. For group 3, a huge number is given as the highest value. This assumes that the salary will not be greater than 30,000.

```
The GROUPS table:

NO  LOW  HIGH
--  ---  -----
 1    0    150
 2  151    200
 3  201  30000
```

The SELECT statement then becomes:

```
SELECT    NO, NAME, AMOUNT
FROM      GROUPS, SALARIES
WHERE     AMOUNT BETWEEN LOW AND HIGH
ORDER BY NO, NAME
```

The result is the same.

One advantage of this method is that it is easier to alter the boundaries of the groups. Adding a new group (for example, from 301 up to and including 400) is also no problem now. If these types of changes occurred in the first solution, the SELECT statement would need to be altered or extended. A second advantage is that the SELECT statement does not become longer as more groups are added to the data. Work out what the statement from the first solution would look like if there were twenty groups!

Example 14.13: Order the SALARIES table by NAME and give each row a sequence number. The desired result is:

```
ROWNO  NAME   AMOUNT
-----  -----  ------
    1  Jan       100
    2  Karen     400
    3  Keith     200
    4  Pete      200
    5  Thea      150
```

The SELECT statement for this is:

```
SELECT    COUNT(*), S1.NAME, S1.AMOUNT
FROM      SALARIES S1, SALARIES S2
WHERE     S1.NAME >= S2.NAME
GROUP BY S1.NAME, S1.AMOUNT
ORDER BY 1
```

We will not show the intermediate result from the FROM clause, but will begin with the WHERE clause:

S1.NAME	S1.AMOUNT	S2.NAME	S2.AMOUNT
Jan	100	Jan	100
Pete	200	Jan	100
Pete	200	Pete	200
Pete	200	Keith	200
Pete	200	Karen	400
Thea	150	Jan	100
Thea	150	Pete	200
Thea	150	Thea	150
Thea	150	Keith	200
Thea	150	Karen	400
Keith	200	Jan	100
Keith	200	Karen	400
Keith	200	Keith	200
Karen	400	Jan	100
Karen	400	Karen	400

By performing a GROUP BY on the columns S1.NAME and S1.AMOUNT we get a table that shows the number of S2.NAME values for every name:

S1.NAME	S1.AMOUNT	S2.NAME	S2.AMOUNT
Jan	100	Jan	100
Pete	200	Jan, Pete, Keith, Karen	100, 200, 200, 400
Thea	150	Jan, Pete, Thea, Keith, Karen	100, 200, 150, 200, 400
Keith	200	Jan, Keith, Karen	100, 200, 400
Karen	400	Jan, Karen	100, 400

The number of S2.NAME values can now be used as a row number:

```
COUNT(*)   S1.NAME   S1.AMOUNT
--------   -------   ---------
       1   Jan             100
       4   Pete            200
       5   Thea            150
       3   Keith           200
       2   Karen           400
```

If this intermediate result is ordered by the data in the second column, the desired result is achieved.

Example 14.14: Get the three highest league numbers. If you want simply to find the highest league number, then the following SELECT statement suffices:

```
SELECT   MAX(LEAGUENO)
FROM     PLAYERS
```

Result:

```
MAX(LEAGUENO)
-------------
8467
```

You cannot, however, use this statement with the MAX function to determine the *three* highest league numbers. Instead, the following statement is necessary:

```
SELECT    LEAGUENO
FROM      PLAYERS P1
WHERE     3 >
          (SELECT    COUNT(*)
          FROM      PLAYERS P2
          WHERE     P1.LEAGUENO < P2.LEAGUENO)
ORDER BY LEAGUENO DESC
```

Result:

```
LEAGUENO
--------
8467
7060
6524
```

Explanation: There is no higher league number than the highest! The second highest number recognizes one number that is higher and the third highest recognizes only two higher numbers. With the subquery we count, for each league number, the number of league numbers that are higher. If this shows fewer than three league numbers, then the league number concerned appears in the end result. Determining the three lowest league numbers is now very simple:

```
SELECT    LEAGUENO
FROM      PLAYERS P1
WHERE     3 >
          (SELECT   COUNT(*)
          FROM      PLAYERS P2
          WHERE     P1.LEAGUENO > P2.LEAGUENO)
ORDER BY LEAGUENO DESC
```

These two examples both pertain to a column that contains *no* duplicate values. Neither statement is appropriate for the three highest (or lowest) values in a column in which duplicate values *are* present. Such a question cannot be answered directly with interactive SQL.

Exercises

14.2 Use the table shown below to complete the following exercises. The primary key of the ORDERROW table is formed by the ORDERNO and ROWNO columns.

The ORDERROW table:

ORDERNO	ROWNO	COSTS
1	1	100
1	2	300
2	1	200
2	2	400
2	3	400

For some of the following exercises you will have to store an intermediate result in a table.

Give, for each order-row combination, the order number, the row number, the costs, and for each order, the cumulative costs. The desired result is:

ORDERNO	ROWNO	COSTS	CUMULATIVE
1	1	100	100
1	2	300	400
2	1	200	200
2	2	400	600
2	3	400	1000

14.3 Give, for each order-row combination, the order number, the row number, the costs, and for each row, the percentage of total costs for the order concerned that the costs represent.

ORDERNO	ROWNO	COSTS	SUM
1	1	100	25
1	2	300	75
2	1	200	20
2	2	400	40
2	3	400	40

14.4 Give, for each order, the order number, the total costs from all order-row combinations that relate to the order concerned, and the percentage that these costs represent of the sum of the costs of all orders.

14.5 Sort the ORDERROW table by order number and within that by row number. Provide a row number before the ORDERNO column.

14.6 Find, for each order, the order-row combination with the highest costs.

14.7 Find the order with the highest total costs.

14.3 The join

You have already seen the join used in many examples in the previous chapters. In a *join* of tables, rows from these tables are combined. The result is, as always, a table. A SELECT statement can be called a join if the FROM clause names two or more table identifiers and the WHERE clause has at least one condition that compares columns from the different tables.

The columns in a SELECT statement that define the join are called, predictably, the *join columns*. In the following SELECT statement these are the PLAYERS.PLAYERNO and TEAMS.PLAYERNO columns.

```
SELECT   PLAYERS.PLAYERNO, TEAMNO
FROM     PLAYERS, TEAMS
WHERE    PLAYERS.PLAYERNO = TEAMS.PLAYERNO
```

Between join columns there always exists a certain type of relationship. If C1 and C2 are two columns, then four types of relationship between C1 and C2 are possible:

1.   The populations of C1 and C2 are *equal*.
2.   The population of C1 is a *subset* of that of C2 (or C2 or C1).
3.   The populations of C1 and C2 are *conjoint* (they have some values in common).
4.   The populations of C1 and C2 are *disjoint* (they have no values in common).

If C1 and C2 are considered to be sets with values, the following relationships can be defined using set theory terminology:

1. $C1 = C2$
2. $C1 \subset C2$ (or $C2 \subset C1$)
3. $C1 - C2 \neq \emptyset$ AND $C2 - C1 \neq \emptyset$
4. $C1 - C2 = C1$ AND $C2 - C1 = C2$

This section is going to look in great detail at how the relationship between the join columns influences the result of the SELECT statement in which the join appears.

Just like 'primary key' and 'row', 'join' is a term from the relational model. The relational model differentiates between types of joins. This section will cover the following types of joins and their characteristics:

- theta join
- equijoin
- natural join

The general join or *theta join* takes this form in SQL:

```
SELECT    *
FROM      PLAYERS, TEAMS
WHERE     PLAYERS.PLAYERNO ? TEAMS.PLAYERNO
```

The question mark stands for any comparison operator. PLAYERS.PLAYERNO and TEAMS.PLAYERNO are the join columns. When the comparison operator is '=' we speak of an *equijoin*. Example:

```
SELECT    *
FROM      PLAYERS, TEAMS
WHERE     PLAYERS.PLAYERNO = TEAMS.PLAYERNO
```

The *natural join* looks like the equijoin. The difference is, however, that in the SELECT clause only one of the join columns is given in the end result. By using the asterisk (*) in the example above the user gets both join columns presented. A natural join is achieved by explicitly specifying all the required columns in the SELECT clause:

```
SELECT    PLAYERS.*, TEAMS.TEAMNO, TEAMS.DIVISION
FROM      PLAYERS, TEAMS
WHERE     PLAYERS.PLAYERNO = TEAMS.PLAYERNO
```

The join column TEAMS.PLAYERNO is not included in the SELECT clause, although the other join column PLAYERS.PLAYERNO is mentioned. An equivalent way of formulating this is:

```
SELECT    TEAMS.*, PLAYERS.NAME, PLAYERS.INITIALS, ...,
          PLAYERS.LEAGUENO
FROM      PLAYERS, TEAMS
WHERE     PLAYERS.PLAYERNO = TEAMS.PLAYERNO
```

Two forms of the equijoin exist: the *inner equijoin* and the *outer equijoin*. You will discover the difference between them by following the next example.

Example 14.15: Find, for each player, the name, player number and the penalties incurred.

```
SELECT    PLAYERS.PLAYERNO, NAME, AMOUNT
FROM      PLAYERS, PENLTIES
WHERE     PLAYERS.PLAYERNO = PENLTIES.PLAYERNO
```

Result:

```
PLAYERNO  NAME         AMOUNT
--------  ---------    ------
       6  Parmenter    100.00
      44  Baker         75.00
      27  Collins      100.00
     104  Moorman       50.00
      44  Baker         25.00
       8  Newcastle     25.00
      44  Baker         30.00
      27  Collins       70.00
```

Indeed, this is the result of the above SELECT statement, but does it satisfy our requirements? The answer is no! This SELECT statement gives only the player number and the name of players who have incurred at least one penalty (that is, those who appear in the PENLTIES table). Because SQL is only presenting data about this subset of all players, this join is called an *inner* equijoin.

The result required can be achieved by extending the SELECT statement:

```
SELECT    PLAYERS.PLAYERNO, NAME, AMOUNT
FROM      PLAYERS, PENLTIES
WHERE     PLAYERS.PLAYERNO = PENLTIES.PLAYERNO
UNION
SELECT    PLAYERNO, NAME, 0.00
FROM      PLAYERS
WHERE     PLAYERNO NOT IN
          (SELECT  PLAYERNO
           FROM    PENLTIES)
```

Result:

PLAYERNO	NAME	AMOUNT
6	Parmenter	100.00
44	Baker	75.00
27	Collins	100.00
104	Moorman	50.00
44	Baker	25.00
8	Newcastle	25.00
44	Baker	30.00
27	Collins	70.00
83	Hope	0.00
2	Everett	0.00
7	Wise	0.00
57	Brown	0.00
39	Bishop	0.00
112	Bailey	0.00
100	Parmenter	0.00
28	Collins	0.00
95	Miller	0.00

This type of equijoin is called an *outer equijoin*.

A subset relationship exists between the populations of the two join columns, PENLTIES.PLAYERNO being a subset of PLAYERS.PLAYERNO.

The influence that the relationship type has on the result of an inner equijoin and an outer equijoin will now be shown, for each type of relationship between the join columns. For this, modified versions of the PLAYERS and PENLTIES tables will be used. PLAYERS.PLAYERNO and PENLTIES.PLAYERNO are the join columns.

14.3.1   The populations of the join columns are the same

Suppose that the two tables look like this:

The PLAYERS table:

PLAYERNO	TOWN
6	Stratford
44	Inglewood
104	Eltham

The PENLTIES table:

PLAYERNO	AMOUNT
6	100
44	75
44	25
44	30
104	50

The inner equijoin:

```
SELECT    P.PLAYERNO, TOWN, AMOUNT
FROM      PLAYERS P, PENLTIES PN
WHERE     P.PLAYERNO = PN.PLAYERNO
```

Result:

```
PLAYERNO   TOWN          AMOUNT
--------   ---------     ------
       6   Stratford       100
      44   Inglewood        75
      44   Inglewood        25
      44   Inglewood        30
     104   Eltham           50
```

An outer equijoin returns the same result because neither of the two tables contains a row with a player number that does not appear in the other table.

14.3.2   The population of one join column is a subset

Suppose that the two tables have the following contents (the PENLTIES.PLAYERNO column is a subset of the PLAYERS.PLAYERNO column):

```
The PLAYERS table:                The PENLTIES table:

PLAYERNO   TOWN                    PLAYERNO   AMOUNT
--------   ---------               --------   ------
       6   Stratford                     6      100
      44   Inglewood                   104       50
     104   Eltham
```

The inner equijoin:

```
SELECT    P.PLAYERNO, TOWN, AMOUNT
FROM      PLAYERS P, PENLTIES PN
WHERE     P.PLAYERNO = PN.PLAYERNO
```

Result:

```
PLAYERNO   TOWN          AMOUNT
--------   ---------     ------
       6   Stratford       100
     104   Eltham           50
```

Only players who appear in both tables (and therefore in the intersection of the two populations) are included in the result. Player 44 does not occur in this intersection, so does not appear in the result.

The outer equijoin:

```
SELECT    P.PLAYERNO, TOWN, AMOUNT
FROM      PLAYERS P, PENLTIES PN
WHERE     P.PLAYERNO = PN.PLAYERNO
UNION
SELECT    PLAYERNO, TOWN, 0
FROM      PLAYERS
WHERE     PLAYERNO NOT IN
          (SELECT    PLAYERNO
           FROM      PENLTIES)
```

Result:

```
PLAYERNO  TOWN        AMOUNT
--------  ---------   ------
       6  Stratford      100
     104  Eltham          50
      44  Inglewood        0
```

14.3.3 The populations of the join columns are conjoint

Suppose that for this example we include player 8 in the PENLTIES table. Actually, this is not really possible because player 8 does not even appear in the PLAYERS table. But we can change the rules of our database design to illustrate the point. The tables now look like this:

```
The PLAYERS table:          The PENLTIES table:

PLAYERNO  TOWN             PLAYERNO  AMOUNT
--------  ---------        --------  ------
       6  Stratford               6     100
      44  Inglewood             104      50
     104  Eltham                  8      25
```

The inner equijoin:

```
SELECT    P.PLAYERNO, TOWN, AMOUNT
FROM      PLAYERS P, PENLTIES PN
WHERE     P.PLAYERNO = PN.PLAYERNO
```

Result:

```
PLAYERNO  TOWN        AMOUNT
--------  ---------   ------
       6  Stratford      100
     104  Eltham          50
```

Only the players who appear in both tables are picked out for the result. In order to formulate an outer equijoin the SELECT statement must be extended with two subqueries.

The outer equijoin:

```
SELECT    P.PLAYERNO, TOWN, AMOUNT
FROM      PLAYERS P, PENLTIES PN
WHERE     P.PLAYERNO = PN.PLAYERNO
UNION
SELECT    PLAYERNO, TOWN, 0
FROM      PLAYERS
WHERE     PLAYERNO NOT IN
          (SELECT    PLAYERNO
           FROM      PENLTIES)
UNION
SELECT    PLAYERNO, '           ', AMOUNT
FROM      PENLTIES
WHERE     PLAYERNO NOT IN
          (SELECT    PLAYERNO
           FROM      PLAYERS)
```

Result:

```
PLAYERNO  TOWN         AMOUNT
--------  ----------   ------
       6  Stratford       100
     104  Eltham           50
      44  Inglewood         0
       8                   25
```

14.3.4   The populations of the join columns are disjoint

The two tables have the following contents:

The PLAYERS table:			The PENLTIES table:	
PLAYERNO	TOWN		PLAYERNO	AMOUNT
--------	----------		--------	------
6	Stratford		27	100
44	Inglewood		8	25
104	Eltham		27	75

The inner equijoin returns absolutely no rows because the two clauses have no value in common.

The outer equijoin of two columns with disjoint populations seldom occurs in practice. If it is really the intention to combine this data in one result, the join is not appropriate. It is best done with a UNION:

```
SELECT    PLAYERNO, TOWN, 0
FROM      PLAYERS
UNION
SELECT    PLAYERNO, '           ', AMOUNT
FROM      PENLTIES
```

Result:

```
PLAYERNO   TOWN         AMOUNT
--------   ---------    ------
       6   Stratford         0
      44   Inglewood         0
     104   Eltham            0
      27                   100
       8                    25
      27                    75
```

Conclusion: When you formulate a join statement you must know precisely what sort of the relationship the join columns have. Do not make any assumptions about the populations of the join columns at any given point, because you may have a false impression. Determine the relationship in advance, therefore, and you can be sure of avoiding mistakes.

Exercises

14.8 Give, for *each* player, the player number and total number of matches won.

14.9 Give, for each player, the player number and the sum of all penalties incurred by him or her.

14.10 Give, for each player, the player number and a list of teams for which they have ever played.

14.4   Conditions with negation

A *condition with negation* is a condition with a NOT operator. Formulating SELECT statements with negative conditions can often cause problems. A negative condition can be made by placing a NOT before a positive condition. This is often compared with the situation of replacing an equal sign with a not equal sign. And herein lies the problem, because that comparison does not always hold true. Here are some examples to demonstrate this.

Example 14.16: Give the player number for every player who lives in Stratford.

```
SELECT   PLAYERNO
FROM     PLAYERS
WHERE    TOWN = 'Stratford'
```

Result:

```
PLAYERNO
--------
       6
      83
       2
       7
      57
      39
     100
```

By placing a NOT operator before the condition, we get a SELECT statement with a negative condition:

```
SELECT    PLAYERNO
FROM      PLAYERS
WHERE     NOT TOWN = 'Stratford'
```

Result:

```
PLAYERNO
--------
      44
      27
     104
     112
       8
      28
      95
```

In this example we can also specify a negative condition using the comparison operator <> (not equal to):

```
SELECT    PLAYERNO
FROM      PLAYERS
WHERE     TOWN <> 'Stratford'
```

The not equal to operator, however, is not always an alternative to the NOT operator. In this example, everything went well because the SELECT clause named the entire primary key of the PLAYERS table. Problems arise if the SELECT clause contains only part of the primary key (naturally, this occurs only if the primary key is made up of more than one column), or if it contains only columns which are not part of the primary key. Let us look at an example.

Example 14.17: Get the number of each player who has incurred a penalty of $25.

As far as structure goes, the question and corresponding SELECT statement appear similar to those of the previous example:

```
SELECT    PLAYERNO
FROM      PENLTIES
WHERE     AMOUNT = 25
```

But, in fact, the SELECT clause of this statement does not mention the primary key of the PENLTIES table (that is, the PAYMENTNO column). If, now, the not equal to sign is substituted for the equal to sign, then the statement looks like this:

```
SELECT    PLAYERNO
FROM      PENLTIES
WHERE     AMOUNT <> 25
```

Result:

```
PLAYERNO
--------
       6
      44
      27
     104
      44
      27
```

If you examine the PENLTIES table, you will see that player 44 has incurred a penalty of $25. In other words, the SELECT statement with its not equal to sign as an alternative to the equal to sign does not give the required negative result. The correct answer is obtained by using the NOT operator along with a subquery:

```
SELECT    PLAYERNO
FROM      PLAYERS
WHERE     PLAYERNO NOT IN
          (SELECT    PLAYERNO
           FROM      PENLTIES
           WHERE     AMOUNT = 25)
```

In the subquery, dBASE IV determines which players have a $25 penalty. In the main query, it looks to see which players do *not* appear in the result of the subquery. But watch out; the main query does not search the PENLTIES table, but the PLAYERS table. If the FROM clause in this statement had named the PENLTIES table, we would have received a list of all players who had incurred *at least one* penalty which was not $25, and that was not the original question.

The statement could also be formulated with NOT EXISTS:

```
SELECT    PLAYERNO
FROM      PLAYERS
WHERE     NOT EXISTS
          (SELECT   *
          FROM      PENLTIES
          WHERE     AMOUNT = 25
          AND       PLAYERS.PLAYERNO = PLAYERNO)
```

Now that we have a negative statement defined using NOT IN, we can also create the positive version of the SELECT statement with a comparable structure:

```
SELECT    PLAYERNO
FROM      PLAYERS
WHERE     PLAYERNO IN
          (SELECT   PLAYERNO
          FROM      PENLTIES
          WHERE     AMOUNT = 25)
```

Conclusion: If a SELECT clause does not contain the whole of the primary key of the table named in the FROM clause, and if the WHERE clause has a negative condition, beware! The following section will discuss still more examples with negative conditions.

Exercises

14.11 Give the number of each player who has won neither 5 nor 6 games.

14.12 Give the division of each team for which player 6 has not played.

14.13 Give the number of each player who has played in teams in which player 57 has never competed.

14.5   The correlated subquery

In Chapter 8 we began to look at subqueries and correlated subqueries. A correlated subquery was defined as a subquery naming a column that belongs to a table which is specified in another query block. This section presents more complex examples of this form of the SELECT statement.

Example 14.18: Get the team number and division of each team in which player 44 has played.

```
SELECT    TEAMNO, DIVISION
FROM      TEAMS
WHERE     EXISTS
          (SELECT  *
          FROM     GAMES
          WHERE    PLAYERNO = 44
          AND      TEAMNO = TEAMS.TEAMNO)
```

Result:

```
TEAMNO  DIVISION
------  --------
     1  first
```

Explanation: Look in the GAMES table to check whether, for each team, there is at least one row in which the TEAMNO value equals the team number of the team concerned and the player number equals 44. We will rewrite this statement in the pseudo-language already used in other parts of this book.

```
RESULT := [];
FOR EACH T IN TEAMS DO
   RESULT_SUB := [];
   FOR EACH G IN GAMES DO
      IF (G.PLAYERNO = 44)
      AND (T.TEAMNO = G.TEAMNO) THEN
         RESULT_SUB :+ G;
   OD;
   IF RESULT_SUB <> [] THEN
      RESULT :+ T;
OD;
```

Example 14.19: Get the number of each player who has incurred more than one penalty.

```
SELECT    DISTINCT PLAYERNO
FROM      PENLTIES PN
WHERE     PLAYERNO IN
          (SELECT  PLAYERNO
          FROM     PENLTIES
          WHERE    PAYMENTNO <> PN.PAYMENTNO)
```

Result:

```
PLAYERNO
--------
      44
      27
```

Explanation: For each row in the PENLTIES table dBASE IV checks whether there is another row in this table with the same player number, but another payment number. If so, then these players have incurred at least two penalties. You can also write this query using a GROUP BY:

```
SELECT    PLAYERNO
FROM      PENLTIES
GROUP BY PLAYERNO
HAVING    COUNT(*) > 1
```

If you are accessing tables whose primary key contains more than one column, you may strike difficulties in formulating SELECT statements. The next question explores this in more detail. Again, the structure and contents of the PLAYERS and PENLTIES tables from the sports database need to be adapted. We assume that the primary key in the PLAYERS table is formed by a combination of the NAME and INITIALS columns, while the primary key in the PENLTIES table remains the PAYMENTNO column.

The PLAYERS table:

NAME	INITIALS	TOWN
Parmenter	R	Stratford
Parmenter	P	Stratford
Miller	P	Douglas

The PENLTIES table:

PAYMENTNO	NAME	INITIALS	AMOUNT
1	Parmenter	R	100
2	Miller	P	200

Example 14.20: Give the name, initials, and town of each player who has incurred at least one penalty. The following SELECT statement does not return the correct answer:

```
SELECT    NAME, INITIALS, TOWN
FROM      PLAYERS
WHERE     NAME IN
          (SELECT    NAME
           FROM      PENLTIES)
AND       INITIALS IN
          (SELECT    INITIALS
           FROM      PENLTIES)
```

Result:

```
NAME        INITIALS  TOWN
---------   --------  ---------
Parmenter   R         Stratford
Parmenter   P         Stratford
Miller      P         Douglas
```

Naturally, the result answers the SELECT statement, but *not* the original question. According to the PENLTIES table, P. Parmenter has incurred *no* penalties. A correct formulation for this question is:

```
SELECT    NAME, INITIALS, TOWN
FROM      PLAYERS, PENLTIES
WHERE     PLAYERS.NAME = PENLTIES.NAME
AND       PLAYERS.INITIALS = PENLTIES.INITIALS
```

Result:

```
NAME        INITIALS  TOWN
---------   --------  ---------
Parmenter   R         Stratford
Miller      P         Douglas
```

Example 14.21: Give the name, initials and town of each player who has incurred *no* penalties.

You cannot solve this question by using the 'good' SELECT statement from the previous example and replacing = with <>. The following join does *not* return the desired result.

```
SELECT    NAME, INITIALS, TOWN
FROM      PLAYERS, PENLTIES
WHERE     PLAYERS.NAME <> PENLTIES.NAME
AND       PLAYERS.INITIALS <> PENLTIES.INITIALS
```

We have to use NOT EXISTS here:

```
SELECT    NAME, INITIALS, TOWN
FROM      PLAYERS
WHERE     NOT EXISTS
          (SELECT   *
          FROM      PENLTIES
          WHERE     PENLTIES.NAME = PLAYERS.NAME
          AND       PENLTIES.INITIALS = PLAYERS.INITIALS)
```

Explanation: The data for a player in the PLAYERS table is only included in the result if no rows in the PENLTIES table can be found with the same NAME and INITIALS combination as that of the corresponding player in the PLAYERS table.

Result:

```
NAME          INITIALS  TOWN
---------     --------  ---------
Parmenter  P            Stratford
```

So, for joining two tables in which a primary key has multiple columns we must take care over our choice of operators.

The previous example can also be solved using the SELECT statement immediately above if NOT EXISTS is replaced by EXISTS:

```
SELECT    NAME, INITIALS, TOWN
FROM      PLAYERS
WHERE     EXISTS
          (SELECT   *
          FROM      PENLTIES
          WHERE     PENLTIES.NAME = PLAYERS.NAME
          AND       PENLTIES.INITIALS = PLAYERS.INITIALS)
```

Yet another correct solution for this example is shown here using the IN operator.

```
SELECT    NAME, INITIALS, TOWN
FROM      PLAYERS
WHERE     NAME IN
          (SELECT   NAME
          FROM      PENLTIES
          WHERE     PLAYERS.INITIALS = PENLTIES.INITIALS)
```

Explanation: In the subquery each row in the main query (therefore in the PLAYERS table) is compared with each row in the PENLTIES table for the same initials. After that, dBASE IV checks whether the NAME of the player also appears in these rows (WHERE NAME IN ...).

And now we return to the original database.

Example 14.22: Give the number of each team in which player 57 has *not* played.

```
SELECT    TEAMNO
FROM      TEAMS
WHERE     NOT EXISTS
          (SELECT   *
          FROM      GAMES
          WHERE     PLAYERNO = 57
          AND       TEAMNO = TEAMS.TEAMNO)
```

Result:

```
TEAMNO
------
     2
```

Explanation: Give the numbers of the teams for which in the GAMES table there is no row with that team number and the player number 57.

Example 14.23: Which players have competed for all teams named in the TEAMS table?

```
SELECT  PLAYERNO
FROM    PLAYERS P
WHERE   NOT EXISTS
        (SELECT *
        FROM    TEAMS T
        WHERE   NOT EXISTS
                (SELECT *
                FROM    GAMES G1
                WHERE   T.TEAMNO = G1.TEAMNO
                AND     P.PLAYERNO = G1.PLAYERNO))
```

Result:

```
PLAYERNO
--------
       8
```

Explanation: We can put the original question in another way using a double negative structure: Find each player for whom no team exists in which the player concerned has never played. The two subqueries produce a list of teams for whom a given player has not played. The main query presents those players for whom the result table of the subquery is empty. dBASE IV determines for each player, separately, whether the subquery yields *no* result. Let us take player 27 as an example. dBASE IV checks whether the following statement has a result for this player.

```
SELECT  *
FROM    TEAMS T
WHERE   NOT EXISTS
        (SELECT *
        FROM    GAMES G1
        WHERE   T.TEAMNO = G1.TEAMNO
        AND     G1.PLAYERNO = 27)
```

This statement has a result if there is a team in which player 27 has never played. Player 27 has not played for team 1, but has for team 2. We conclude that the result of this statement consists of the data from team 1. This means that player 27 does not appear in the end result, because the WHERE clause specifies players for whom the result of the subquery is empty (NOT EXISTS).

We can do the same with player number 8. The result of the subquery, in this case, is empty, because he has played for team 1 as well as team 2. So, the condition in the main query is true and player 8 is included in the end result.

Example 14.24: Give the number of each player who has played for at least all the teams in which player 57 has ever played.

```
SELECT    PLAYERNO
FROM      PLAYERS
WHERE     NOT EXISTS
          (SELECT    *
          FROM       GAMES G1
          WHERE      PLAYERNO = 57
          AND        NOT EXISTS
                     (SELECT    *
                     FROM       GAMES G2
                     WHERE      G1.TEAMNO = G2.TEAMNO
                     AND        PLAYERS.PLAYERNO = G2.PLAYERNO))
```

Result:

```
PLAYERNO
--------
       6
      44
      83
       2
      57
       8
```

Explanation: This statement is similar to the previous one. But the question was not asking for players who have played for *all* teams, but for those teams in which player 57 has also played. This difference is apparent in the first subquery. Here, dBASE IV does not check all teams (in contrast to the subquery in the previous example), but only teams in which player 57 has played.

Example 14.25: Give the number of each player who has played for the same teams as player 57.

This question can also be put differently: Give the number of each player who, first, has played for all the teams in which player 57 has played and, second, has not played for teams in which player 57 has not played. The first part of the question is like the previous one; the second part of the question can be answered with the SELECT statement below. This statement finds all players who have competed in teams in which player 57 has not competed.

```
SELECT    PLAYERNO
FROM      GAMES
WHERE     TEAMNO IN
          (SELECT    TEAMNO
          FROM       TEAMS
          WHERE      TEAMNO NOT IN
                     (SELECT    TEAMNO
                     FROM       GAMES
                     WHERE      PLAYERNO = 57))
```

Combining this statement with that of the previous question supplies us with our answer:

```
SELECT    PLAYERNO
FROM      PLAYERS P
WHERE     NOT EXISTS
          (SELECT   *
          FROM      GAMES G1
          WHERE     PLAYERNO = 57
          AND       NOT EXISTS
                    (SELECT   *
                    FROM      GAMES G2
                    WHERE     G1.TEAMNO = G2.TEAMNO
                    AND       P.PLAYERNO = G2.PLAYERNO))
AND       PLAYERNO NOT IN
          (SELECT   PLAYERNO
          FROM      GAMES
          WHERE     TEAMNO IN
                    (SELECT   TEAMNO
                    FROM      TEAMNS
                    WHERE     TEAMNO NOT IN
                              (SELECT   TEAMNO
                              FROM      GAMES
                              WHERE     PLAYERNO = 57)))
```

Example 14.26: Get, for each player who has incurred at least one penalty, the player number, the highest penalty and the date on which this penalty was incurred.

```
SELECT    PLAYERNO, AMOUNT, PEN_DATE
FROM      PENLTIES PN
WHERE     AMOUNT =
          (SELECT   MAX(AMOUNT)
          FROM      PENLTIES P
          WHERE     P.PLAYERNO = PN.PLAYERNO)
```

Result:

```
PLAYERNO  AMOUNT  PEN_DATE
--------  ------  --------
       6  100.00  12/08/80
       8   25.00  12/08/80
      27  100.00  09/10/83
      44   75.00  05/05/81
     104   50.00  12/08/84
```

Exercises

14.14 Find the number and name of each player who has incurred at least one penalty; use a correlated subquery.

14.15 Find the number and name of each player who has won more games than lost for at least two teams.

14.16 Give the name and initials of each player who has incurred no penalties between 1 January 1980 and 31 December 1980.

14.17 Give the number of each player who has incurred at least one penalty that is equal to an amount which has occurred at least two other times.

15

Updating tables

SQL has various statements for updating the contents (rows) of tables. There are statements for inserting new rows, for changing column values and for deleting rows. You will note, then, that we use the term update to refer to different processes that add, change or remove data. Each type of update is dealt with in a separate section.

15.1 Inserting new rows

SQL's *INSERT statement* is used to add new rows to a table. This statement comes in two different forms; the first form is covered in this section, and the second in the following section. The first form of the INSERT statement allows you to add only one row to a table, while the second allows you to populate a table with rows taken from another table.

```
<insert statement> ::=
    INSERT INTO <table identifier>
            [ <column list> ]
    VALUES ( <expression> [ {,<expression>}... ] )

<table identifier> ::= <table name>

<column list> ::=
    ( <column name> [ {,<column name>}... ] )
```

Example 15.1: A new team has enrolled in the league. This third team will be captained by player 100 and will compete in the third division.

```
INSERT INTO TEAMS
        (TEAMNO, PLAYERNO, DIVISION)
VALUES (3, 100, 'third')
```

You don't have to specify the column names. If they are omitted, dBASE IV assumes that the order in which the values are entered is the same as the default sequence of the columns (see COLNO in the SYSCOLS table). The following statement is, therefore, equivalent to the previous one:

```
INSERT INTO TEAMS
VALUES (3, 100, 'third')
```

You are not obliged, however, to specify columns in the default sequence. So the next statement is equivalent to the previous two statements:

```
INSERT INTO TEAMS (PLAYERNO, DIVISION, TEAMNO)
VALUES (100, 'third', 3)
```

If the columns had *not* been specified in this statement, the result would have been entirely different. dBASE IV would have considered the value 100 to be a team number, 'third' a player number and the value 3 a division. Of course, the insertion would not have been performed at all because the value 'third' is an alphanumeric literal and the PLAYERNO column has a numeric data type.

15.2 Populating one table with rows from another table

In Section 15.1 we looked at the first form of the INSERT statement with which one row could be added to a table. The second form does not add new rows, but fills the table with rows from another table (or tables). You could say that data is *copied* from one table to another. The definition for this is:

```
<insert statement> ::=
   INSERT INTO <table identifier>
   [ <column list> ]
   <select statement>

<table identifier> ::= <table name>

<column list> ::=
   ( <column name> [ {,<column name>}... ] )
```

Example 15.2: Make a separate table to record the number, name, town and telephone number of each non-competition player.

First create a table, and then define a unique index on it:

```
CREATE TABLE RECREATE
        (PLAYERNO  SMALLINT ,
         NAME      CHAR(15) ,
         TOWN      CHAR(10) ,
         PHONENO   CHAR(10) )

CREATE UNIQUE INDEX REC_PRIM ON
        RECREATE (PLAYERNO)
```

The following INSERT statement populates the RECREATE table with data about recreational players registered in the PLAYERS table.

```
INSERT   INTO RECREATE
         (PLAYERNO, NAME, TOWN, PHONENO)
SELECT   PLAYERNO, NAME, TOWN, PHONENO
FROM     PLAYERS
WHERE    LEAGUENO = ''
```

The contents of the table now look like this:

PLAYERNO	NAME	TOWN	PHONENO
7	Wise	Stratford	070-347689
39	Bishop	Stratford	070-393435
28	Collins	Midhurst	071-659599
95	Miller	Douglas	070-867564

Explanation: The first part of the INSERT statement follows the pattern of the first type of INSERT statement. The second part does not consist of a row of values, but a SELECT statement. We know already that the result of a SELECT statement can be viewed as a number of rows with values. However, these rows are not projected onto the screen as the statement executes, but are stored directly in the RECREATE table.

The same rules which apply for the first form of the INSERT statement apply here also. The next two statements, then, have an equivalent result to the previous one:

```
INSERT   INTO RECREATE
SELECT   PLAYERNO, NAME, TOWN, PHONENO
FROM     PLAYERS
WHERE    LEAGUENO = ''
```

```
INSERT    INTO RECREATE
          (TOWN, PHONENO, NAME, PLAYERNO)
SELECT    TOWN, PHONENO, NAME, PLAYERNO
FROM      PLAYERS
WHERE     LEAGUENO = ' '
```

At the same time, there are several other rules:

- The SELECT statement may *not* refer to the table into which the new rows are being inserted.

- The SELECT statement is a fully fledged SELECT statement and therefore may include subqueries, joins, GROUP BY, functions, and so on.

- The number of columns in the INSERT INTO clause must equal the number of expressions in the SELECT clause.

- The data types of the columns in the INSERT INTO clause must conform to the data types of the expressions in the SELECT clause.

Here are two examples which contravene the first rule by referring to tables into which rows are to be added.

```
INSERT    INTO PLAYERS
SELECT    *
FROM      PLAYERS
```

and

```
INSERT    INTO RECREATE
SELECT    *
FROM      PLAYERS
WHERE     JOINED >
          (SELECT    AVG(JOINED)
           FROM      RECREATE)
```

15.3   Updating values in rows

The UPDATE statement is used to change values in a table. The definition of this
statement reads:

```
<update statement> ::=
   UPDATE <table identifier>
   SET    <object column> [ {,<object column>}... ]
   [ WHERE  <condition> ]

<table identifier> ::= <table name>

<object column> ::=
   <column name> = <expression>
```

Example 15.3: Update the league number for players 95 to 2000.

```
UPDATE PLAYERS
SET    LEAGUENO = '2000'
WHERE  PLAYERNO = 95
```

Explanation: The LEAGUENO must be changed to 2000 (SET LEAGUENO =
'2000') for *every* row where the player number equals 95 (WHERE PLAYERNO =
95) in the PLAYERS table (UPDATE PLAYERS).

An UPDATE statement always refers to a table. The WHERE clause
names rows which are to be updated and the SET clause attributes the new values
to one or more columns.

Example 15.4: Increase all penalties by 5 per cent.

```
UPDATE    PENLTIES
SET       AMOUNT = AMOUNT * 1.05
```

Because the WHERE clause has been omitted, the update is performed on all
rows in the table concerned. In this example, the AMOUNT in each row of the
PENLTIES table is increased by 5 per cent.

Example 15.5: Set the number of matches won to zero for all competitors resident in Stratford.

```
UPDATE    GAMES
SET       WON = 0
WHERE     PLAYERNO IN
          (SELECT  PLAYERNO
          FROM    PLAYERS
          WHERE   TOWN = 'Stratford')
```

Example 15.6: The Parmenter family has moved house to 83 Palmer Street in Inglewood; the post code has become 1234 UU and the telephone number is unknown.

```
UPDATE    PLAYERS
SET       STREET   = 'Palmer Street',
          HOUSENO  = '83',
          TOWN    = 'Inglewood',
          POSTCODE = '1234UU',
          PHONENO = ''
WHERE     NAME     = 'Parmenter'
```

Explanation: An UPDATE statement can update multiple columns in a row in the same operation. Remember the comma between each item in the SET clause.

15.4   Complex updates

In this section we discuss a number of updates which look simple, but which require a few statements in order to be completed.

Example 15.7: Increase all player numbers by 1. You might expect the statement to read like this:

```
UPDATE    PLAYERS
SET       PLAYERNO = PLAYERNO + 1
```

But this does not run correctly, because the PLAYERNO column is the primary key of the PLAYERS table and has a unique index defined on it. This index is at the root of the problem. With the UPDATE statement above, dBASE IV will try, for every row, to increase the PLAYERNO value by 1. dBASE IV executes this process row by row. This leads to a problem in the first row (in our example). The player number in the first row is 6. If this number is increased by 1 it becomes 7. But number 7 already exists, the player number for Wise. Therefore, because this update is being performed on the index column, the index ceases to be unique, and dBASE IV immediately stops processing the statement.

For this update to execute correctly, the unique index concerned must be dropped. Once the UPDATE statement has been processed successfully the index must, of course, be created again.

In order to maintain full data consistency the update must be applied to all other tables in which the player numbers are recorded.

An UPDATE on a key column is not necessarily going to be problematic. Dropping and recreating a unique index on a key column, as described above, is sometimes superfluous, apart from influencing the execution time. Using a SELECT statement you can check to see whether such an update on a key column will cause difficulties. Let us take, for example, the UPDATE statement from above:

```
SELECT    COUNT(*)
FROM      PLAYERS
WHERE     PLAYERNO + 1 IN
          (SELECT   PLAYERNO
          FROM      PLAYERS)
```

Result:

```
COUNT(*)
--------
       3
```

Explanation: The result of the COUNT indicates that three rows will be affected by such an update. These are, in fact, where the player numbers are 6, 7 and 27.

If, during the processing of an UPDATE statement, it looks as though something has gone wrong, dBASE IV rolls back all the changes which have already occurred.

Example 15.8: Set all penalties which are lower than the average penalty to $10.

Just as with the INSERT statement, subqueries in the WHERE clause of the UPDATE statement may not contain references to the table that is being updated. The following solution for this question, then, is *not* acceptable.

```
UPDATE    PENLTIES
SET       AMOUNT = 10
WHERE     AMOUNT <
          (SELECT   AVG(AMOUNT)
          FROM      PENLTIES)
```

This update must take place in steps.

1.   Calculate the average penalty and save it in a specially created HELP table:

```
      SELECT    AVG(AMOUNT)
      FROM      PENLTIES
      SAVE TO   TEMP HELP (AVERAGE)
```

2.   Process the update:

```
      UPDATE    PENLTIES
      SET       AMOUNT = 10
      WHERE     AMOUNT <
                (SELECT   AVERAGE
                FROM      HELP)
```

Exercises

15.1   Change the value F in the SEX column of the PLAYERS table to W.

15.2   Increase each team number in the TEAMS and GAMES tables by 1.

15.3   Increase all penalties which are higher than the average penalty by 20 per cent.

15.5   Deleting rows from a table

The DELETE statement is used to remove rows from a table. The definition of the DELETE statement reads:

```
<delete statement> ::=
   DELETE
   FROM    <table identifier>
   [ WHERE <condition> ]

<table identifier> ::= <table name>
```

Example 15.9: Delete all penalties incurred by player 44.

```
DELETE
FROM    PENLTIES
WHERE   PLAYERNO = 44
```

If the WHERE clause is omitted, all rows for the named table are deleted. This is not the same as dropping a table with the DROP statement. DELETE removes the contents, leaving the structure of the table intact, whereas the DROP statement deletes the contents and also removes the definition of the table from the catalog.

It is also true for the DELETE statement that subqueries in the WHERE clause may not refer to the table from which rows are to be deleted. The following statement is incorrect, therefore:

```
DELETE
FROM    PLAYERS
WHERE   PLAYERNO IN
        (SELECT  PLAYERNO
         FROM    PLAYERS
         WHERE   TOWN = 'Stratford')
```

Exercises

15.4   Delete all penalties incurred by player 44 in 1980.

15.5   Delete all penalties incurred by players who have ever played for a team in the second division.

15.6   Delete all players who live in the same town as player 44, but keep the data about player 44.

16
Optimization of statements

Some SQL statements have a reasonably constant or predictable execution time. Examples include the CREATE TABLE and GRANT statements. SQL has no way of influencing their execution time; there is no way of reducing their execution time. Nevertheless, this is not the case for all statements. The time required to process SELECT, UPDATE and DELETE statements varies from one statement to the next. One SELECT statement may be processed in two seconds, while another could take minutes. You can influence the time SQL needs to execute these types of statements. Broadly speaking, there are four techniques available for decreasing the execution time of SELECT, UPDATE and DELETE statements (known as *optimization*):

- creating indexes
- alternative ways of formulating statements
- compiling statements
- use of statistical data in the catalog

Sections 16.1 to 16.5 discuss creating indexes and how they work. Section 16.6 discusses the second technique. The third technique has already been covered in Chapter 2, so we will not repeat it, and Section 16.7 deals with the last technique.

16.1 How an index works

Preliminary remark: This section does not so much cover an SQL statement, but provides insight into how dBASE IV uses indexes. You should view this section as background information.

dBASE IV has two methods of accessing rows in a table: the *sequential access* method and the *direct access* method

Sequential access is best described as 'browsing through a table row by row'. dBASE IV reads each row in the table. If only one row is sought, and if the table has many rows, this method is, of course, very time consuming and inefficient. It is comparable to going through a telephone book page by page. If you are looking for the number of someone whose name begins with an L, you certainly don't want to start looking in the As.

When dBASE IV uses the direct access method, it reads only the rows that exhibit the required characteristics. To do this, however, an *index* is necessary. An index is a type of alternative access to a table and can be compared with an index in a book.

An index in dBASE IV is built like a *tree*, consisting of a number of *nodes*. Figure 16.1 is a pictorial representation of an index. On the left of the figure is the index structure itself, and on the right, two columns from the PLAYERS table. The nodes of the index are represented by the rectangles. The node on the far left forms the beginning point of the index and is known as the *root*. Each node contains a maximum of three ordered values from the PLAYERNO column. Each value in a node points to another node or to a row in the PLAYERS table (Figure 16.1 does not include every 'pointer') and each row in the table is referenced through at least one node. A node that points to a row is called a *leaf page*. The values in a node are ordered. For each node, apart from the root, the values are always less than or equal to the value that pointed to that node. Leaf pages are themselves linked to one another; a leaf page has a pointer to the leaf page with the next set of values. In Figure 16.1 we represent these pointers with the thick vertical arrows.

Broadly speaking, dBASE IV has two algorithms available for use with indexes. One of the algorithms is for searching for rows in which a particular value occurs, and the other is for browsing through a whole table or a part of a table via an ordered column. We will illustrate these two algorithms with two examples. First, here is an example of how dBASE IV uses the index to select a particular row.

Example 16.1: Suppose that all rows with player number 44 must be found.

Step 1   Search the root of the index. This root becomes the active node.

Step 2   Is the active node a leaf page? If so, continue with step 4; if not, continue with step 3.

Step 3   Does the active node contain the value 44? If so, the node to which this value points becomes the active node; go back to step 2. If not, choose the lowest value that is higher than 44 in the active node. The node to which this value points becomes the active node; go back to step 2.

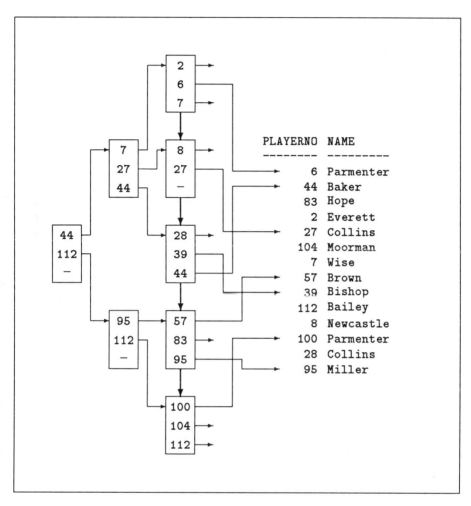

Figure 16.1: Pictorial representation of an index tree

Step 4   Search for the value 44 in the active node. This value now points to all
the rows in the PLAYERS table where the PLAYERNO column equals
44. Retrieve all these rows from the database for further processing.

Without browsing through all the rows, dBASE IV has found the desired row(s).
In most cases, the time spent searching for rows can be reduced considerably if
dBASE IV can use an index.

In this next example dBASE IV uses the index to retrieve ordered rows
from a table.

Example 16.2: Give all players ordered by the player number.

Step 1   Search the leaf page with the lowest value. This leaf page becomes the active node.

Step 2   Retrieve all rows to which the values in the active node are pointing for further processing.

Step 3   If there is a subsequent leaf page, make this the active node and continue with step 2.

Updating values in rows, or adding or deleting rows means that dBASE IV must automatically alter the index. So the index tree is always consistent with the contents of the table.

You can define an index on a non-unique column like the NAME column. The result of this is that values in a leaf page point to multiple rows; there is one pointer for each row in which the value occurs.

Indexes can also be defined on combinations of values. Each value in a node is then, in fact, a concatenation of the individual values. The leaf pages point to rows in which that combination of values appears.

There are two other important observations to note about the use of indexes:

• Index rows are just like rows in tables and are stored in files. So, an index takes up physical storage space (just like an index in a book).

• Updates to tables can lead to updates to indexes. When an index must be updated, dBASE IV tries, where it can, to fill the gaps in the nodes in order to complete the process as quickly as possible. But an index can become so 'full' that a new index must be created and this can necessitate a total *reorganization* of the index. Such a reorganization can be very time consuming.

This section presents a very simplified picture of the workings of an index. In practice, for example, a node in an index tree can accommodate not just three, but many values. For a more detailed description we refer you to Date (1985).

16.2   Processing a SELECT statement: the six steps

Chapter 6 described the six clauses of a SELECT statement and how they are processed one after another. These clauses provide the 'structure' around which dBASE IV builds a *basic strategy* for processing a statement. By basic strategy we are assuming sequential access of the data. This section discusses how the use of an index can change the basic strategy to an *optimized strategy*.

dBASE IV tries to choose the most efficient strategy for processing each statement. This analysis is performed by a dBASE IV module called the *optimizer*. (The analysis of statements is also referred to as *query optimization*.) The optimizer defines a number of alternative strategies for each statement. It estimates which strategy is likely to be the most efficient, on the basis of such factors as the expected execution time, the number of rows and the presence of indexes (in the absence of indexes, this can be the basic strategy). dBASE IV then executes the statement according to its chosen strategy.

Here are some illustrations of optimized processing strategies.

Example 16.3: Get all information about player 44. (We assume that there is an index defined on the PLAYERNO column.)

```
SELECT    *
FROM      PLAYERS
WHERE     PLAYERNO = 44
```

The FROM clause: Normally, dBASE IV would retrieve all rows from the PLAYERS table. Speeding up the processing by using an index means that only the rows where the value in the PLAYERNO column equals 44 are fetched.

Intermediate result:

```
PLAYERNO  NAME   ...
--------  -----  ---
      44  Baker  ...
```

The WHERE clause: In this example, this clause was processed at the same time as the FROM clause.

The SELECT clause: All columns are presented.

The difference between the basic strategy and this optimized strategy can be represented in another way.

Basic strategy:

```
RESULT := [];
FOR EACH P IN PLAYERS DO
   IF P.PLAYERNO = 44 THEN
      RESULT :+ P;
OD;
```

Optimized strategy:

```
RESULT := [];
FOR EACH P IN PLAYERS WHERE PLAYERNO = 44 DO
   RESULT :+ P;
OD;
```

With the first strategy all rows are fetched by the FOR EACH statement. The second strategy works much more selectively. When an index is used, only those rows where the player number equals 44 are retrieved.

Example 16.4: Give the number and town of each player whose number is lower than 10 and who lives in Stratford; order the result by number.

```
SELECT    PLAYERNO, TOWN
FROM      PLAYERS
WHERE     PLAYERNO < 10
AND       TOWN = 'Stratford'
ORDER BY  PLAYERNO
```

The FROM clause: Fetch all rows where the player number is smaller than 10. Again, use the index on the PLAYERNO column. Fetch the rows in ascending order, thus accounting for the ORDER BY clause. This is simple, because the values in an index are always ordered.

Intermediate result:

```
PLAYERNO  ...  TOWN          ...
--------  ---  ---------     ---
       2  ...  Stratford     ...
       6  ...  Stratford     ...
       7  ...  Stratford     ...
       8  ...  Inglewood     ...
```

The WHERE clause: The WHERE clause specifies two conditions. Each row in the intermediate result satisfies the first condition that has already been evaluated in the FROM clause. Now, only the second condition must be evaluated.

Intermediate result:

```
PLAYERNO  ...  TOWN          ...
--------  ---  ---------     ---
       2  ...  Stratford     ...
       6  ...  Stratford     ...
       7  ...  Stratford     ...
```

The SELECT clause: Two columns are selected.

Intermediate result:

```
PLAYERNO  TOWN
--------  ---------
       2  Stratford
       6  Stratford
       7  Stratford
```

The ORDER BY clause: Thanks to the use of an index during the processing of the FROM clause, no extra sorting needs to be done. The end result, then, is the same as the table shown above.

Here are the basic strategy and the optimized strategy for this example, as well:

Basic strategy:

```
RESULT := [];
FOR EACH P IN PLAYERS DO
   IF (P.PLAYERNO < 10)
   AND (P.TOWN = 'Stratford') THEN
      RESULT :+ P;
OD;
```

Optimized strategy:

```
RESULT := [];
FOR EACH P IN PLAYERS WHERE PLAYERNO < 10 DO
   IF P.TOWN = 'Stratford' THEN
      RESULT :+ P;
OD;
```

Example 16.5: Give the name and initials of each player who lives in the same place as player 44.

```
SELECT    NAME, INITIALS
FROM      PLAYERS
WHERE     TOWN =
          (SELECT  TOWN
          FROM     PLAYERS
          WHERE    PLAYERNO = 44)
```

Here are the two strategies.

Basic strategy:

```
RESULT := [];
FOR EACH P IN PLAYERS DO
   HELP := FALSE;
   FOR EACH P44 IN PLAYERS DO
      IF (P44.TOWN = P.TOWN)
      AND (P44.PLAYERNO = 44) THEN
         HELP := TRUE;
   OD;
   IF HELP = TRUE THEN
      RESULT :+ P;
OD;
```

Optimized strategy:

```
RESULT := [];
FIND P IN PLAYERS WHERE PLAYERNO = 44;
FOR EACH S IN PLAYERS WHERE TOWN = P DO
   RESULT := S;
OD;
```

These were relatively simple examples. As the statements become more complex, so too is it more difficult for dBASE IV to determine the optimal strategy, and this adds to processing time as well, of course.

If you want to know more about the optimization of SELECT statements, refer to Kim (1985). You don't, however, need this knowledge to understand SQL statements. That is why we have only given a summary of the topic in this book.

Exercise

16.1   Write, for the following two statements, the basic strategy and an optimized strategy; assume that there is an index defined on each column.

```
SELECT    *
FROM      TEAMS
WHERE     TEAMNO > 1
AND       DIVISION = 'second'

SELECT    P.PLAYERNO
FROM      PLAYERS P, GAMES G1
WHERE     P.PLAYERNO = G1.PLAYERNO
AND       BIRTH > 1963
```

16.3   Creating and dropping indexes

The definition of the CREATE INDEX statement is as follows:

```
<create index statement> ::=
   CREATE [ UNIQUE ] INDEX <index name>
   ON     <table identifier>
   ( <column in index> [ {,<column in index>}... ] )

<table identifier> ::= <table name>

<column in index> ::=
   <column name> [ ASC | DESC ]
```

Two examples of non-unique indexes:

```
CREATE    INDEX PLAY_PC
ON        PLAYERS (POSTCODE ASC)

CREATE    INDEX GAM_WL
ON        GAMES (WON, LOST)
```

Chapter 5 looked at some examples defining unique indexes. Here is another:

```
CREATE    UNIQUE INDEX NAMEINIT
ON        PLAYERS (NAME, INITIALS)
```

Once this statement has been processed, dBASE IV prevents any two identical combinations of name and initials from being inserted into the PLAYERS table.

dBASE IV creates a file for each index, the file name being the same as the table name on which the index is based and the file type being 'MDX'. In cases where such a file already exists, because an index has already been created on that table, the new index is also stored in that file. In other words, all indexes belonging to a given table are stored together in a single file.

The index name must satisfy certain conditions. It can be up to 8 characters long, contain only letters, digits and the underscore character, and must begin with a letter. As well as this, the name of a new index cannot be the same as the name of another, already created index in the same database. It is also important to avoid the use of key words such as CREATE and SELECT when naming indexes. In Appendix B we give a list of reserved or key words.

You cannot create an index on a column whose data type is LOGICAL. In addition, the total length of the column or combination of columns on which the index is defined cannot be more than 100 characters. For example, you could never define an index on a column whose data type is CHAR(110).

The addition of ASC or DESC enables you to specify whether the index should be built in ASCending or DESCending order. If neither is specified dBASE IV chooses ASC as a default. If an index is built on two or more columns, all the columns must be defined as ASC or DESC. Therefore, ASC and DESC may not be used together in the same index. If a SELECT statement requires a particular column to be sorted in ascending order, the execution time will be shorter if there is also an ascending index defined on this column.

Indexes can be created at any time. You don't have to create all the indexes for a table as soon as the CREATE TABLE statement has finished executing. You can also create indexes on tables that already have data in them. But, creating a unique index on a table where the column concerned already contains duplicate values can be problematic. dBASE IV notes this and does not create the index. The duplicate values have to be removed by the user first before the index can be created. The SELECT statement will help locate the duplicate values (where C is the column on which the index must be defined):

```
SELECT    C
FROM      T
GROUP BY  C
HAVING    COUNT(*) > 1
```

The DROP INDEX statement is used to remove indexes.

```
<drop index statement> ::=
   DROP INDEX <index name>
```

Examples:

    DROP INDEX PLAY_PC

    DROP INDEX P_LEAGNO

When you drop a unique index you do not need to refer to the word UNIQUE.

16.4   Recording indexes in the catalog

Just as with tables and columns, indexes are also recorded in a catalog table, the SYSIDXS table. Below we give the descriptions of the columns of this table. The IXNAME column is the primary key of the SYSIDXS table.

SYSIDXS	
IXNAME	Name of the index
CREATOR	Name of the user who created the index
TBNAME	Name of the table on which the index is defined
TBCREATOR	Name of the owner of the table on which the index is defined
UNIQUERULE	Whether the index is U(nique) or contains D(uplicate) values
COLCOUNT	The number of columns in the index
CLUSTERING	Not used
CLUSTERED	Statistical data
FIRSTKCARD	The number of different values in the first column of the index
FULLKCARD	The number of different values in the whole index
NLEAF	The number of nodes in the index tree
NLEVELS	The number of levels in the index tree

The columns on which the index is defined are stored in a separate table, the SYSKEYS table, the primary key of this table being formed by the IXNAME and COLNAME columns.

SYSKEYS	
IXNAME	Name of the index
IXCREATOR	Name of the user who created the index
COLNAME	Name of the column on which the index is defined
COLNO	Sequence number of the column in the index
COLSEQ	Relative position of index values in the index
ORDERING	Whether the index is built in A(scending) or D(escending) order

The examples of indexes from this section would be recorded in the SYSIDXS and SYSKEYS tables as follows (we are assuming that SQLDBA created all the tables and indexes):

```
IXNAME     CREATOR    TBNAME    TBCREATOR   UNIQUERULE   COLCOUNT
--------   --------   -------   ---------   ----------   --------
PLAY_PC    SQLDBA     PLAYERS   SQLDBA      D                   1
GAM_WL     SQLDBA     GAMES     SQLDBA      D                   2
NAMEINIT   SQLDBA     PLAYERS   SQLDBA      U                   2


IXNAME     IXCREATOR   COLNAME    COLNO   COLSEQ   ORDERING
--------   ---------   --------   -----   ------   --------
PLAY_PC    SQLDBA      POSTCODE      10        1   A
GAM_WL     SQLDBA      WON            3        1   A
GAM_WL     SQLDBA      LOST           4        2   A
NAMEINIT   SQLDBA      NAME           2        1   A
NAMEINIT   SQLDBA      INITIALS       3        2   A
```

16.5　Choosing columns for indexes

In order to be absolutely sure that every SELECT statement will be efficiently processed, you could create an index on every column and combination of columns. And if you were going to be entering only SELECT statements against the data, this could well be a good approach. But such a solution does raise a number of problems, not the least of them being the cost of index storage space. Another important disadvantage is that each data update (via an INSERT, UPDATE or DELETE statement) requires a corresponding index update. The update will take significantly longer if many indexes also need to be updated. So, a choice has to be made. Here are some guidelines.

16.5.1　A unique index on primary keys and candidate keys

It is important for the primary key and all candidate keys not to contain duplicate values. Many statements and programs depend on this. The only way in which dBASE IV can guarantee uniqueness of values in columns is to use a unique index. Therefore, you should always create a unique index on each primary and candidate key.

16.5.2   An index on foreign keys

Joins can take a long time to execute if there are no indexes defined on the join columns. For a large percentage of joins, the join columns are also, in fact, keys of the tables concerned. They can be primary and candidate keys, but also foreign keys. According to the first rule of thumb, you should already have an index on the primary and candidate key columns. What remains now is to define indexes on the foreign keys. In the sample database, then, you would define the following indexes for the TEAMS and GAMES tables:

```
CREATE     INDEX TSNO
ON         TEAMS (PLAYERNO)

CREATE     INDEX GMNO
ON         GAMES (PLAYERNO)

CREATE     INDEX GTNO
ON         GAMES (TEAMNO)
```

16.5.3   An index on columns included in selection criteria

SELECT, UPDATE, and DELETE statements execute faster if there is an index defined on the columns named in the WHERE clause.

Example:

```
SELECT     *
FROM       PLAYERS
WHERE      TOWN = 'Stratford'
```

dBASE IV selects rows on the basis of the value in the TOWN column and processing this statement is more efficient if there is an index on this column. This was discussed extensively in the earlier sections of this chapter.

Nevertheless, you should only place an index on a column which has many different values, and not on one like SEX in the PLAYERS table which has only two different values, F and M. If, via a SELECT statement, we search for all players of a particular sex, we will probably find a normal distribution of half men and half women in the rows. If dBASE IV uses an index in this case, the processing time will probably be longer than if the rows are read sequentially.

An index is not just worthwhile when the = operator is used, but also for <, <=, > and >=. (Note that the <> operator does not appear in this list.) But this is only true when the number of rows selected is much smaller than the number of rows not selected.

If a WHERE clause contains an AND operator, an index should be defined on the two columns to ensure more efficient execution.

Example:

```
SELECT    *
FROM      PLAYERS
WHERE     NAME = 'Collins'
AND       INITIALS = 'DD'
```

Associated index:

```
CREATE    INDEX NAMEINIT
ON        PLAYERS (NAME, INITIALS)
```

In some cases, when you are executing such a query, it can suffice to have an index on only one of the columns. Suppose that duplicate names occur seldom in the NAME column and suppose that this is the only column with an index. dBASE IV will find all the rows that satisfy the condition NAME = 'Collins' by using this index. Only infrequently will it retrieve a few too many rows. In this case, an index on the combination of columns will take up more storage space than necessary, and will not significantly improve the processing of the SELECT statement.

Indexes defined on combinations of columns are also used for selections in which only the first column (or columns) of the index are specified. Therefore, the NAMEINIT index above is used by dBASE IV to process the condition, NAME = 'Collins', but not for INITIALS = 'DD'. The INITIALS column is not the first one in the NAMEINIT index.

16.5.4 An index on columns used for ordering

If dBASE IV needs to order the result of a SELECT statement by a column that has no index, a separate (time consuming) sort process must be performed. This extra sorting can be avoided if you define an index on the relevant column. When dBASE IV fetches the rows from the database (with the FROM clause) this index can then be used. The intermediate result from the FROM clause is already ordered by the correct column. After that, no extra sorting is necessary.

16.5.5 An index on columns used for grouping

To group columns (using the GROUP BY clause) dBASE IV must first order all the rows. The previous rule is again applicable: dBASE IV will be able to process a GROUP BY clause more quickly when the rows are already ordered.

Closing remark: Naturally, it makes little sense to define two indexes on the same column or combination of columns. Consult the SYSIDXS table to check whether by creating a new index you are simply replicating an existing one.

16.6 Reformulating statements

We have proposed that the presence of an index can improve the execution time of particular statements. The question remains, though, as to whether the dBASE

IV optimizer can, in fact, develop the best processing strategy for all statements. Unfortunately, the answer is 'No'! Some statements are written in such a way that the optimizer is in no position to develop the fastest processing strategy. This occurs principally when WHERE clause conditions are too complex or when the optimizer is taken up a 'false trail'. In addition, even when indexes are available, dBASE IV sometimes chooses a sequential processing strategy.

In practice, it appears that certain forms of SQL statements are not easily optimized and give rise to longer processing times. By reformulating such statements you give dBASE IV a better chance of developing an optimal processing strategy. In this section we give you a number of guidelines for formulating statements with faster execution in mind. So, we are giving the optimizer a 'helping hand'.

Note: In new versions of dBASE IV the optimizer will improve, of course, and will be able to develop good processing strategies for still more statements. Therefore, the following guidelines will have to be tested for validity against each new version of the product.

16.6.1   Avoid the OR operator

In most cases dBASE IV will not use an index if the condition in the WHERE clause contains the OR operator. These statements can be rewritten in two ways. In certain circumstances we can replace the condition with one containing an IN operator, or replace the whole statement with two SELECT statements linked with UNION.

Example 16.6: Give the names and initials of players 6, 83 and 44.

```
SELECT    NAME, INITIALS
FROM      PLAYERS
WHERE     PLAYERNO = 6
OR        PLAYERNO = 83
OR        PLAYERNO = 44
```

Even if there is an index on the PLAYERNO column, dBASE IV will not use it. The condition in the SELECT statement can, however, be simply replaced by the IN operator, so that now dBASE IV will use the index.

```
SELECT    NAME, INITIALS
FROM      PLAYERS
WHERE     PLAYERNO IN (6, 83, 44)
```

For UPDATE and DELETE statements the same applies.

Example 16.7: Get the players who were born in 1963 plus the players who live in Stratford.

```
SELECT    *
FROM      PLAYERS
WHERE     BIRTH = 1963
OR        TOWN = 'Stratford'
```

dBASE IV will develop a sequential processing strategy irrespective of the presence of indexes on the TOWN and BIRTH columns. But in this example we cannot replace the OR operator with an IN operator. What we can do is replace the whole statement with two SELECT statements linked with UNION.

```
SELECT    *
FROM      PLAYERS
WHERE     BIRTH = 1963
UNION
SELECT    *
FROM      PLAYERS
WHERE     TOWN = 'Stratford'
```

UPDATE and DELETE statements like this can *not* be adapted using the UNION operator. In such a case, two separate statements are necessary:

Example 16.8: Update penalties of $100 or those incurred on 1 December 1980 to $150.

```
UPDATE    PENLTIES
SET       AMOUNT = 150
WHERE     AMOUNT = 100
OR        PEN_DATE = {12/01/80}
```

Another formulation:

```
UPDATE    PENLTIES
SET       AMOUNT - 150
WHERE     AMOUNT = 100
```

and

```
UPDATE    PENLTIES
SET       AMOUNT = 150
WHERE     PEN_DATE = {12/01/80}
```

Let us return to the example with the SELECT statement. With UNION, dBASE IV automatically removes duplicate rows (that is, DISTINCT is assumed). In fact, in this case there are no duplicate rows because the SELECT clause names the primary key of the PLAYERS table.

If the original SELECT statement had looked like the next one shown (no primary key columns in the SELECT clause), the alternative construction with UNION would not have been possible. Why? Because this statement could produce duplicate rows that would, with the UNION operator, be deleted (and that is not the intention). The two versions would give different results.

```
SELECT    NAME
FROM      PLAYERS
WHERE     BIRTH = 1963
OR        TOWN = 'Stratford'
```

By adding DISTINCT the duplicate rows are legitimately removed and the use of UNION becomes possible.

16.6.2   Isolate columns in conditions

When an index is defined on a column that occurs in a calculation or scalar function, that index is not used.

Example 16.9: Find the players who were born ten years before 1979.

```
SELECT    *
FROM      PLAYERS
WHERE     BIRTH + 10 = 1979
```

On the left of the = comparison operator you see an expression that contains both a column name and a literal. To the right of the same operator there is another literal. The index on the BIRTH column will not be used. You could expect, however, a faster execution with the next statement, which reformulates the previous one:

```
SELECT    *
FROM      PLAYERS
WHERE     BIRTH = 1969
```

Now the expression to the left of the comparison operator contains only a column name. In other words, the column has been isolated.

16.6.3   Use the BETWEEN operator

dBASE IV will generally not use an index when a WHERE clause specifies values in a particular range using the AND operator. In such cases, we can replace the AND operator with the BETWEEN operator.

Example 16.10: Find the numbers of the players born in the period 1962 - 1965.

```
SELECT    PLAYERNO
FROM      PLAYERS
WHERE     BIRTH >= 1962
AND       BIRTH <= 1965
```

An index on the BIRTH column will not be used here, whereas in the next example with the condition adapted it will be considered:

```
SELECT    PLAYERNO
FROM      PLAYERS
WHERE     BIRTH BETWEEN 1962 AND 1965
```

16.6.4   Avoid particular forms of the LIKE operator

In some cases, when an index is defined on a column used with the LIKE operator in a WHERE clause condition, the index will not be considered. If the mask in the LIKE operator begins with a percent sign or an underscore character, the index cannot be used.

Example 16.11: Find the players whose name ends with the letter *n*.

```
SELECT    *
FROM      PLAYERS
WHERE     NAME LIKE '%n'
```

The index will not be used, but unfortunately there is no alternative solution for this example.

16.7   Working with statistical data

We have seen that the presence of indexes can positively influence the processing time of some SQL statements. To do this, the optimizer queries the catalog to see whether there is an index or not, and whether it can be used. As well as this, the optimizer studies the *statistical data*. Statistical data shows how much data exists in the database and what the structure of it is. This data is stored in catalog tables. For example, the SYSTABLS table contains the CARD column which tells how many rows there are in each of the tables. You can probably see why an optimizer might develop a different processing strategy for a table with two rows from one for a table with twenty thousand rows. In the table below we show which columns in catalog tables contain statistical data.

table name	column name
SYSCOLS	COLCARD HIGH2KEY LOW2KEY
SYSIDXS	FIRSTKCARD FULLKCARD NLEAF NLEVELS
SYSTABLS	UPDATED CARD NPAGES

This statistical data is not automatically updated by dBASE IV. For example, if a new row is added to a table with an INSERT statement, the value in the CARD column (in the SYSTABLS catalog table) for the table concerned is not increased by one. The immediate update of all statistical data when any table update occurred would lead to unacceptable response times. Therefore, there is a separate process which enables the statistical data to be brought up to date as required. This is achieved with the *RUNSTATS statement*.

```
<runstats statement> ::=
    RUNSTATS [ <table identifier> ]

<table identifier> ::= <table name>
```

The following statement updates all statistical data in the associated database.

```
RUNSTATS
```

If you want to update the data for only one table in the database, you must specify the table name.

Example 16.12: See first whether the statistical data for the PLAYERS is current. If not, update them:

```
SELECT    CARD, NPAGES, UPDATED
FROM      SYSTABLS
WHERE     TBNAME = 'PLAYERS'
```

Result:

```
CARD   NPAGES   UPDATED
----   ------   --------
   0        0   08/10/88
```

The statistical data is clearly not current!

```
RUNSTATS
```

And then:

```
SELECT    CARD, NPAGES, UPDATED
FROM      SYSTABLS
WHERE     TBNAME = 'PLAYERS'
```

Result:

```
CARD   NPAGES   UPDATED
----   ------   --------
  14        2   08/12/88
```

When should you use the RUNSTATS statement? The data should present a reasonably accurate picture of the table contents at all times. If a table has 2000 rows, it should not appear that it has only 10 rows, otherwise the optimizer may develop an incorrect processing strategy. Then, while the statement is executing, it will become clear that it was not the most efficient strategy. However, the data does not have to be exactly correct; a deviation of about 10% is acceptable. Here are some guidelines for using RUNSTATS:

- Use RUNSTATS periodically for the whole database, say, at the end of each week.

- Use RUNSTATS directly after inserting many new rows into a table, after deleting many, or after many updates.

- Use RUNSTATS immediately after executing the LOAD statement (see Chapter 21).

17

Views

dBASE IV recognizes two types of tables: real tables, generally known as *base tables*, and derived tables, also called *views*. Base tables are created with CREATE TABLE statements, and of the two table types, are the only ones in which data can be stored. Familiar examples are the PLAYERS and TEAMS tables from the sports club database.

A derived table, or view, stores *no* rows itself. Rather, it exists, and can be seen, as a prescription or formula for combining data from base tables to make a 'virtual' table. The word virtual is used because a view only exists when it is named in an SQL statement. At that moment, dBASE IV takes the prescription that makes up the *view formula*, executes it and presents the user with what seems to be a real table.

This chapter describes how views are created and how they can be used. Some useful applications include the simplification of routine statements and the reorganization of data structures in and between tables. The last section looks at restrictions on querying and updating views.

17.1 Creating views

Views are created with the *CREATE VIEW statement*.

```
<create view statement> ::=
   CREATE VIEW <view name>
      [ <column list> ] AS
      <select statement>
      [ WITH CHECK OPTION ]

<column list> ::=
   ( <column name> [ {,<column name>}... ] )
```

Examples:

```
CREATE    VIEW TOWNS AS
SELECT    DISTINCT TOWN
FROM      PLAYERS

CREATE    VIEW COMPPLAY AS
SELECT    PLAYERNO, LEAGUENO
FROM      PLAYERS
WHERE     LEAGUENO <> ''
```

These two CREATE VIEW statements, then, create two views: TOWNS and
COMPPLAY. The contents of each view are defined by a SELECT statement.
So the view formula comprises a normal SELECT statement. These two views
now exist to be queried as though they were base tables. The COMPPLAY view
can even be updated.

Example 17.1: Get all information about competition players whose numbers
run from 6 to 44 inclusive.

```
SELECT    *
FROM      COMPPLAY
WHERE     PLAYERNO BETWEEN 6 AND 44
```

Result:

```
PLAYERNO  LEAGUENO
--------  --------
      6   8467
     44   1124
     27   2513
      8   2983
```

Without the COMPPLAY view you would need a longer SELECT statement to
retrieve the same information.

```
SELECT    PLAYERNO, LEAGUENO
FROM      PLAYERS
WHERE     LEAGUENO <> ''
AND       PLAYERNO BETWEEN 6 AND 44
```

Example 17.2: Remove the competition player whose league number is 7060.

```
DELETE
FROM      COMPPLAY
WHERE     LEAGUENO = '7060'
```

When this statement is executed, the row in the base table, the PLAYERS table, is deleted where the LEAGUENO column equals 7060.

The contents of a view are not stored, but derived the moment the view is referenced. This means that the view contents, by definition, always concur with the contents of the base table. Every change made to the data in a base table is immediately visible in a view that accesses that data. Users need never be concerned about the integrity of view data, as long as the integrity of the base tables is maintained.

A view formula may specify another view. Example:

```
CREATE    VIEW SEVERAL AS
SELECT    *
FROM      COMPPLAY
WHERE     PLAYERNO BETWEEN 6 AND 44

SELECT    *
FROM      SEVERAL
```

Result:

```
PLAYERNO  LEAGUENO
--------  --------
       6  8467
      44  1124
      27  2513
       8  2983
```

Note: Not all forms of the SELECT statement are permitted in view formulas; the two restrictions are:

- the UNION operator is *not* allowed;
- the ORDER BY clause is *not* allowed.
- the SAVE clause is *not* allowed.

CREATE SYNONYM statements can also be applied to views (see also Section 5.10). Here, views and tables can be regarded as equivalent.

The *DROP VIEW statement* is used to delete a view.

```
<drop view statement> ::=
   DROP VIEW <table identifier>

<table identifier> ::= <table name>
```

Every other view that refers to the dropped view also disappears. The automatic dropping of these views, can, of course, lead to the dropping of still more views. If a base table is dropped, all views directly or indirectly derived from this table are also dropped.

17.2 The column names of views

The column names in a view are the same as the column names in the SELECT clause. The two columns in the SEVERAL view are called PLAYERNO and LEAGUENO. A view, therefore, inherits the column names. You can also explicitly define column names for views.

Example:

```
CREATE   VIEW SFD_FOLK (PNO, NAME, INIT, BORN) AS
SELECT   PLAYERNO, NAME, INITIALS, BIRTH
FROM     PLAYERS
WHERE    TOWN = 'Stratford'

SELECT   *
FROM     SFD_FOLK
WHERE    PNO > 90
```

Result (note the column names):

```
PNO  NAME        INIT  BORN
---  ----------  ----  ----
100  Parmenter   P     1963
```

These new column names are permanent. You can no longer refer to the columns PLAYERNO or BIRTH in the SFD_FOLK view.

If an expression in the SELECT clause of a view formula does *not* consist of a column identifier, but is a function or calculation, then it is mandatory to provide names for the columns. In the following view definition, then, you may not leave out the column names TOWN and NUMBER.

```
CREATE   VIEW RESIDENT (TOWN, NUMBER) AS
SELECT   TOWN, COUNT(*)
FROM     PLAYERS
GROUP BY TOWN
```

Exercises

17.1 Create a view called NUMBPLAY that contains all the team numbers and the number of players who have played for that team. (Assume that at least one player has competed for each team.)

17.2   Create a view called WINNERS that contains the number and name of each player who, for a given team, has won more games than lost.

17.3   Create a view called TOTALS that records the total amount of penalties for each player who has incurred at least one penalty.

17.3   Recording views in the catalog

Information about views is recorded in various tables. The view formula is stored in the SYSVIEWS catalog table (see below). The primary key of this table is formed by the VIEWNAME and SEQNO columns.

SYSVIEWS	
VIEWNAME	Name of the view
CREATOR	Name of the owner (or creator) of the view
SEQNO	If the view formula is too long for the SQLTEXT column it is stored in multiple rows, the SEQNO column showing which row in the sequence it is
VCHECK	Has the value Y if the view is defined with the WITH CHECK OPTION, otherwise N
READONLY	Has the value Y if the view is updatable, otherwise N
JOIN	Has the value Y if the view can be used in a join, otherwise N
SQLTEXT	The view formula (SELECT statement)

The columns of the view inherit the data type of the column expression from the SELECT clause of the view formula.

    The SYSVDEPS table records which tables or views appear in the view formula. This table has the following structure:

SYSVDEPS	
VIEWNAME	Name of the view
TBLNO	Relative position of the table in the view formula
TBNAME	Name of the table or view on which the view is defined
CREATOR	Name of the owner (or creator) of the view

The SYSVDEPS table is filled with the following data after the creation of the RESIDENT view (we assume that the PLAYERS table was created by SQLDBA and the RESIDENT view by DIANE):

```
VIEWNAME  TBLNO  TBNAME   CREATOR
--------  -----  -------  -------
RESIDENT     1   PLAYERS  DIANE
```

The primary key of the SYSVDEPS table is formed by the VIEWNAME and TBLNO columns.

Example:

```
CREATE   VIEW YOUTH AS
SELECT   P2.PLAYERNO
FROM     PLAYERS P1, PLAYERS P2
WHERE    P1.BIRTH > P2.BIRTH
AND      P1.PLAYERNO = 6
```

Contents of the SYSVDEPS table:

```
VIEWNAME  TBLNO  TBNAME   CREATOR
--------  -----  -------  -------
YOUTH        1   PLAYERS
YOUTH        2   PLAYERS
```

17.4   Updating views: the WITH CHECK OPTION

We have already looked at a number of examples of views being updated. In fact, what is happening is that the underlying tables are being updated. Nevertheless, updating views can have unexpected results. Let us illustrate this with a few examples.

Example 17.3: Create a view of all players born before 1950.

```
CREATE   VIEW VETERAN AS
SELECT   *
FROM     PLAYERS
WHERE    BIRTH < 1950
```

Now we would like to alter the year of birth of the veteran whose player number is 2 from 1948 to 1960. The update statement reads:

```
UPDATE   VETERAN
SET      BIRTH = 1960
WHERE    PLAYERNO = 2
```

This is a correct update. The year of birth of player number 2 in the PLAYERS table is altered. The unexpected or undesired effect of this update, though, is that if we look at the *view* using a SELECT statement, player 2 no longer appears. This is because when the update occurred the player ceased to satisfy the condition specified in the view formula.

If you extend the view definition with the so-called *WITH CHECK OP-TION*, dBASE IV will ensure that such an unexpected effect does not arise.
The view definition then becomes:

```
CREATE    VIEW VETERAN AS
SELECT    *
FROM      PLAYERS
WHERE     BIRTH < 1950
WITH      CHECK OPTION
```

If a view includes the 'WITH CHECK OPTION' clause all changes via UPDATE and INSERT statements are controlled for validity:

- An UPDATE statement is correct if the rows that are updated still belong to the (virtual) contents of the view after the update.

- An INSERT statement is correct if the new rows belong to the (virtual) contents of the view.

The WITH CHECK OPTION clause can only be used in conjunction with views updatable according to the rules mentioned in Section 17.6.

17.5   Limitations of views with querying

SELECT, INSERT, UPDATE and DELETE statements may be applied to views. There are a number of limitations, though. For example, some views may not be queried in particular ways and rows of some views may not be deleted. This section contains a summary of all these limitations. Let us begin with the restrictions that apply to the querying of views (with the SELECT statement).

Limitation 1: When a column in a view is derived from a function in the SELECT clause of the view formula, this column may be named in only the SELECT or ORDER BY clauses of the SELECT statement that queries the view, and not, for example, in the WHERE clause.
Example:

```
CREATE    VIEW TOTALS
          (PLAYERNO, TOT_PEN) AS
SELECT    PLAYERNO, SUM(AMOUNT)
FROM      PENLTIES
GROUP BY PLAYERNO
```

The next SELECT statement is not permitted because the TOT_PEN column is based on a function in the view formula and therefore cannot be used in the WHERE clause.

```
SELECT    *
FROM      TOTALS
WHERE     TOT_PEN > 100
```

Limitation 2: When a column in a view is derived from a function in the view formula, this column may *not* be used in a function in the SELECT clause of the statement that accesses the view.

Take the TOTALS view again. The following statement is unacceptable because the MAX function operates on the TOT_PEN column from the TOTALS view. TOT_PEN, itself, is derived from a function, (SUM(AMOUNT)):

```
SELECT    MAX(TOT_PEN)
FROM      TOTALS
```

Limitation 3: When a view formula contains a GROUP BY clause, the view may not be joined with another view or table.

To illustrate this we turn to the TOTALS view again which has a GROUP BY clause. The following join, then, is not permitted:

```
SELECT    NAME, TOT_PEN
FROM      PLAYERS, TOTALS
WHERE     PLAYERS.PLAYERNO = TOTALS.PLAYERNO
```

17.6   Limitations of views with updating

As we mentioned, there are also restrictions placed on updating views (that is, updating tables through views). A view can only be updated if the view formula satisfies the following conditions. Note that the first five conditions apply to all update statements.

- the SELECT clause may not contain DISTINCT
- the SELECT clause may not contain statistical functions
- the FROM clause may specify only one table
- the WHERE clause may not contain a correlated subquery
- the SELECT statement may not contain a GROUP BY clause (and therefore also no HAVING clause)

In addition, the following restriction holds for the UPDATE statement:

- A virtual column may not be updated.

The BEG_AGE column in the following view may not be updated (though the PLAYERNO column may be updated):

```
CREATE    VIEW AGES
          (PLAYERNO, BEG_AGE) AS
SELECT    PLAYERNO, JOINED - BIRTH
FROM      PLAYERS
```

Exercise

17.4 This chapter has shown many examples of views. For each of these views say whether an UPDATE, INSERT or DELETE statement may be performed on them:

1. TOWNS
2. COMPPLAY
3. SEVERAL
4. SFD_FOLK
5. RESIDENT
6. YOUTH
7. VETERAN
8. TOTALS
9. AGES

17.7 Processing view statements

How does dBASE IV process statements which refer to views? The six processing steps (see Chapter 6) cannot be executed one by one as happens for tables. As soon as dBASE IV reaches the FROM clause and attempts to fetch rows from the database, it stumbles onto a problem, as a view contains no stored rows. So which rows must be retrieved when a statement refers to a view? dBASE IV knows that it is dealing with a view (thanks to a routine look in the catalog). Therefore, in order to make processing possible, it executes an extra step before moving on to the six other steps. In this first step, the view formula is included in the statement. Suppose that you create the following view:

```
CREATE    VIEW COSTLY AS
SELECT    *
FROM      PLAYERS
WHERE     PLAYERNO IN
          (SELECT   PLAYERNO
          FROM      PENLTIES)
```

Example 17.4: Get the number of each player who has incurred at least one penalty and lives in Stratford.

```
SELECT    PLAYERNO
FROM      COSTLY
WHERE     TOWN = 'Stratford'
```

The first step comprises the merging of the view formula into the SELECT statement. This step produces the following statement:

```
SELECT    PLAYERNO
FROM      PLAYERS
WHERE     TOWN = 'Stratford'
AND       PLAYERNO IN
          (SELECT   PLAYERNO
          FROM      PENLTIES)
```

Now dBASE IV can process this statement moving through the six steps. In short, there emerges a seventh step which must be executed before the other six steps.
Final result:

```
PLAYERNO
--------
       6
```

Here is another example, using the SFD_FOLK view from Section 17.2.

Example 17.5: Delete all Stratford people born after 1965.

```
DELETE
FROM      SFD_FOLK
WHERE     BORN > 1965
```

After the inclusion of the view formula the statement reads:

```
DELETE
FROM      PLAYERS
WHERE     BIRTH > 1965
AND       TOWN = 'Stratford'
```

17.8   Useful applications with views

Views can be used in a great variety of ways and in this section we look at some of those. There is no special significance in the order in which they are discussed.

17.8.1   Simplification of routine statements

Statements that are executed frequently, or are structurally similar, can be simplified through the use of views.

Example 17.6: Suppose that these two statements are frequently entered:

```
SELECT    *
FROM      PLAYERS
WHERE     PLAYERNO IN
          (SELECT   PLAYERNO
          FROM      PENLTIES)
AND       TOWN = 'Stratford'
```

and

```
SELECT    TOWN, COUNT(*)
FROM      PLAYERS
WHERE     PLAYERNO IN
          (SELECT    PLAYERNO
           FROM      PENLTIES)
GROUP BY TOWN
```

Both players are concerned only with the players who have incurred a penalty, so this subset of players can be accessed via a view:

```
CREATE    VIEW PEN_PLAY AS
SELECT    *
FROM      PLAYERS
WHERE     PLAYERNO IN
          (SELECT    PLAYERNO
           FROM      PENLTIES)
```

Now these two SELECT statements can be greatly simplified by using instead the PEN_PLAY view:

```
SELECT    *
FROM      PEN_PLAY
WHERE     TOWN = 'Stratford'
```

and

```
SELECT    TOWN, COUNT(*)
FROM      PEN_PLAY
GROUP BY TOWN
```

Example 17.7: Suppose that the PLAYERS table is often joined with the GAMES table:

```
SELECT    ...
FROM      PLAYERS, GAMES
WHERE     PLAYERS.PLAYERNO = GAMES.PLAYERNO
AND       ...
```

In this case the SELECT statement becomes simpler if the join is defined as a view:

```
CREATE    VIEW PLAY_GAM AS
SELECT    *
FROM      PLAYERS, GAMES
WHERE     PLAYERS.PLAYERNO = GAMES.PLAYERNO
```

What was a join statement now takes this simplified form:

```
SELECT   ...
FROM     PLAY_GAM
WHERE    ...
```

17.8.2   Reorganizing tables

The structure of a database is designed and implemented on the basis of a particular situation. This situation can change from time to time which means that the structure may also have to change. For example, a new column is added to a table, or two tables are joined to make a single table. In most cases, the reorganization of a database requires the alteration of already developed and operational statements. Such alterations can be time consuming and expensive. Appropriate use of views can keep this time and cost to a minimum. Let us see how.

Example 17.8: Give the name and initials of each competition player and also the divisions in which he or she has played.

```
SELECT   NAME, INITIALS, DIVISION
FROM     PLAYERS P, GAMES G1, TEAMS T
WHERE    P.PLAYERNO = G1.PLAYERNO
AND      G1.TEAMNR = T.TEAMNR
```

Result:

NAME	INITIALS	DIVISION
Parmenter	R	first
Baker	E	first
Hope	PK	first
Everett	R	first
Collins	DD	second
Moorman	D	second
Brown	M	first
Bailey	IP	second
Newcastle	B	first
Newcastle	B	second

Assume that the database structure has to be reorganized: the TEAMS and GAMES tables have been combined to form the RESULTS table shown below:

TEAMNO	PLAYERNO	WON	LOST	CAPTAIN	DIVISION
1	6	9	1	6	first
1	44	7	5	6	first
1	83	3	3	6	first
1	2	4	8	6	first
1	57	5	0	6	first
1	8	0	1	6	first
2	27	11	2	27	second
2	104	8	4	27	second
2	112	4	8	27	second
2	8	4	4	27	second

The CAPTAIN column in the RESULTS table is the former PLAYERNO column from the TEAMS table. This column has been given another name otherwise there would have been two columns called PLAYERNO. All statements that refer to the two tables now have to be rewritten, including the SELECT statement above. One solution, which renders a total rewrite unnecessary, is to define two views on the results table. These two views represent the former TEAMS and GAMES tables respectively:

```
CREATE   VIEW TEAMS (TEAMNO, PLAYERNO, DIVISION) AS
SELECT   DISTINCT TEAMNO, CAPTAIN, DIVISION
FROM     RESULTS
```

and

```
CREATE   VIEW GAMES AS
SELECT   TEAMNO, PLAYERNO, WON, LOST
FROM     RESULTS
```

The virtual contents of each of these two views is the same as the contents of the two original tables. Not one statement has to be rewritten, including the SELECT statement from the beginning of this section.

Of course, you cannot manage every reorganization of the database structure with views. It has been decided, for example, to store data about male and female players in separate tables. Each new table acquires the same columns as the PLAYERS table, but omits the SEX column. It is no longer possible to construct the original PLAYERS table with a view, because the UNION operator is necessary, and this operator cannot be specified in a view formula.

17.8.3   Stepwise building of SELECT statements

Suppose you have to answer the following question: Give the name and initials of each Stratford player who has incurred a penalty which is higher than the average penalty for players from the second team, and who played for at least one first division team. You could write a huge SELECT statement to answer this, but you could also build a query in a stepwise fashion.

First of all, create a view of all the players who have incurred a penalty which is greater than the average penalty for players from the second team:

```
CREATE    VIEW GREATER AS
SELECT    DISTINCT PLAYERNO
FROM      PENLTIES
WHERE     AMOUNT >
          (SELECT    AVG(AMOUNT)
           FROM      PENLTIES
           WHERE     PLAYERNO IN
                     (SELECT    PLAYERNO
                      FROM      GAMES
                      WHERE     TEAMNO = 2))
```

Then create a view of all players who have competed for a team in the first division:

```
CREATE    VIEW FIRST AS
SELECT    DISTINCT PLAYERNO
FROM      GAMES
WHERE     TEAMNO IN
          (SELECT    TEAMNO
           FROM      TEAMS
           WHERE     DIVISION = 'first')
```

Using these two views, answering the original question is quite simple:

```
SELECT    NAME, INITIALS
FROM      PLAYERS
WHERE     TOWN = 'Stratford'
AND       PLAYERNO IN
          (SELECT    PLAYERNO
           FROM      GREATER)
AND       PLAYERNO IN
          (SELECT    PLAYERNO
           FROM      FIRST)
```

The problem is, so to speak, split into 'mini-problems' and executed in steps. In this way, you can, if you want to, avoid writing a complex and long SELECT statement.

17.8.4 Specifying integrity rules

By using the WITH CHECK OPTION clause, it is possible to lay down rules for determining which values may be entered into columns.

Example 17.9: The SEX column in the PLAYERS table can contain either the value M or the value F, and nothing else. You can use the WITH CHECK OPTION clause to provide an automatic control for this. The following view should be defined:

```
CREATE    VIEW PLAY_SEX AS
SELECT    *
FROM      PLAYERS
WHERE     SEX IN ('M', 'F')
WITH      CHECK OPTION
```

To follow this up we give nobody the possibility of updating the PLAYERS table directly; instead they have to do so via the PLAY_SEX view. The WITH CHECK OPTION clause tests every update (that is, every UPDATE and INSERT statement) to see whether the new value falls into the permitted range.

17.8.5   Unit conversion

Suppose that you use the following table to record prices of articles. The prices are given in pounds.

```
The ARTICLE table:

ARTICLE     PRICE
---------   -----
pen          1.50
scrap pad    3.75
pencil       1.00
```

Imagine, now, that you want to give the price in dollars. You simply create a view:

```
CREATE    VIEW DOLLARS
          (ARTICLE, NEW_VAL) AS
SELECT    ARTICLE, PRICE / 0.5
FROM      ARTICLE
```

The virtual contents of this view are:

```
SELECT    *
FROM      DOLLARS
```

Result:

```
ARTICLE     NEW_VAL
---------   -------
pen          3.00
scrap pad    7.50
pencil       2.00
```

If the exchange rate changes, then you need only alter the view formula.

17.8.6   Data security

Views can also be used to protect or screen parts of tables. Chapter 18 deals with
this topic in detail.

Exercise

17.5   Decide whether or not the following reorganizations of the database structure are possible through the use of views.

1.   The LEAGUENO column is removed from the PLAYERS table and
placed in a separate table with a PLAYERNO column. If a player has
no league number he or she does not appear in this new table.

2.   The NAME column is added to the PENLTIES table but also remains in the PLAYERS TABLE.

3.   The TOWN column is removed from the PLAYERS table and
placed together with the PLAYERNO column in a separate table.

18
User and data security

In Chapter 4 we discussed the fact that dBASE IV recognizes multiple users. Now we need to look at how new users and their privileges are entered in the catalog. We will also describe how privileges are withdrawn and how users can be removed from the catalog.

18.1 Security with PROTECT

Access to all data in a dBASE IV database is open to anyone if it has not been explicitly protected. Anyone who can type the letters DBASE and who knows some SQL can look at the data and possibly change it. To limit access to the data to particular people we need to ensure that everyone who starts dBASE IV identifies him or herself with a name and password. As well as this, we must grant the registered users privileges to use the data appropriately. For example, we could give the user JAN the privilege of reading the data in the PLAYERS table but not updating it. If a user attempts to perform an action he or she is not authorized for, dBASE IV prevents it.

But how do we set up dBASE IV to ask for a name and password when it is started? Very simply. If, during startup, dBASE IV comes across a file called *DBSYSTEM.DB* in the \DBASE directory, it asks automatically which data is to be used. If this file does not exist, anyone can start dBASE IV and read or change all the data.

So, in order to secure the data, you need to create a DBSYSTEM.DB file and this is done with the *PROTECT command*. This command performs, among other things, the following tasks:

- introducing and removing users
- attributing passwords to users
- dividing users into groups
- listing existing users
- attributing access levels to users
- specifying access levels for dBASE IV files

The first four tasks are applicable to SQL tables and dBASE IV files, whereas the other tasks are only relevant to dBASE IV files. They are outside the scope of this book.

The PROTECT command creates the DBSYSTEM.DB file directly after the first user is introduced. The security mechanism is still not immediately in force; dBASE IV has to be stopped and restarted. In fact, userids (or names) and passwords are stored in the DBSYSTEM.DB file by the PROTECT program, and not in normal DBF files.

To specify access to SQL tables there is a special SQL statement; we will discuss it in Section 18.3.

The protection can be extended by the DBSYSTEM.DB file, for example, to remove or add names.

18.2   Introducing new users

The *PROTECT command* is used to introduce or enter new users.

```
PROTECT
```

The *dBASE IV Password Security System screen* appears and a password must be entered (see the screen in Figure 18.1). Each time PROTECT is used, this password must be provided. If PROTECT is being used for the first time, dBASE IV asks for the password to be entered twice. This is for your benefit to be sure that you have typed in the password you intended. After the password has been entered (the password itself does not show up as it is being typed in), the screen shown in Figure 18.2 appears. There are four menu options here (see the top of the screen): Users, Files, Reports and Exit. PROTECT assumes that you will choose the Users option where a user can be entered.

For each user you can enter a *Login name* (userid), the *Password*, the *Group name* to which the user belongs, a *Full name* and an *Access level*. For SQL use it is mandatory to enter the userid, password and group to which the user belongs. The other two entries are not necessary for SQL. In fact, the Group name is not important for SQL itself, but is used for starting dBASE IV. At start time a group *must* be specified along with a userid and password.

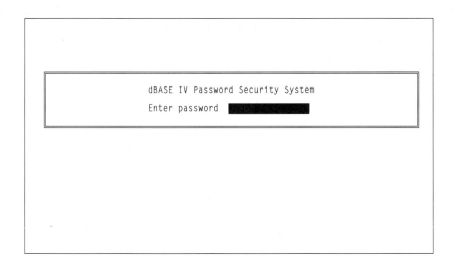

Figure 18.1: Securing data with PROTECT

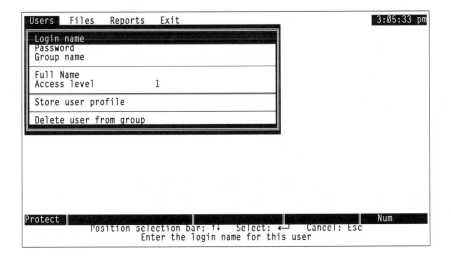

Figure 18.2: Introducing users with PROTECT

After the three mandatory items have been filled in for a new user, you move to the field which holds the Store user profile. When you press the Enter key the user is added to this list of those registered.

Once you have entered all the users you go to the Exit menu. From there, you have three options: Save, Abandon or Exit. Choose the Save option if you want to keep all the new users registered, the Abandon option if you don't, and Exit if you want to end PROTECT. Should this be the first time that you have used PROTECT and you choose the Save option, then the DBSYSTEM.DB file is created. Choosing the Exit option means that you leave PROTECT and return automatically to SQL. As we mentioned in the previous section, you must stop dBASE IV and restart it to activate the security mechanism.

When dBASE IV is restarted, the screen with the familiar Ashton-Tate logo no longer appears first, but one into which you must enter a group, a userid and a password. If you happen to enter a combination which does not occur in the DBSYSTEM.DB file, dBASE IV stops again.

Every user must have a userid. A given userid can occur in two or more groups. Two users in the same group cannot have the same userid and for each userid there is one password. Note that if two users have the same userid, but belong to different groups, SQL does not distinguish between them. Within SQL, privileges are principally connected to userids. The group is not considered.

Data about users is not focused on a special database, but is system-wide. This is because before a database is started you have to provide a userid and password.

The userid and name of the group can be up to 8 characters long, while the password can be up to 16 characters. All can use any characters.

A registered user is automatically accorded the following privileges:

- (s)he may create and drop databases
- (s)he may create tables and access these tables using all the other SQL statements
- (s)he may create synonyms for all tables, even those not created by him- or herself
- (s)he may query the catalog
- (s)he may use the SHOW DATABASE statement
- (s)he may use all other trivial statements, such as HELP

Users may not automatically access tables created by someone else. For this, they need to receive an explicit privilege, and this is what we cover in the next section.

One user with special privileges is the one with the userid *SQLDBA*. This user is in a position to access tables created by someone else, and even to drop them without having received the privilege to do so. You enter this user via the PROTECT command in the normal way.

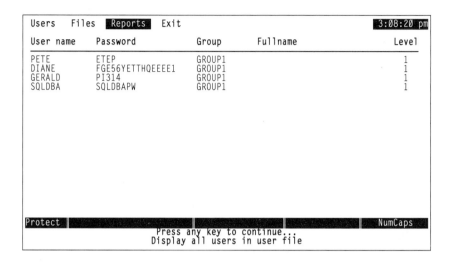

Figure 18.3: List of all registered users

It is possible to get a list of all registered users by choosing the option called User information from the Reports menu. Figure 18.3 is an example of what such a list might look like.

18.3 Granting privileges

Note: In this chapter we are assuming, unless otherwise mentioned, that the user called SQLDBA enters the statements.

Suppose that we have entered the users, JAN and PETE, using the PROTECT command. Now they are allowed to create and access their own tables, among other things. So far, they have no authority to access tables created by others, even with the SELECT statement. The *GRANT statement* must be used to grant privileges to these two users. These types of privileges are called *table privileges*. SQL recognizes the following seven table privileges:

- SELECT: This privilege gives a user the right to access the table concerned with the SELECT and UNLOAD statements. (S)he can also include the table in a view formula. In fact, a user must have the SELECT privilege for every table (or view) specified in a view formula.

- INSERT: This privilege gives a user the right to add rows to the table concerned with the INSERT and LOAD statements.

- DELETE: This privilege gives a user the right to remove rows from the table concerned with the DELETE statement.

- UPDATE: This privilege gives a user the right to change values in the table concerned with the UPDATE statement.

- INDEX: This privilege gives a user the right to create and drop indexes on the table concerned.

- ALTER: This privilege gives a user the right to add new columns to the table concerned.

- ALL or ALL PRIVILEGES: This privilege is a shortened form for all the privileges named above.

```
<grant statement> ::=
    GRANT         <privileges>
    ON [ TABLE ] <table identifier>
    TO            <grantees>
    [ WITH  GRANT OPTION ]

<privileges> ::=
    ALL [ PRIVILEGES ] |
    <table privilege>

<table privilege> ::=
    SELECT |
    INSERT |
    DELETE |
    UPDATE [ <column list> ] |
    INDEX  |
    ALTER

<column list> ::=
    ( <column name> [ {,<column name>}... ] )

<table identifier> ::= <table name>

<grantees> ::=
    PUBLIC |
    <userid> [ {,<userid>}... ]
```

Here are a few examples of how table privileges must be granted.

Example 18.1: Give JAN the SELECT privilege on the PLAYERS table.

```
GRANT   SELECT
ON      PLAYERS
TO      JAN
```

After this GRANT statement has been processed JAN may use any acceptable SELECT statement to query the PLAYERS table, irrespective of who has created the table.

With the UPDATE privilege you can state which columns may be updated. Specifying no columns implies that the privilege extends to *all* columns in the table.

Example 18.2: Give JAN the INSERT and UPDATE privileges for all columns in the TEAMS table:

```
GRANT     INSERT, UPDATE
ON        TEAMS
TO        JAN
```

Example 18.3: Give PETE the UPDATE privilege for the PLAYERNO and DIVISION columns of the TEAMS table:

```
GRANT     UPDATE (PLAYERNO, DIVISION)
ON        TEAMS
TO        PETE
```

A privilege can be granted to one user, a number of users or to PUBLIC. If a privilege is granted to PUBLIC, each user who has been introduced now has that privilege. It applies to all users introduced after the granting of the privilege and means that once a user is entered into the system, (s)he automatically receives all the privileges granted to PUBLIC.

Example 18.4: Give all users the SELECT and INDEX privileges on the PENL-TIES table:

```
GRANT     SELECT, INDEX
ON        PENLTIES
TO        PUBLIC
```

A table privilege can only be granted by the owner of the table or the user called SQLDBA.

18.4   Passing on privileges: WITH GRANT OPTION

A GRANT statement can be concluded with the WITH GRANT OPTION clause. This means that all users named in the TO clause can *themselves* pass on the privilege or (part of the privilege) to other users.

Example 18.5: Give JAN the INDEX privilege on the TEAMS table, and allow her to pass it on to other users:

```
GRANT    INDEX
ON       TEAMS
TO       JAN
WITH     GRANT OPTION
```

Because of the WITH GRANT OPTION clause, JAN can pass this privilege on to PETE, say:

```
GRANT    INDEX
ON       TEAMS
TO       PETE
```

JAN can herself extend the statement with WITH GRANT OPTION, so that PETE, in turn, can pass on the privilege.

If a user is given a table privilege via the WITH GRANT OPTION clause, (s)he can grant that privilege on the table without being the owner of it.

18.5   Recording privileges in the catalog

All privileges are stored in the SYSAUTH and SYSCOLAU tables of the catalog. The first contains data about privileges on tables and the second about the privileges granted on columns.

The SYSAUTH table holds one row for each privilege granted to a user on a table. The primary key of this table is formed by the GRANTOR, TNAME and USERID columns.

SYSAUTH	
GRANTOR	User who granted the privilege
TNAME	Table or view on which the privilege was granted
USERID	User to whom the privilege was granted
TBTYPE	Type of table on which the privilege was granted: T(able) or V(iew)
PSELECT	A sequence number reflecting when the privilege to query the table was granted; the value equals zero if the user does not have this privilege
PINSERT	A sequence number reflecting when the privilege to add new rows to the table was granted; the value equals zero if the user does not have this privilege
PDELETE	A sequence number reflecting when the privilege to delete rows from the table was granted; the value equals zero if the user does not have this privilege
PALTER	A sequence number reflecting when the privilege to add new columns to the table was granted; the value equals zero if the user does not have this privilege
PINDEX	A sequence number reflecting when the privilege to define indexes on the table was granted; the value equals zero if the user does not have this privilege
PUPDATE	Represents the privilege to update values in the table; ALL means all columns, SOME means some columns and NONE means the user does not have this privilege
GRANTOPT	If this column is filled with the value G, the user may pass the privilege on to other users; otherwise the value is Y

The columns on which UPDATE privileges are held are recorded in a separate catalog table, the SYSCOLAU table. The primary key of this column is formed by the GRANTOR, TNAME, GRANTEE and COLNAME columns. The table has the following structure:

SYSCOLAU	
GRANTOR	User who granted the privilege
TNAME	Table or view on which the privilege was granted
GRANTEE	User to whom the privilege was granted
COLNAME	Column name on which the UPDATE privilege was granted
AUTHTIME	A sequence number reflecting when the privilege was granted; the value equals zero if the user does not have this privilege
GRANTOPT	If this column is filled with the value G, the user may pass the privilege on to other users; otherwise the value is Y

The GRANT statements that we entered as examples in the previous sections result in the following updates to the SYSAUTH and SYSCOLAU tables. (The names of the last columns are shortened; S = PSELECT, I = PINSERT, D = PDELETE, A = PALTER, X = PINDEX, UPDATE = PUPDATE and GRANT = GRANTOPT.):

GRANTOR	TNAME	USERID	TYPE	S	I	D	A	X	UPDATE	GRANT
SQLDBA	PLAYERS	JAN	T	2	0	0	0	0	NONE	Y
SQLDBA	TEAMS	JAN	T	0	3	0	0	0	ALL	Y
SQLDBA	TEAMS	PETE	T	0	0	0	0	0	SOME	Y
SQLDBA	PENLTIES	PUBLIC	T	5	0	0	0	5	NONE	Y
SQLDBA	TEAMS	JAN	T	0	0	0	0	6	NONE	G
JAN	TEAMS	PETE	T	0	0	0	0	7	NONE	Y

GRANTOR	TNAME	GRANTEE	COLNAME	AUTHTIME	GRANTOPT
SQLDBA	TEAMS	PETE	PLAYERNO	4	Y
SQLDBA	TEAMS	PETE	DIVISION	4	Y

Exercise

18.1 What does the SYSAUTH table look like after the following GRANT statements have been issued? The first two statements have been entered by SQLDBA.

```
GRANT    SELECT
ON       PLAYERS
TO       PUBLIC

GRANT    INSERT
ON       PLAYERS
TO       OLGA
WITH     GRANT OPTION
```

OLGA enters these statements:

```
GRANT   INSERT
ON      PLAYERS
TO      REGINA

GRANT   INSERT
ON      PLAYERS
TO      SUSAN
WITH    GRANT OPTION
```

SUSAN enters these statements:

```
GRANT   INSERT
ON      PLAYERS
TO      REGINA
```

18.6   Deleting users

The PROTECT command is used to remove users from the system. Enter the command and choose the Users option, just as you would for entering new users. Fill in the userid, password and group of the user to be deleted. Shift the cursor to the area which says Delete user from group and press the Enter key. The user is then deleted from the list of those who are registered. In fact, the user is really only deleted when you go to the Exit menu and choose the Save option.

The table privileges of deleted users remain and must be deleted using the SQL REVOKE statement. We will look at this statement in the next section. As well as the table privileges, all the tables and indexes created by deleted users remain too. The only thing that can't be done is starting dBASE IV with that userid and associated password.

18.7   Revoking privileges

You use the *REVOKE statement* to withdraw privileges from users. This statement has the opposite effect to the GRANT statement.

```
<revoke statement> ::=
   REVOKE        <privileges>
   ON [ TABLE ] <table identifier>
   FROM          <grantees>

<privileges> ::=
   ALL [ PRIVILEGES ] |
   <table privilege>

<table privilege> ::=
   SELECT |
   INSERT |
   DELETE |
   UPDATE [ <column list> ] |
   INDEX  |
   ALTER

<column list> ::=
   ( <column name> [ {,<column name>}... ] )

<table identifier> ::= <table name>

<grantees> ::=
   PUBLIC |
   <userid> [ {,<userid>}... ]
```

Example 18.6: JAN's SELECT privilege on the PLAYERS table is to be withdrawn (we assume that the situation is as it was at the end of Section 18.5):

```
REVOKE    SELECT
ON        PLAYERS
FROM      JAN
```

The record of that privilege is now deleted from the SYSAUTH table.

Example 18.7: JAN's INDEX privilege on the TEAMS table is withdrawn:

```
REVOKE    INDEX
ON        TEAMS
FROM      JAN
```

This privilege is revoked, along with all the privileges directly or directly dependent on it. In this example PETE also loses his INDEX privilege on the TEAMS table.

The SYSAUTH table looks like this after the two REVOKE statements have executed:

GRANTOR	TNAME	USERID	TYPE	S	I	D	A	X	UPDATE	GRANT
SQLDBA	TEAMS	JAN	T	0	3	0	0	0	ALL	Y
SQLDBA	TEAMS	PETE	T	0	0	0	0	0	SOME	Y
SQLDBA	PENLTIES	PUBLIC	T	5	0	0	0	5	NONE	Y

Exercises

18.2 These exercises take the results of Exercise 18.1 as a starting point. What does the SYSAUTH table look like after the following REVOKE statement is executed?

```
REVOKE   INSERT
ON       PLAYERS
FROM     OLGA
```

18.3 The SYSAUTH table has the following contents:

GRANTOR	TNAME	USERID	S	I	D	A	X	UPDATE	GRANT
SQLDBA	TEAMS	DIANE	1	1	1	1	1	NONE	Y
DIANE	TEAMS	KAREN	2	0	0	0	0	ALL	Y
RONALD	PLAYERS	DIANE	3	3	0	0	0	NONE	G
RONALD	PLAYERS	LUKE	4	4	0	0	0	NONE	Y
DIANE	PLAYERS	CORINE	5	0	0	0	0	NONE	Y
DIANE	TEAMS	CORINE	6	0	0	0	0	NONE	Y

How does the table differ after this statement is processed?

```
REVOKE   SELECT, INSERT
ON       PLAYERS
FROM     RONALD
```

18.8   Security of and through views

GRANT statements can refer to tables, but also to views (see the definition of the GRANT statement). Let us look at this more closely.

Because privileges can also be granted for views, it is possible to provide users with access to only a part of a table, or to only derived or summarized information. Here are examples of both features.

Example 18.8: Give DIANE the privilege to read only the names and addresses of non-competitive players.

First, DIANE must be introduced to the system via the PROTECT command. Second, a view is created specifying which data she may see:

```
CREATE    VIEW NAR AS
SELECT    NAME, INITIALS, STREET, HOUSENO,
          TOWN
FROM      PLAYERS
WHERE     LEAGUENO = ' '
```

The last step is to grant DIANE the SELECT privilege on the NAR view:

```
GRANT    SELECT
ON       NAR
TO       DIANE
```

With this statement DIANE has access to only that part of the PLAYERS table defined in the view formula.

Example 18.9: Ensure that GERARD can look only at the number of players in each town. First, we introduce GERARD.
    The view which limits his access is:

```
CREATE    VIEW RESIDENT (TOWN, NUMBER) AS
SELECT    TOWN, COUNT(*)
FROM      PLAYERS
GROUP BY TOWN
```

Now we give GERARD the privilege for the view above:

```
GRANT    SELECT
ON       RESIDENT
TO       GERARD
```

Four types of privileges can be applied to views: INSERT, UPDATE, DELETE and SELECT. The INDEX and ALTER privileges are not permissible because the CREATE INDEX and ALTER statements cannot refer to a view.

19
Catalog tables

A *catalog table* is a table in which dBASE IV maintains data about the database. There are ten catalog tables, collectively known as the *catalog*. dBASE IV keeps different types of data in the catalog. This includes which columns occur in which tables, which indexes have been defined, who created the tables or views and so on. All this data is updated by dBASE IV. Say, for example, a column is added to a table; at this point dBASE IV automatically updates the catalog to reflect the change. The contents of the catalog, then, are always consistent with the actual contents of the database.

The previous chapters have described the catalog tables more or less independently of one another. This chapter places the emphasis more on the catalog as a whole, and the relationship existing between the tables. We give examples of how to query the catalog using SELECT statements. Section 19.3 covers protection of the catalog.

19.1 Overview of the catalog tables

During the creation of a new database dBASE IV builds a new directory and places a number of tables in it. The name of the directory is the same as that of the database. Therefore, for our sports club, it is SPORTDB. For each user–created table dBASE IV records the owner; for the catalog tables the owner is SYSTEM.

We continue now with a description of the columns in each catalog table and make further remarks on the tables.

19.1.1   SYSAUTH table

The SYSAUTH table contains one row for each table privilege granted to a user.
Notes:

- The primary key of this table is formed by the GRANTOR, TNAME and USERID columns.

- The number in the PSELECT, PINSERT, PDELETE, PALTER, PINDEX and PUPDATE columns is a sequence number dependent on the time when the privilege was granted. Each time an privilege is granted dBASE IV looks for the highest value appearing in these six columns. The new privilege then gets a number which is one higher. dBASE IV is not interested in the actual dates on which these occurred, but in the sequence.

- Each table privilege belongs to a table. The set of table names from the SYSAUTH table is a subset of the set of table names from the SYSTABLS table.

column name	data type	length	description
GRANTOR	CHAR	10	User who granted the privilege
TNAME	CHAR	10	Table or view on which the privilege was granted
USERID	CHAR	10	User to whom the privilege was granted
TBTYPE	CHAR	1	Type of table on which the privilege was granted: T(able) or V(iew)
PSELECT	NUM	8	A sequence number reflecting when the privilege to query the table was granted; the value equals zero if the user does not have this privilege
PINSERT	NUM	8	A sequence number reflecting when the privilege to insert rows into a table was granted; the value equals zero if the user does not have this privilege
PDELETE	NUM	8	A sequence number reflecting when the privilege to delete rows from a table was granted; the value equals zero if the user does not have this privilege
PALTER	NUM	8	A sequence number reflecting when the privilege to add new columns to a table was granted; the value equals zero if the user does not have this privilege
PINDEX	NUM	8	A sequence number reflecting when the privilege to define an index on the table was granted; the value equals zero if the user does not have this privilege
PUPDATE	CHAR	4	Represents the privilege to update values in the table; ALL means all columns, SOME means some columns and NONE means the user does not have this privilege
GRANTOPT	CHAR	1	If this column is filled with the value G, the user may pass this privilege on to other users; otherwise, the value in the column is Y

19.1.2 SYSCOLAU table

The SYSCOLAU table contains one row for each column on which the UPDATE privilege has been granted to a user.
Notes:

- The primary key of this table is formed by the GRANTOR, TNAME, GRANTEE and COLNAME columns.

- The sequence number in the AUTHTIME column reflects when the privilege was granted.

- Each UPDATE privilege in a column belongs to an UPDATE privilege on a table. The set of combinations of table names and column names from the SYSCOLAU table is a subset of the set of table names and column names from the SYSCOLS table.

column name	data type	length	description
GRANTOR	CHAR	10	User who granted the privilege
TNAME	CHAR	10	Table or view on which the privilege was granted
GRANTEE	CHAR	10	User to whom the privilege was granted
COLNAME	CHAR	10	Column name on which the UPDATE privilege was granted
AUTHTIME	NUM	8	A sequence number reflecting when the privilege was granted; the value equals zero if the user does not have this privilege
GRANTOPT	CHAR	1	If this column is filled with the value G, the user may pass the privilege on to other users; otherwise the value is Y

19.1.3 SYSCOLS table

The SYSCOLS table contains one row for each column in a table or view.
Notes:

- The primary key of this table is formed by the TBNAME and COLNAME columns.

- The COLCARD, HIGH2KEY and LOW2KEY columns are filled when the RUNSTATS statement is processed.

- Each column belongs to a table. The set of table names from the SYSCOLS table is a subset of the set of table names from the SYSTABLS table.

column name	data type	length	description
COLNAME	CHAR	10	Name of the column
TBNAME	CHAR	10	Name of the table in which the column is found
TBCREATOR	CHAR	10	Name of the owner (or creator) of the table in which the column is found
COLNO	NUM	3	Sequence number of the column within the table; this sequence is the same as the sequence of the columns in the CREATE TABLE statement
COLTYPE	CHAR	1	Data type of the column: C(har), D(ate), F(loat), L(ogical) or N(umeric)
COLLEN	NUM	3	Length of the column if the COLTYPE is C(har), F(loat) or N(umeric); D(ate) has a fixed length of 8 and L(ogical) of 1
COLSCALE	NUM	2	If the value in COLTYPE is F(loat) or N(umeric) the number of figures after the decimal point is given
NULLS	CHAR	1	Not used
COLCARD	NUM	10	The number of different values in the column
UPDATES	CHAR	1	Set to Y if the column can be updated; otherwise set to N
HIGH2KEY	CHAR	8	Second highest value in the column
LOW2KEY	CHAR	8	Second lowest value in the column

19.1.4 SYSDBS table

The SYSDBS table contains one row for each database created.
Notes:

- The NAME column is the primary key of this table.

- As opposed to the other catalog tables, the SYSDBS table is stored in the \SQLHOME directory. Another way in which this table differs from the other catalog tables is that all databases share the same SYSDBS table. Because of this, the SYSDBS table has no relationship to other catalog tables.

- The SYSDBS table cannot be queried with SELECT statements.

column name	data type	length	description
NAME	CHAR	8	Name of the database
CREATOR	CHAR	10	Owner of the database
CREATED	DATE	8	Date on which the database was created
PATH	CHAR	64	The specification of the directory path in which the database was created

19.1.5   SYSIDXS table

The SYSIDXS table contains one row for each index created.
Notes:

- The IXNAME column is the primary key of the table.

- The CLUSTERED, FIRSTKCARD, FULLKCARD, NLEAF and NLEV-
  ELS columns are filled when the RUNSTATS statement is executed.

- Each index is defined on a table. The set of table names from the SYSIDXS
  table is a subset of the set of table names from the SYSTABLS table.

column name	data type	length	description
IXNAME	CHAR	10	Name of the index
CREATOR	CHAR	10	Name of the user who created the index
TBNAME	CHAR	10	Name of the table on which the index is defined
TBCREATOR	CHAR	10	Name of the owner of the table on which the index is defined
UNIQUERULE	CHAR	1	Whether the index is U(nique) or contains D(uplicate) values
COLCOUNT	NUM	3	The number of columns in the index
CLUSTERING	CHAR	1	Not used
CLUSTERED	CHAR	1	Statistical data
FIRSTKCARD	NUM	5	The number of different values in the first column of the index
FULLKCARD	NUM	5	The number of different values in the whole index
NLEAF	NUM	5	The number of nodes in the index tree
NLEVELS	NUM	3	The number of levels in the index tree

19.1.6   SYSKEYS table

The SYSKEYS table contains one row for each column belonging to an index.
Notes:

- The primary key of this table is formed by the IXNAME and COLNAME columns.

- Each column in an index is a column from a table. The set of combinations of table name and column name from the SYSKEYS table is a subset of the set of combinations of table name and column name from the SYSCOLS table.

- Each column in an index belongs to an index. The set of index names from the SYSKEYS table is a subset of the set of index names from the SYSIDXS table.

column name	data type	length	description
IXNAME	CHAR	10	Name of the index
IXCREATOR	CHAR	10	Owner of the index
COLNAME	CHAR	10	Name of the column on which the index is defined
COLNO	NUM	3	Sequence number of the column in the table
COLSEQ	NUM	3	Sequence number of the column in the index
ORDERING	CHAR	1	The column has the value A(scending) if the column values are increasing; otherwise, D(escending)

19.1.7   SYSSYNS table

The SYSSYNS table contains one row for each synonym.
Notes:

- The SYNAME column is the primary key of this table.

- Each synonym belongs to a table. The set of table names from the SYS-SYNS table is a subset of the set of table names from the SYSTABLS table.

column name	data type	length	description
SYNAME	CHAR	10	Synonyn for the table name
CREATOR	CHAR	10	Name of the user who created the synonym
TBNAME	CHAR	10	Name of the table on which the synonym is defined
TBCREATOR	CHAR	10	Name of the owner (or creator) of the table

19.1.8   SYSTABLS table

The SYSTABLS table contains one row for each table and view.
Notes:

- The TBNAME is the primary key of this table.

- The UPDATED, CARD and NPAGES columns are filled when the RUN-STATS statement is executed.

column name	data type	length	description
TBNAME	CHAR	10	Name of the table or view (depending on the TYPE column)
CREATOR	CHAR	10	Name of the owner (or creator) of the table or view
TBTYPE	CHAR	1	The type of table; T for real table, V for view, D for a table created by the SAVE clause of a SELECT statement (without the KEEP option) and K for a table created by the SAVE clause of a SELECT statement (with the KEEP option)
COLCOUNT	NUM	3	The number of columns in the table or view
CLUSTERRID	NUM	10	Not used
INDXCOUNT	NUM	3	The number of indexes defined on the table; in the case of a view this value is set to zero
CREATED	DATE	8	Date on which the table or view was created
UPDATED	DATE	8	Date on which the last ALTER TABLE or RUN-STATS statement was executed against the table
CARD	NUM	10	The number of rows in the table; in the case of a view this value is set to zero
NPAGES	NUM	10	The number of physical pages this table takes up on the disk

19.1.9 SYSVDEPS table

The SYSVDEPS table contains one row for each table and view on which another view is defined. The short form VDEPS stands for view dependencies.
    Notes:

- The primary key of this table is formed by the VIEWNAME and TBLNO columns.

- Each view dependency belongs to a view. The set of view names from the SYSVDEPS table is a subset of the set of view names from the SYSVIEWS table.

- Each view dependency belongs at the same time to a table. The set of table names from the SYSVDEPS table is a subset of the set of table names from the SYSTABLS table.

column name	data type	length	description
VIEWNAME	CHAR	10	Name of the view
TBLNO	NUM	5	Relative position of the table in the view formula
TBNAME	CHAR	10	Name of the table or view on which the view is defined
CREATOR	CHAR	10	Name of the owner (or creator) of the view

19.1.10 SYSVIEWS table

The SYSVIEWS table contains one row for each view.
Notes:

- The primary key of this table is formed by the VIEWNAME and SEQNO columns.

- Each view is itself a table. The set of table names from the SYSVIEWS table is a subset of the set of table names from the SYSTABLS table.

column name	data type	length	description
VIEWNAME	CHAR	10	Name of the view
CREATOR	CHAR	10	Name of the owner (or creator) of the view
SEQNO	NUM	1	In cases where the view formula is too long for the SQLTEXT column, it is stored in multiple rows. The SEQNO column represents the sequence number of these rows.
VCHECK	CHAR	1	Has the value Y if the view is defined with the WITH CHECK OPTION, otherwise N
READONLY	CHAR	1	Has the value Y if the view is updateable, otherwise N
JOIN	CHAR	1	Has the value Y if the view can be used in a join, otherwise N
SQLTEXT	CHAR	200	The view formula (SELECT statement)

19.2 Querying the catalog tables

Every database management system records data about tables. In other words, every database management system has a catalog. Otherwise it would be impossible for the system to decide whether a question from a user may, or can, be answered. Not every database management system makes the catalog available to users, though; some have it for internal use only. With dBASE IV the user does have access to the catalog. In terms of querying, these tables in dBASE IV are seen simply as ordinary tables that can be accessed using the SELECT statement. Consulting the catalog has many uses. Here are three of them:

- As a *help function* for new users to determine, for example, which tables there are in the database and what columns exist in these tables.

- As a *control function* to see, for example, which indexes, views and privileges would be deleted if a particular table were dropped.

- As a *processing function* for dBASE IV itself when it executes statements (as a help function for dBASE IV).

In this section we look a few examples of SELECT statements against the catalog tables.

Example 19.1: Give the name, data type and length of each column in the
PLAYERS table.

```
SELECT    COLNO, COLNAME, COLTYPE, COLLEN
FROM      SYSCOLS
WHERE     TBNAME = 'PLAYERS'
```

Result:

```
COLNO  CNAME        COLTYPE  LENGTH
-----  ----------   -------  ------
    1  PLAYERNO     N             1
    2  NAME         C            15
    3  INITIALS     C             3
    5  BIRTH        N             1
    6  SEX          C             1
    7  JOINED       N             1
    8  STREET       C            15
    9  HOUSENO      C             4
   10  POSTCODE     C             6
   11  TOWN         C            10
   12  PHONENO      C            10
   13  LEAGUENO     C             4
```

Example 19.2: May the user JIM create a table called ADVICE or has he already used the name for another table, view or synonym?

```
SELECT    TBNAME
FROM      SYSTABLS
WHERE     TBNAME = 'ADVICE'
UNION
SELECT    SYNAME
FROM      SYSSYNS
WHERE     SYNAME = 'ADVICE'
```

Explanation: The SELECT statement checks whether there is an existing table
or synonym called ADVICE.

Example 19.3: Which views are based on more than one base table or view?

```
SELECT    VIEWNAME, COUNT(*)
FROM      SYSVDEPS
GROUP BY  VIEWNAME
HAVING    COUNT(*) > 1
```

Explanation: If a particular view appears twice or more in the SYSVDEPS table
it implies that it is based on more than one base table or view.

Example 19.4: For each table in the sports club database, find the number of rows, the number of columns and the total number of rows and columns in the four tables together.

```
SELECT    'PLAYERS  ', COUNT(*), COLCOUNT
FROM      PLAYERS, SYSTABLS
WHERE     TBNAME = 'PLAYERS'
GROUP BY  TBNAME, COLCOUNT
UNION
SELECT    'TEAMS    ', COUNT(*), COLCOUNT
FROM      TEAMS, SYSTABLS
WHERE     TBNAME = 'TEAMS'
GROUP BY  TBNAME, COLCOUNT
UNION
SELECT    'PENLTIES ', COUNT(*), COLCOUNT
FROM      PENLTIES, SYSTABLS
WHERE     TBNAME = 'PENLTIES'
GROUP BY  TBNAME, COLCOUNT
UNION
SELECT    'GAMES    ', COUNT(*), COLCOUNT
FROM      GAMES, SYSTABLS
WHERE     TBNAME = 'GAMES'
GROUP BY  TBNAME, COLCOUNT
ORDER BY  1
```

Result:

TABLE	NUMBER ROWS	NUMBER COLUMNS
PENLTIES	8	4
PLAYERS	14	13
TEAMS	2	3
GAMES	10	4

Example 19.5: Which base table has no unique index (that is, which table has no primary key defined)?

```
SELECT    CREATOR, TBNAME
FROM      SYSTABLS TAB
WHERE     NOT EXISTS
          (SELECT   *
          FROM      SYSIDXS
          WHERE     TAB.TBNAME = TBNAME
          AND       UNIQUERULE = 'U')
AND       TYPE = 'T'
```

Explanation: The extra condition is necessary to cull out all views from the result table as you can never define an index on a view.

Example 19.6: Which is the table which has never been updated by RUNSTATS?

```
SELECT   *
FROM     SYSTABLS
WHERE    CARD = -1;
```

Explanation: When a table is created, the UPDATED, CARD and NPAGES columns are set to -1.

Exercises

19.1 For each view defined *directly* on the PLAYERS table, find the column names and data types.

19.2 How many indexes has JAKE defined on the PLAYERS table?

19.3 Give the view formulas of the views defined on the PLAYERS table.

19.4 Give the names of the indexes which have been created by users who are the owners of the tables on which these indexes have been defined.

19.3   Protecting the catalog tables

Within each database a network of privileges ought to be set up using the GRANT statement. This network serves to protect the users' data in the tables and the catalog tables themselves as they contain important information that certainly should not be available to everyone.

Below we show how simply access to the catalog tables can be protected.

Example 19.7: In the SPORTDB database no users can directly access the catalog tables. They may see only the data related to the tables created by themselves and the columns belonging to those tables.

First we create two views: the TABLES view and the COLUMNS view. The TABLES view contains all columns from the SYSTABLS table minus CREATOR. The COLUMNS view contains all columns from the SYSCOLS table also minus the TBCREATOR column.

```
CREATE   VIEW TABLES AS
SELECT   TBNAME, TYPE, COLCOUNT, CLUSTERRID, INDXCOUNT,
         CREATED, UPDATED, CARD, NPAGES
FROM     SYSTABLS
WHERE    TBCREATOR = USER
```

```
CREATE    VIEW COLUMNS AS
SELECT    TBNAME, COLNAME, COLTYPE, COLLEN, COLSCALE,
          COLNO, NULLS, COLCARD, UPDATES, HIGH2KEY, LOW2KEY
FROM      SYSCOLS
WHERE     TBCREATOR = USER
```

Two GRANT statements are used to grant the privileges:

```
GRANT    SELECT
ON       TABLES
TO       PUBLIC

GRANT    SELECT
ON       COLUMNS
TO       PUBLIC
```

By using the system variable USER in the view formulas (see Chapter 6 for an explanation of this), and by granting the privilege to PUBLIC, the intended authorization structure is created. For each user, the virtual contents of the two views are different. Anyone who starts dBASE IV and queries the TABLES or COLUMNS view sees only the data about tables and columns for which he or she has a privilege. One advantage of this design is that if existing privileges or tables change, the TABLES and COLUMNS views automatically accommodate the new situation.

When a database is set up, dBASE IV grants the SELECT privilege on all catalog tables to PUBLIC. If we want to protect them against illegal use we must revoke this privilege. To do this, dBASE IV must be started up under the userid SQLDBA and the SELECT privileges withdrawn with REVOKE statements. Here is an example.

```
REVOKE    SELECT
ON        SYSTABLS
FROM      PUBLIC
```

Note, after this only SQLDBA is still able to access the catalog tables directly!

20
Application development with SQL

SQL can be used in two ways: *interactively* (that is, at a terminal) and *embedded* (in a program). The previous chapters have more or less always assumed the former use. Interactive means that statements are processed as soon as they are entered, whereas with embedded SQL statements are included in a dBASE IV program. Results of these SQL statements are not immediately visible to the user, but are processed by an *enveloping* program.

Embedded SQL is used primarily in programs developed for users who need not learn the SQL language, but instead work with data via menus and screens.

Most of the SQL statements discussed in earlier chapters can be used in embedded SQL. Apart from a few minor additions, embedded SQL is the same as interactive SQL. This chapter describes statements in their embedded SQL environment. The way in which SQL statements can be used in a program depends, in a sense, on the type of statement. We differentiate between the following groups of statements:

- DDL statements (such as CREATE TABLE and CREATE INDEX) and DCL statements (such as GRANT)
- update statements (such as UPDATE and DELETE)
- SELECT statements whose result is shown immediately
- SELECT statements whose result consists of one row
- SELECT statements whose result consists of an unknown number of rows

We will discuss each group, along with examples, in the following sections. The accent in these programs will fall on the integration of the SQL statements and the dBASE IV commands. We made as much use as possible of commands that were available in dBASE III when we wrote the programs. For example, we have not used commands for the presentation of *windows*. This should enable users who do not yet know the new dBASE IV commands to understand the programs.

Note: In this chapter we are using dBASE IV commands which do not form a part of SQL, and we assume that you are familiar with them. If not, then we refer you to the Ashton-Tate manuals listed in Appendix F.

20.1   General rules for embedded SQL

Before we begin with the description of how SQL statements are incorporated into a dBASE IV program, we need to outline a few general rules.

- The name of a file that contains a program with SQL statements must have a file type of PRS.

- Program files can be altered with the MODIFY COMMAND statement or any text editor that creates ASCII files.

- Every embedded SQL statement must end with a semi-colon.

- An embedded SQL statement can extend over multiple lines.

The semi-colon with SQL statements, therefore, has a different meaning than with dBASE IV commands. In the latter case, it does not signify the end of a command, but that the command will continue on the following line.

The following dBASE IV commands may not be used in a program which contains SQL statements:

APPEND [BLANK]	APPEND FROM	APPEND MEMO
AVERAGE	CALCULATE	CONTINUE
CONVERT TO	COPY INDEXES/TAG	COPY MEMO
COPY STRUCTURE	COPY TO ARRAY	COUNT
CREATE FROM	DELETE/DELETE TAG	DISPLAY
DISPLAY STRUCTURE	EXPORT TO	FIND
GO/GOTO [GOTO] <exp>	IMPORT FROM	INDEX
INSERT	JOIN	LST
LIST STRUCTURE	LOCATE	PACK
RECALL	REINDEX	REPLACE
RESET	ROLLBACK	SCAN
SEEK	SET BLOCKSIZE	SET CARRY
SET FIELDS	SET FILTER	SET INDEX
SET MEMOWIDTH	SET NEAR	SET ORDER
SET RELATION	SET SKIP	SET UNIQUE
SET VIEW	SKIP	SORT
SUM	UNLOCK	TOTAL ON
UPDATE	ZAP	

20.2 DDL and DCL statements

SQL recognizes these DDL statements (Data Definition Language):

- ALTER TABLE
- CREATE INDEX
- CREATE SYNONYM
- CREATE TABLE
- CREATE VIEW
- DROP INDEX
- DROP SYNONYM
- DROP TABLE
- DROP VIEW

and these DCL statements (Data Control Language):

- GRANT
- REVOKE

The inclusion of DDL and DCL statements in a program is simple. There is no difference between the functions and the syntax of these two types of statements for interactive or embedded use.

Example 20.1: Develop a program that creates or drops the index on the PLAY-ERS table, depending on what choice the user makes.

```
***** Program: PLAYINDX.PRS *****
* This program creates or drops the PLAY index
* on the PLAYERS table
*
DO INIT.PRS
*
WAIT "Do you want to create (C) or drop (D)"+;
   "the PLAY index ? " TO choice
* Dependent on choice, create or drop the index
DO CASE
   CASE UPPER(choice) = 'C'
      CREATE UNIQUE INDEX PLAY ON
         PLAYERS (PLAYERNO);
      ? "PLAY index is created!"
   CASE UPPER(choice) = 'D'
      DROP INDEX PLAY;
      ? "PLAY index is dropped!"
   OTHERWISE
      ? "Unknown choice!"
ENDCASE
RETURN
```

Result:

```
Do you want to create (C) or drop (D) the PLAY index? C
PLAY index is created!
```

Explanation: You can see from this program that the embedded SQL statement is the same as its interactive counterpart. There is a semi-colon following each SQL statement, which has not been included in any of the previous chapters. This is because we have been stressing the SQL statements themselves, and not how they should be entered. In the next program we invoke another program called INIT.PRS. INIT.PRS executes the following commands: SET ECHO OFF, SET TALK OFF and CLEAR.

Example 20.2: Develop a program that confers the SELECT privilege on PUBLIC for the four tables from the sample database.

```
***** Program: GRANT.PRS *****
* This program grants the SELECT privilege to everyone
* (PUBLIC) for the four tables from the sample database.
*
DO INIT.PRS
*
GRANT SELECT ON PLAYERS  TO PUBLIC;
GRANT SELECT ON TEAMS    TO PUBLIC;
GRANT SELECT ON GAMES    TO PUBLIC;
GRANT SELECT ON PENLTIES TO PUBLIC;
? "Ready!"
RETURN
```

20.3   Update statements

SQL recognizes three statements for changing the data in tables: DELETE, INSERT and UPDATE. These statements are included in a dBASE IV program in the same way as DDL and DCL statements.

Example 20.3: Develop a program that deletes all rows from the PENLTIES table.

```
***** DELPEN.PRS *****
* This program deletes all rows from the PENLTIES table.
*
DO INIT.PRS
* Should all rows be deleted?
WAIT "Do you want to delete all rows from PENLTIES (Y/N)? ";
   TO choice
* Determine what the answer is.
IF UPPER(choice) = 'Y'
   DELETE FROM PENLTIES;
   ? "The rows are deleted!"
ELSE
   ? "The rows are not deleted!"
ENDIF
RETURN
```

We mentioned memory variables in Chapter 6. Up until now, we have shown few examples of their use, because they are mainly applicable to embedded SQL. Here are some examples.

Example 20.4: Develop a program that increases the number of matches won by a given player in a team by one.

```
***** RAISE.PRS *****
* This program raises the number of matches won by a given player
*in a team by one.
*
DO INIT.PRS
* Ask for the player number and team number
pno = '    '
ACCEPT "Enter the player number: " TO pno
pno = VAL(pno)
tno = '    '
ACCEPT "Enter the team number: " TO tno
tno = VAL(tno)
* Increase the number of matches
UPDATE    GAMES
SET       WON = WON + 1
WHERE     PLAYERNO = pno
AND       TEAMNO = tno;
? "Ready!"
RETURN
```

Explanation: To make it clearer we show the memory variables in lower case letters. Of course it is not mandatory.

If memory variables are specified in an SQL statement, the data types of these variables must already be known. Another important rule is that if a memory variable is used in a condition, for example, its data type must coincide with that of the column with which it is being compared. If we look at the example,

we see that the values of the memory variables PNO and TNO are read in via
ACCEPT commands. At that moment they are attributed a data type. However,
because ACCEPT can only read alphanumeric values, the PNO and TNO variables have to be converted to numeric values by the VAL function. If this were
not done, the data types would not be the same (the PLAYERNO and TEAMNO
columns are, of course, numeric).

Example 20.5: Develop a program for entering data about a penalty.

```
***** ENTER.PRS *****
* Data about a penalty can be entered via this program.
*
*
DO INIT.PRS
* Initialize the variables
payno = 0
pno = 0
m_date  = DATE()
m_amount = 0
* Have the user enter the data
@4,5 SAY "Payment number: " GET payno PICTURE "999"
@5,5 SAY "Player number : " GET pno PICTURE "999"
@6,5 SAY "Date incurred : " GET m_date
@7,5 SAY "Penalty amount: " GET m_amount PICTURE "9999.99"
READ
* Add the new data to the PENLTIES table
INSERT  INTO PENLTIES
    (PAYMENTNO, PLAYERNO, PEN_DATE , AMOUNT)
VALUES (payno, pno, m_date, m_amount);
? "Ready!"
RETURN
```

Explanation: Here we use the SAY GET command to read the data into the memory variables. Just as with SQL statements, it is necessary to know the data type of
the relevant memory variable before using the SAY GET statement. Therefore,
we give the variable a value first and then a data type. The variables acquire the
data type that pertains to that value. We attribute the value zero to the PAYNO,
PNO and M_AMOUNT variables, and through this they are given a NUMERIC
data type. The M_DATE variable is set to the system date; it takes the DATE data
type. After reading in the values, the program enters them into the table with the
INSERT statement.

20.4   The SQLCNT memory variable

The RAISE.PRS program from the previous section used an UPDATE statement
to increase the value in the WON column by one. But how do we know if this
increase has actually taken place? Perhaps there was no row in the GAMES table

corresponding to the player number and team number entered. We can test for this using the value in the *SQLCNT memory variable*.

After each DML statement dBASE IV shows how many rows were processed via the SQLCNT variable. This means that after an UPDATE statement SQLCNT shows how many rows were updated, after a DELETE statement how many rows were deleted and after each INSERT statement how many rows were added.

Example 20.6: We extend the RAISE program to include a test on SQLCNT:

```
***** RAISE2.PRS *****
* This program increases the number of matches won by
* a player for a team by one.
*
DO INIT.PRS
* Ask for the player number and the team number
pno = '   '
ACCEPT "Enter the player number: " TO pno
pno = VAL(pno)
tno = '   '
ACCEPT "Enter the team number: " TO tno
tno = VAL(tno)
* Increase the number of matches won
UPDATE    GAMES
SET       WON = WON + 1
WHERE     PLAYERNO = pno
AND       TEAMNO = tno;
* Determine if it has executed successfully
IF sqlcnt > 0
   ? "Update has occurred"
ELSE
   ? "The player entered has played no matches for"
   ? "that team"
ENDIF
? "Ready!"
RETURN
```

Example 20.7: Develop a program that deletes all rows from the PENLTIES table for a given player.

```
***** PENPLAY.PRS *****
* This program deletes all penalties from the
* PENLTIES table for a given player.
*
DO INIT.PRS
* Read the player number in
pno = '    '
ACCEPT "Enter the player number: " TO pno
pno = VAL(pno)
* Delete all this player's penalties
DELETE FROM PENLTIES
WHERE  PLAYERNO = pno;
? "There have been "+LTRIM(STR(sqlcnt))+" penalties deleted."
RETURN
```

Explanation: At the end of the execution of the program the user gets a message about how many penalties have been deleted.

20.5   SELECT statements

The inclusion of SELECT statements in a program is simple, as long as the result of the particular statement does *not* have to be processed further within the program, but can be directly sent to the screen or printer. We discuss examples where the result *is* processed by the program in the following sections. This section describes inclusion of SELECT statements in programs in a simplified way.

Example 20.8: Develop a program that presents all the penalty data for a player after that player's number is entered.

```
***** SELPEN.PRS *****
* This program prints all the penalty data for a player
* sorted by the payment number.
*
DO INIT.PRS
* Ask for the player number
pno = '    '
ACCEPT "Enter the player number: " TO pno
pno = VAL(pno)
* Print all the penalties incurred by this player
SELECT  PAYMENTNO, AMOUNT, PEN_DATE
FROM    PENLTIES
WHERE   PLAYERNO = pno
ORDER BY PAYMENTNO;
RETURN
```

Result:

```
Enter the player number: 44

        PAYMENTNO    AMOUNT PEN_DATE
                2     75.00 05/05/81
                5     25.00 12/08/80
                7     30.00 12/30/82
```

20.6 SELECT statements with one row

In many cases you will want to capture the result of a SELECT statement in the program instead of sending it to display on the screen. This can be done by saving the result in a memory variable. Here, we need to distinguish between SELECT statements which always return one row, and those whose result consists of an indeterminate number of rows. The topic of this section is the former type; the next section discusses the latter.

Embedded SQL recognizes a variant on the SELECT statement intended for those statements whose result table consists of one row. A new clause is added to these SELECT statements: the *INTO clause*. In this clause we specify one memory variable for each expression in the SELECT clause. These types of SELECT statements are known as *SELECT INTO statements*. The reason for differentiating them from 'normal' SELECT statements is that, apart from the new INTO clause, there are a number of other constraints:

- the GROUP BY clause is not permitted (and therefore also the HAVING clause)
- the ORDER BY clause is not permitted
- UNION is not permitted

```
<select into statement> ::=
   <select clause>
   <into clause>
   <from clause>
   [ <where clause> ]

<into clause> ::=
   INTO <memory variable> [ {,<memory variable>}... ]
```

Example 20.9: Develop a program that prints a player's address data line by line, after a particular player number is entered.

```
***** ADDRESS.PRS *****
* This program presents all address data for a player
*
DO INIT.PRS
* Ask for the player number
pno = '    '
ACCEPT "Enter the player number: " TO pno
pno = VAL(pno)
* Search for address data
SELECT   NAME, INITIALS, HOUSENO,
         STREET, TOWN, POSTCODE
INTO     m_name, m_init, m_houseno
         m_street, m_town, m_postcode
FROM     PLAYERS
WHERE    PLAYERNO = pno;
IF sqlcnt > 0
   * Present address data
   CLEAR
   ? "Player number :"+LTRIM(STR(pno))
   ? "Surname        :"+m_name
   ? "Initials       :"+m_init
   ? "Street         :"+m_houseno+" "+RTRIM(m_street)"
   ? "Town           :"+m_town
   ? "Postcode       :"+m_postcode
ELSE
   ? "There is no player with number "+LTRIM(STR(pno))
ENDIF
RETURN
```

Result:

```
Enter the player number: 27

Player number :27
Surname       :Collins
Initials      :DD
Street        :804 Long Drive
Town          :Eltham
Postcode      :8457DK

Enter the player number: 112

Player number :112
Surname       :Bailey
Initials      :IP
Street        :8 Vixen Road
Town          :Plymouth
Postcode      :6392LK
```

Explanation: The SELECT statement retrieves the data about the player whose number has been entered. This SELECT statement can return a maximum of one row, because the PLAYERNO column is the primary key of the PLAYERS table. By using the SQLCNT variable we can test whether the player number indeed appears in the table.

Note: In Section 20.3 we stated that every memory variable used in an SQL statement must first have a data type assigned to it. This is, however, not true for those memory variables which occur only in an INTO clause. Here, the statement itself assigns the memory variables a value and a data type.

Example 20.10: Develop a program which prints the number of players who live in a given town which is entered by the user.

```
***** NUMBER.PRS *****
* This program gives the number of players who live
* in a given town
*
DO INIT.PRS
* Ask for the town
m_town - SPACE(10)
ACCEPT "Enter the town: " TO m_town
* Determine the number of players
number = 0
SELECT   COUNT(*)
INTO     number
FROM     PLAYERS
WHERE    TOWN = m_town;
? "+LTRIM(STR(number))+" players live in "+RTRIM(m_town)
RETURN
```

Explanation: First, the NUMBER variable is set to zero. We do this because it is possible that the SELECT statement could return no rows. After the statement has been processed the NUMBER memory variable has a numeric data type.

Example 20.11: With the ENTER program from Section 20.3, the user has to enter a payment number him- or herself. Of course, we can let the program itself decide on the next payment number using a SELECT statement.

```
***** ENTER2.PRS *****
* This program is used to enter data about a penalty
*
DO INIT.PRS
* Initializee the variables
pno = 0
m_date = DATE()
m_amount = 0
* Have the user enter the data
@5,5 SAY "Player number  : " GET pno PICTURE "999"
@6,5 SAY "Date incurred  : " GET m_date
@7,5 SAY "Penalty amount : " GET m_amount PICTURE "9999.99"
READ
* Determine the highest payment number already entered
payno = 1
SELECT   MAX(PAYMENTNO) + 1
INTO     payno
FROM     PENLTIES;
* Add the new data to the PENLTIES table
INSERT  INTO PENLTIES
    (PAYMENTNO, PLAYERNO, PEN_DATE, AMOUNT)
VALUES (payno, pno, m_date, m_amount);
? "Ready!"
RETURN
```

Explanation: The SELECT statement finds the highest payment number in the table and adds one to it. This becomes the new payment number. We assign the PAYNO variable with the value one. The SELECT statement returns no result if the PENLTIES table is empty, and in that case the PAYNO variable would have no value.

Note: Beware of using SELECT * with embedded SQL! Such a SELECT clause returns all columns from a given table. It still holds that a memory variable has to be specified for every column in the INTO clause. The number of columns in a table can increase, though, with the ALTER statement. If this happens, the SELECT statement will no longer work because there will not be enough memory variables available in the INTO clause. So, avoid the * in SELECT clauses in this embedded SQL environment.

20.7   The SQLCODE memory variable

We have established, then, that SQLCNT is a memory variable that gets a value after every DML statement is processed. SQL recognizes another such variable: *SQLCODE*. What is SQLCODE? SQLCODE is also a memory variable to which a given value is attributed after any SQL statement, not just after DML statements. If the value of SQLCODE is zero, it means that the SQL statement has executed correctly. The value 100 means that no rows have been found.

To illustrate we will expand the ADDRESS program from the previous section with the SQLCODE variable.

```
***** ADDRESS2.PRS *****
* This program presents all address information for a
* player
*
DO INIT.PRS
* Ask for the player number
pno = '    '
ACCEPT "Enter the player number: " TO pno
pno = VAL(pno)
* Find address data
SELECT   NAME, INITIALS, HOUSENO,
         STREET, TOWN, POSTCODE
INTO     m_name, m_init, m_houseno,
         m_street, m_town, m_postcode
FROM     PLAYERS
WHERE    PLAYERNO = pno;
* Test whether the player exists
IF sqlcnt > 0
   * Present address data
   CLEAR
   ? "Player number :"+LTRIM(STR(pno))
   ? "Surname       :"+m_name
   ? "Initials      :"+m_init
   ? "Street        :"+m_houseno+" "+RTRIM(m_street)"
   ? "Town          :"+m_town
   ? "Postcode      :"+m_postcode
ELSE
   IF sqlcode = 100
      ? "There is no player with number "+LTRIM(STR(pno))
   ELSE
      ? "Something is wrong"
      ? "sqlcode :"+STR(sqlcode)
   ENDIF
ENDIF
RETURN
```

20.8   SELECT statements with multiple rows

The SELECT statements discussed in the previous section return only one row. SELECT statements which *can* return more than one row require a different approach. We will give an example and work through it in detail afterwards. But try to understand the program yourself before reading the explanation.

Example 20.12: Develop a program that gives an ordered list of all player numbers and surnames. For each row, print a row number alongside.

```
***** ALLPLAY.PRS *****
* This program gives an ordered list of all
* player numbers, surnames and a row number.
*
DO INIT.PRS
* Cursor declaration
DECLARE  cplayers CURSOR FOR
SELECT   PLAYERNO, NAME
FROM     PLAYERS
ORDER BY PLAYERNO;
* Initialize variables
pno = 0
aname = ' '
* Print a report heading
? "ROWNO  PLAYER NUMBER  SURNAME  "
? "=====  =============  ========="
* Start the SELECT statement
OPEN cplayers;
* Look for the first player
counter = 0
FETCH cplayers INTO pno, aname;
DO WHILE sqlcode = 0
   counter = counter + 1
   ? SUBSTR(STR(counter),4,7)+"       "+STR(pno)+"  "+aname
   * Look for the next player
   FETCH cplayers INTO pno, aname;
ENDDO
CLOSE cplayers;
RETURN
```

Result:

ROWNO	PLAYER NUMBER	SURNAME
1	2	Everett
2	6	Parmenter
3	7	Wise
4	8	Newcastle
5	27	Collins
6	28	Collins
7	39	Bishop
8	44	Baker
9	57	Brown
10	83	Hope
11	95	Miller
12	100	Parmenter
13	104	Moorman
14	112	Bailey

The *DECLARE statement* is used to declare a SELECT statement. In some senses this is comparable to declaring variables. The declaration of the SELECT statement defines a *cursor*, in this example called *cplayers*. Now, via the cursor name we can refer to the SELECT statement in other statements. It will become clear later why we call this a cursor. Note that even though the cursor has been declared, the SELECT statement is not yet processed at that point.

The cursor name, cplayers, is mentioned again in the *OPEN statement*. The OPEN statement executes the SELECT statement which is associated with the cursor. When the OPEN statement has executed, the result of the SELECT statement becomes available. dBASE IV stores this result away, probably in the internal memory, and it is still invisible to the program.

The *FETCH statement* is used to step through and process the rows in the result of the SELECT statement one by one. In other words, we use the FETCH statement to render the result visible. The first FETCH statement that is processed, retrieves the first row, the second FETCH the second row, and so on. Because we are stepping through the result table row by row, and there is always one row available for processing, these are called cursors. The values of the retrieved rows are attributed to the memory variables. In our example, these are the PNO and ANAME variables. Note that a FETCH statement can only be used once a cursor has been opened (with an OPEN statement). In the program we step through all rows of the result with a DO WHILE statement. When the FETCH statement has retrieved the last row, the following FETCH statement triggers the SQLCODE variable to be set to 100 (the code for 'no row found' or 'end of file').

The *CLOSE statement* closes the cursor again and the result of the SELECT statement ceases to be available.

Let us have a closer look at the four statements.

```
<declare statement> ::=
    DECLARE <cursor name> CURSOR FOR
    <select block>
    [ { UNION <select block> }... ]
    [ <order by clause> | <for update clause> ]

<select block> ::=
      <select clause>
      <from clause>
    [ <where clause> ]
    [ <group by clause>
    [ <having clause> ] ]

<for update clause> ::=
    FOR UPDATE OF <column name> [ {,<column name>}... ]
```

You declare a cursor with the DECLARE statement. A cursor consists of a name and a SELECT statement. The cursor name can be up to eight characters long and may contain only letters, digits and the underscore character. Remember that the SAVE clause cannot be used in the SELECT statement here. We will explain the meaning of the FOR UPDATE clause in the next section. A DECLARE statement, itself, like typical declarations, does nothing. Only after the OPEN statement does the SELECT statement in the cursor become active. In the OPEN, FETCH and CLOSE statements, the cursor is referred to via the cursor name.

```
<open statement> ::=
   OPEN <cursor name>
```

The OPEN statement takes care of the execution of the SELECT statement associated with the specified cursor. You can open a cursor more than once in a program. If the SELECT statement contains memory variables, they are assigned a value at the time of opening. This means that the result of the cursor after each OPEN statement can differ, depending on whether the values in the memory variables have been updated or not.

```
<fetch statement> ::=
   FETCH <cursor name>
   INTO  <variable list>

<variable list> ::=
   <memory variable> [ {,<memory variable>}... ]
```

The FETCH statement has an INTO clause which has the same significance as the INTO clause in the SELECT INTO statement. The number of memory variables in the INTO clause of a FETCH statement must also coincide with the number of expressions in the SELECT clause of the DECLARE statement. A SELECT statement within a DECLARE statement may contain *no* INTO clause as this function is taken over by the FETCH statement.

```
<close statement> ::=
   CLOSE <cursor name>
```

With the CLOSE statement the result of the cursor disappears and is no longer available. Cursors may be closed before the last row of the result is 'FETCHed'. We advise you to close cursors as quickly as possible because their results take up space in the internal memory of the computer.

We have already mentioned that a cursor may be opened more than once in a program. Before a cursor can be opened for a second time, and before the program ends, it *must* be closed.

We have adapted the ALLPLAY.PRS program so that it asks first from which town it should present its ordered list of players.

```
***** ALLPLAY2.PRS *****
* This program gives an ordered list of player numbers,
* surnames and a row number.
*
DO INIT.PRS
* Cursor declaration
DECLARE  cplayers CURSOR FOR
SELECT   PLAYERNO, NAME
FROM     PLAYERS
WHERE    TOWN = m_town
ORDER BY PLAYERNO;
* Initialize variables
pno = 0
aname = ' '
ready = 'N'
DO WHILE UPPER(ready) = 'N'
   CLEAR
   m_town = SPACE(10)
   @2,1 SAY "From which town do you want to list "+;
       "the players? " GET m_town
   READ
   IF READKEY() = 12
      CLEAR
      RETURN
   ENDIF
   * Print a report heading
   CLEAR
   ? "ROWNO  PLAYER NUMBER  SURNAME  "
   ? "=====  =============  ========="
   OPEN cplayers;
   * Look for the first player
   counter = 0
   FETCH cplayers INTO pno, aname;
   DO WHILE sqlcode = 0
      counter = counter + 1
      ? SUBSTR(STR(counter),4,7)+"     "+STR(pno)+"  "+aname
      * Look for the next player
      FETCH cplayers INTO pno, aname;
   ENDDO
   CLOSE cplayers;
   ACCEPT "Do you want to stop? " TO ready
ENDDO
RETURN
```

Once opened, the result of a SELECT statement, does not change. Only when the cursor has been closed and opened again, can the result be different.

Note: In Section 20.6 we mentioned that you should avoid the use of *
in a SELECT clause in embedded SQL. This remark also applies to SELECT
statements in the form of cursors for the same reasons.

20.9   The FOR UPDATE clause

The rows in the result of a cursor cannot be updated; they are *locked*. Because the cursor is using the rows, no other statement can update them at that point. The following program, therefore, is not correct (we have omitted details to make it easier to read):

```
DECLARE   cplayers CURSOR FOR
SELECT    PLAYERNO, NAME
FROM      PLAYERS;
:
OPEN cplayers;
:
FETCH cplayers INTO pno, aname;
DO WHILE sqlcode = 0
   :
   UPDATE PLAYERS
   SET    ...
   WHERE  PLAYERNO = pno;
   :
   FETCH cplayers INTO pno, aname;
ENDDO
CLOSE cplayers;
```

dBASE IV does not accept this UPDATE statement as it is trying to update a row in the PLAYERS table while that row is being used by the cursor. In other words, the cursor has locked the row and the only way to update the row is via the cursor itself. This is why the DECLARE statement has a *FOR UPDATE clause*. In this clause you specify which columns could be updated, and a special version of the UPDATE statement allows you to update the current row of a given cursor. Here is an extended definition of the UPDATE statement:

```
<update statement> ::=
   UPDATE <table identifier>
   SET    <object in column> [ {,<object in column>}... ]
   [ WHERE  { <condition> | CURRENT OF <cursor name> } ]

<table identifier> ::= <table name>

<object in column> ::=
   <column name> = <expression>
```

Example 20.13: This program is based on the RAISE2 program from Section 20.4. We have made the following changes. The program shows the games information for team 1, row by row. It asks, for each row, whether the number of matches won should be increased by one.

```
***** RAISE3.PRS *****
* This program raises the number of matches
* won by 1.
*
DO INIT.PRS
* Cursor declaration
DECLARE c_gam CURSOR FOR
SELECT   PLAYERNO, WON
FROM     GAMES
WHERE    TEAMNO = 1
FOR      UPDATE OF WON;
*
OPEN c_gam;
FETCH c_gam INTO pno, m_won;
DO WHILE sqlcode = 0
   CLEAR
   ? "Do you want, for player "+LTRIM(STR(pno))
   ? "with number of matches won, ("+LTRIM(STR(m_won))
   ? "to be increased by 1?"
   WAIT "Answer Y or N " TO choice
   IF UPPER(choice) = 'Y'
      UPDATE   GAMES
      SET      WON = WON + 1
      WHERE    CURRENT OF c_gam;
   ENDIF
   FETCH c_gam INTO pno, m_won;
ENDDO
CLOSE c_gam;
? "Ready"
RETURN
```

Explanation: The only change in this program, with regard to the original version, is that the DECLARE statement has been expanded with a FOR UPDATE clause. By doing this we are making provision for the WON column to be updated sometime. In the UPDATE statement we specify in the WHERE clause that in the row which is current for the C_GAM cursor the WON column should be increased by one.

20.10   Deleting rows via cursors

Cursors can be used for deleting individual rows. The DELETE statement has a similar condition to the one we have just discussed for the UPDATE statement.

```
<delete statement> ::=
   DELETE
   FROM    <table identifier>
   [ WHERE { <condition> | CURRENT OF <cursor name> } ]

<table identifier> ::= <table name>
```

Example 20.14: Develop a program that presents all data from the PENLTIES table row by row, and asks whether the row showing should be deleted.

```
***** DELPEN.PRS *****
* This program deletes rows from the PENLTIES table.
*
DO INIT.PRS
* Cursor declaration
DECLARE c_pen CURSOR FOR
SELECT  PAYMENTNO, PLAYERNO, PEN_DATE, AMOUNT
FROM    PENLTIES;
*
OPEN c_pen;
FETCH c_pen INTO payno, pno, m_date, m_amount;
DO WHILE sqlcode = 0
   CLEAR
   ? "Do you want to delete this penalty?"
   ? "Payment number    : "+LTRIM(STR(payno))
   ? "Player number     : "+LTRIM(STR(pno))
   ? "Penalty date      : "+DTOC(m_date)
   ? "Amount            : "+LTRIM(STR(m_amount))
   WAIT "Answer Y or N " TO choice
   :
```

```
      :
   IF UPPER(choice) = 'Y'
      DELETE
      FROM      PENLTIES
      WHERE     CURRENT OF c_pen;
   ENDIF
   FETCH c_pen INTO payno, pno, m_date, m_amount;
ENDDO
CLOSE c_pen;
? "Ready"
RETURN
```

20.11   Validating entered data

The entry and update processes ought always to be controlled for the validity of the new data. For example, the ENTRY2 program from Section 20.6 allows us to enter a penalty for a player who may not exist, a date which lies beyond the present, or a penalty amount which is less than zero. In each of these situations we would end up with an incorrect row in the PENLTIES table. So we must validate data after the user has entered it and before it is stored in the table.

The dBASE IV SAY GET command offers many alternatives for validating entered data, especially the VALID and RANGE options. Nevertheless, the SAY GET command does not offer us the possibility of comparing newly entered data with existing data. Take the PENLTIES table, for example; if a penalty is entered, the program ought to check to see whether the player number occurs in the PLAYERS table. This cannot be done with the VALID or RANGE options.

In the following version of the ENTRY program we have included these controls:

- the player number entered must occur in the PLAYERS table
- the date entered must come before the system date in time
- the penalty amount must lie between 0 and 300 inclusive

```
***** ENTRY3.PRS *****
* This program enables the user to enter and validate
* penalty data
*
DO INIT.PRS
* Initialize the variables
pno = 0
payno = 0
m_date = DATE()
m_amount = 0
number = 0
      :
```

```
:
DO WHILE .T.
   CLEAR
   @5,5 SAY "Player number  : "
   @6,5 SAY "Date incurred  : "
   @7,5 SAY "Penalty amount : "
   goodpno = .F.
   DO WHILE .NOT. goodpno
      @5,23 GET pno PICTURE "999"
      READ
      IF READKEY() = 12
         * Stop the program
         CLEAR
         RETURN
      ENDIF
      * Check whether the player number already exists
      SELECT   COUNT(*)
      INTO     number
      FROM     PLAYERS
      WHERE    PLAYERNO = pno;
      IF sqlcode = 100
         @5,30 SAY "The number "+LTRIM(STR(pno))"+" does not exist"
         LOOP
      ELSE
         goodpno = .T.
      ENDIF
   ENDDO
   @6,23 GET m_date VALID m_date <= DATE() ;
        ERROR "Date cannot lie in the future"
   @7,23 GET m_amount PICTURE "9999.99" RANGE 0,300
   READ
   * Determine the highest payment number allocated so far
   SELECT MAX(PAYMENTNO) + 1
   INTO   payno
   FROM   PENLTIES;
   * Add the new data to the PENLTIES table
   INSERT  INTO PENLTIES
      (PAYMENTNO, PLAYERNO, PEN_DATE, AMOUNT)
   VALUES (payno, pno, m_date, m_amount);
   * Check whether it has processed correctly
   IF sqlcode <> 0
      @9,5 SAY "Data has not been added"
   ELSE
      @9,5 SAY "Data has been added"
   ENDIF
ENDDO
RETURN
```

Explanation: The program stops when the user presses the Esc key, which is controlled by the condition READKEY() = 12. The statements in the innermost DO

WHILE block are executed until the user enters an existing player number, or, of course, presses the Esc key. After that the other two pieces of information are requested with SAY GET commands. You can see also how the other two checks have been implemented.

20.12   Transactions

Some programs consist of a series of update statements, all of which must have executed correctly, or none will. Suppose that a program deletes all data about a given player from the four tables. Three DELETE statements are necessary, as well as an UPDATE statement for the TEAMS table. (If a player is a captain, the team must not be deleted, but only the player number erased.) A program like this cannot stop half-way through, otherwise half of the player's data would be gone, say from the PLAYERS and GAMES tables, while the rest remained in the other tables. The database would then be in a state of *non-integrity*.

We need a structure to check that all updates have executed correctly. If this is not the case, then all the updates processed thus far need to be undone. This can be done with SQL by defining a *transaction*. A transaction consists of one or more updates that shift the database from one state of integrity to another. Here is an example, with an explanation to follow.

Example 20.15: Develop a program that deletes all the data about a given player from the four tables. If the player is a captain, the deletion may not take place.

```
***** DELETE.PRS *****
* This program deletes all data about a
* player
*
DO INIT.PRS
ON ERROR DO BREAK.PRS
* Ask for the player number
pno = '    '
ACCEPT "Enter the player number: " TO pno
pno = VAL(pno)
* Check to see whether the player is a captain
SELECT    COUNT(*)
INTO      number
FROM      TEAMS
WHERE     PLAYERNO = pno;
IF sqlcode = 0
    ? "The player is a captain, and may not be"+;
      "deleted."
ELSE
    BEGIN TRANSACTION
    :
```

```
              :
              DELETE FROM PLAYERS
              WHERE  PLAYERNO = pno;
              DELETE FROM GAMES
              WHERE  PLAYERNO = pno;
              DELETE FROM PENLTIES
              WHERE  PLAYERNO = pno;
              END TRANSACTION
              ? "Ready!"
         ENDIF
         RETURN

         ***** BREAK.PRS *****
         *
         ? "Something has gone wrong!"
         ? "Error number:"+STR(ERROR())
         ? "Error message:"+MESSAGE()
         ROLLBACK WORK;
         ? "The entire transaction has not been executed."
         RETURN
```

Explanation: The three DELETE statements fall between the two dBASE IV commands, BEGIN and END TRANSACTION. The names of these commands speak for themselves; BEGIN TRANSACTION marks the beginning of the transaction. Each update executed from that point on is not permanent until the END TRANSACTION command has processed. In our case, that means that the three updates have only actually occurred once the END TRANSACTION is processed.

What happens now if something goes wrong? In this case, dBASE IV starts the BREAK program specified in the ON ERROR statement. This program begins by printing the error number with its associated message. What is more important is that the ROLLBACK statement is executed. This statement undoes or rolls back all the updates which have not yet been made permanent (that is, the statements executed after the BEGIN TRANSACTION command).

Conclusion: If everything goes well, either all three DELETE statements execute, or none of them.

```
<rollback statement> ::=
    ROLLBACK [ WORK ]
```

Working with transactions naturally offers many advantages. But there are also a number of disadvantages. It costs dBASE IV time and effort to register the permanence or lack of permanence of data. It is like maintaining an extra administrative load. Also, all non-permanent data is blocked until it is made permanent or the transaction rolled back, which leads to extra administration. So, it is always wise to keep the quantity of non-permanent data in a database to a minimum.

21
The database environment

In this chapter we discuss a number of individual topics which have a bearing on the database environment rather than on the management of the database. These are the topics under consideration:

- exporting data to a file
- importing data into an SQL table
- converting a dBASE IV file to an SQL table
- checking the contents of the catalog
- copying tables to another database

21.1 Exporting data

If you want to use data from an SQL table for another purpose (outside dBASE IV), then it must be *exported*. The *UNLOAD statement* rewrites data to a file.

```
<unload statement> ::=
   UNLOAD DATA TO [ <directory path> ] <file>
   FROM TABLE <table identifier>
   [ [ TYPE ] <format identifier> ]

<directory path> ::= \ { <file> \ }...

<file> ::= <filename> [ .<file type> ]

<table identifier> ::= <table name>

<format identifier> ::=
   SDF | DIF | WKS |
   SYLK | FW2 | dBASEII | RPD |
   DELIMITED { WITH BLANK | WITH <separator> }

<separator> ::= <character>
```

The UNLOAD statement can create files with the following formats:

- files created for dBASE III (Plus) or another dBASE IV system are, in fact, files with a file type of DBF
- ASCII files whose values begin in fixed positions, known as Standard Data Format (SDF)
- files created for VisiCalc (DIF)
- files created for Lotus 1-2-3 (WKS)
- files created for Multiplan (SYLK)
- files created for Framework II (FW2)
- files created for RapidFile (RPD)
- files created for dBASE II (dBASEII)
- ASCII files whose values are separated by a special character such as a comma or blank (DELIMITED)

You use the format identifier to state the format that the new file is to get. If it is omitted, dBASE IV creates a DBF file. To give you an idea of what files can be created, here are two examples.

Example 21.1: Create a file to which the contents of the PENLTIES table will be written. The name of the file is PENLTIES.DAT and must be stored in the main directory.

```
UNLOAD    DATA TO \PENLTIES.DAT
FROM      TABLE PENLTIES
TYPE      SDF
```

The PENLTIES.DAT file now looks like this:

```
1       619801208   100.00
2      4419810505    75.00
3      2719830910   100.00
4     10419841208    50.00
5      4419801208    25.00
6       819801208    25.00
7      4419821230    30.00
8      2719841112    75.00
```

Explanation: First, a large number of blanks are printed. That happens because the first column, PAYMENTNO, is defined as INTEGER which equates to NUMERIC(20,0).

Example 21.2: Create a file to which the contents of the PENLTIES table will be rewritten. The name of this file is PENAL2.DAT and must be stored in the \DATA directory.

```
UNLOAD    DATA TO \DATA\PENAL2.DAT
FROM      TABLE PENLTIES
TYPE      DELIMITED WITH ,
```

Again, we print the file, this time with a comma between each value.

```
1,6,19801208,100.00
2,44,19810505,75.00
3,27,19830910,100.00
4,104,19841208,50.00
5,44,19801208,25.00
6,8,19801208,25.00
7,44,19821230,30.00
8,27,19841112,75.00
```

Views are useful if you do not want to export the whole of a table. First, define the view that encompasses precisely the data you want to export. Then, execute the UNLOAD statement on the view instead of on the table.

21.2   Importing data

The INSERT statement is used to add new rows to a table, or to copy data from one table to another, as long as both tables belong to the same database. The LOAD statement can be used to read data from a file into an SQL table. These files can be part of another SQL database, or of other programs such as RapidFile and Lotus 1-2-3. The LOAD statement reads the file and inserts each row into the specified table. We call this process *importing*.

```
<load statement> ::=
   LOAD DATA FROM [ <directory path> ] <file>
   INTO TABLE <table identifier>
   [ [ TYPE ] <format identifier> ]

<directory path> ::= \ { <file> \ }...

<file> ::= <filename> [ .<file type> ]

<table identifier> ::= <table name>

<format identifier> ::=
   SDF | DIF | WKS |
   SYLK | FW2 | dBASEII | RPD |
   DELIMITED { WITH BLANK | WITH <separator> }

<separator> ::= <character>
```

The LOAD statement can be used to load the following types of files:

- files created by dBASE III (Plus) and dBASE IV, in fact, all files with file type DBF
- ASCII files whose values begin in fixed positions (SDF)
- files created by VisiCalc (DIF)
- files created by Lotus 1-2-3 (WKS)
- files created by Multiplan (SYLK)
- files created by Framework II (FW2)
- files created by RapidFile (RPD)
- files created by dBASE II (dBASEII)
- ASCII files whose values are separated by a special character like a comma or a blank (DELIMITED)

Just as with the UNLOAD statement, we use the format identifier to specify the format of the file. Again, if it is omitted, dBASE IV assumes that it is a DBF file.

Note: The LOAD statement only works correctly if the format in the file to be read in matches the one described in the statement.

Example 21.3: Suppose that the PENLTIES table is completely empty and that we must fill it with the contents of the file PENAL2.DAT created in the previous section. This file is stored in the \DATA directory.

```
LOAD     DATA FROM \DATA\PENAL2.DAT
INTO     TABLE PENLTIES
TYPE     DELIMITED WITH ,
```

Note: After you have loaded data into a table, we advise you to use the RUN-STATS statement to update the catalog data about the table.

21.3   Converting files to SQL tables

The dBASE IV database commands like CREATE and APPEND can be used to create and update tables outside SQL. However, these tables cannot be used within SQL; even though they have the same internal format as SQL tables, they are not recorded in the catalog. This means that if such a table *is* required for SQL access (for example, in a SELECT statement) dBASE IV gets an error message.

If you have a table, created by dBASE IV commands, that you want to use within SQL, you need first to involve the catalog. dBASE IV recognizes a special statement to do this: the *DBDEFINE statement*.

```
<dbdefine statement> ::=
    DBDEFINE [ <filename> ]
```

Example 21.4: Suppose that you create a file called TEAMS using dBASE IV statements and you want to use SQL statements to access it. The statement to convert a file to an SQL table is:

```
DBDEFINE TEAMS
```

Explanation: TEAMS has to be the filename of a file with a file type of DBF. Along with this, the file must be stored in the same directory as the database. If the filename is omitted, dBASE IV executes the DBDEFINE statement for each file whose file type is DBF. If an MDX file (where all indexes are stored) is linked to the file, it, too, is converted.

Files created by dBASE IV database commands can contain fields with the MEMO data type which SQL does not recognize. For that reason, DBEFINE misses these fields out, though the MEMO fields do remain in the file. Therefore, if you have converted a file to an SQL table with DBDEFINE and then query it again with dBASE IV database commands, the MEMO fields are still present.

With the dBASE IV DELETE command rows are highlighted with *deletion marks*. A deletion mark on a row indicates that the row is to be deleted. The PACK command is used to actually delete marked rows. DBDEFINE leaves all deletion marks intact. Within SQL they have no significance, though they are presented with SELECT statements.

DBDEFINE must be used in the following situations.

- A table has been created in one SQL database and must be copied to another SQL database.
- A table has been created by dBASE IV database commands or the SAVE option of the SELECT statement.
- The structure of a table has been altered by dBASE IV commands (for example, a column has been added).

Note: Tables created by the SQL CREATE TABLE statement or via DB-DEFINE, can be accessed or updated by dBASE IV commands without problems or extra measures.

21.4   Checking the catalog

It is possible to delete SQL tables from outside dBASE IV with operating system commands. Such an occurrence would result in the contents of the catalog no longer being correct. Therefore, dBASE IV makes use of the *DBCHECK statement* with which it verifies the contents of the catalog. DBCHECK compares the definition of a table with the actual file.

```
<dbcheck statement> ::=
   DBCHECK [ <table identifier> ]

<table identifier> ::= <table name>
```

Example 21.5: The next statement checks whether the TEAMS table is still correct.

```
DBCHECK TEAMS
```

Explanation: When using DBCHECK, if you omit the table name dBASE IV performs the check on every table in the database. Note that with DBDEFINE you must specify a filename and with DBCHECK a table name. This table name must appear in the SYSTABLS table.

21.5   Copying tables

A table can be copied from one database to another using dBASE IV and operating system commands.

Example 21.6: The TEAMS table must be copied from the SPORTDB database to the HELP database. We assume that this HELP database has already been created.

We use the SHOW DATABASE statement first to find out which directories are storing these databases.

```
SHOW DATABASE
```

Result:

```
Existing databases are:
    1 SPORTDB   07/23/88 \DBASE\SPORTDB
    2 HELP      07/31/88 \HELP
```

The dBASE IV RUN command can be used with the MS/DOS COPY command, for example, to copy the table from one directory to another:

```
RUN COPY \DBASE\SPORTDB\TEAMS.DBF \HELP
```

Then we start the HELP database:

```
START DATABASE HELP
```

Finally, we must still cause an entry to be made in the catalog:

```
DBDEFINE TEAMS
```

The TEAMS table is now available. We advise you to execute the RUNSTATS statement against the TEAMS table in order to update the catalog's statistical data.

Appendix A
Answers to exercises

Introduction

Many of the answers are the questions given in the form of SQL statements. In most cases we have provided only one formulation, but this does not mean that it is the only way of answering the question. Nor does it mean that it is necessarily the best way. This book would be huge if we gave every possible answer for every question. If you come up with another answer it does not automatically mean that you are wrong. Compare your answer with the one in the book as they should be equivalent.

As well as this, we advise you to consult Appendix B as you write your statements. Here we describe the syntax of SQL.

Chapter 5

5.1   CREATE TABLE DEPTS
```
        ( DEPTNO   CHAR(5)       ,
          BUDGET   DECIMAL(8,2)  ,
          LOCATION CHAR(30)      )
```

5.2   The SYSTABLS table (not all columns are included):

CREATOR	TBNAME	TYPE	COLCOUNT	...	CREATED	...
SQLDBA	DEPTS	T	3	...	11/05/88	...

The SYSCOLS table (not all columns are included):

TBCREATOR	TBNAME	COLNAME	COLTYPE	COLLEN	COLSCALE	COLNO
SQLDBA	DEPTS	DEPTNO	C	5	0	1
SQLDBA	DEPTS	BUDGET	N	9	2	2
SQLDBA	DEPTS	LOCATION	C	30	0	3

Chapter 6

6.1 1. correct; floating point data type
2. incorrect; because there must be quotation marks before and after the alphanumeric literal
3. correct; alphanumeric data type
4. incorrect; the alphanumeric literal should be enclosed in quotation marks, and the single quotation mark within the literal should be given as a double quotation mark
5. correct; alphanumeric data type
6. correct; integer data type
7. correct; alphanumeric data type
8. correct; alphanumeric data type
9. correct; alphanumeric data type
10. correct; logical data type

6.2 1. 200
2. 3800
3. 200
4. 200
5. Jim's

6.3 A SELECT statement consists of a minimum of two clauses: the SELECT and the FROM clause.

6.4 Yes

6.5 No, if a SELECT statement has a HAVING clause, a GROUP BY clause is mandatory.

6.6 1. There is no FROM clause.
2. The GROUP BY clause must be specified before the HAVING clause.
3. The ORDER BY clause should be the last clause.

6.7   The FROM clause:

PAYMENTNO	PLAYERNO	PEN_DATE	AMOUNT
1	6	12/08/80	100.00
2	44	05/05/81	75.00
3	27	09/10/83	100.00
4	104	12/08/84	50.00
5	44	12/08/80	25.00
6	8	12/08/80	25.00
7	44	12/30/82	30.00
8	27	11/12/84	75.00

The WHERE clause:

PAYMENTNO	PLAYERNO	PEN_DATE	AMOUNT
2	44	05/05/81	75.00
3	27	09/10/83	100.00
4	104	12/08/84	50.00
7	44	12/30/82	30.00
8	27	11/12/84	75.00

The GROUP BY clause:

PAYMENTNO	PLAYERNO	PEN_DATE	AMOUNT
2, 7	44	05/05/81, 12/30/82	75.00, 30.00
3, 8	27	09/10/83, 11/12/84	100.00, 75.00
4	104	12/08/84	50.00

The HAVING clause:

PAYMENTNO	PLAYERNO	PEN_DATE	AMOUNT
2, 7	44	05/05/81, 12/30/82	75.00, 30.00
3, 8	27	09/10/83, 11/12/84	100.00, 75.00

The SELECT clause:

```
PLAYERNO
--------
      44
      27
```

The ORDER BY clause:

```
PLAYERNO
--------
      27
      44
```

Chapter 7

7.1 1. Both tables have a column called PLAYERNO.
2. The SELECT clause refers to the PLAYERS table even though it is not specified in the FROM clause.

7.2 The question: 'Give the name of each player who is captain of a team'. The FROM clause:

TEAMNO	PLAYERNO	DIVISION	PLAYERNO	NAME	...
1	6	first	6	Parmenter	...
1	6	first	44	Baker	...
1	6	first	83	Hope	...
1	6	first	2	Everett	...
1	6	first	27	Collins	...
1	6	first	104	Moorman	...
1	6	first	7	Wise	...
1	6	first	57	Brown	...
1	6	first	39	Bishop	...
1	6	first	112	Bailey	...
1	6	first	8	Newcastle	...
1	6	first	100	Parmenter	...
1	6	first	28	Collins	...
1	6	first	95	Miller	...
2	27	second	6	Parmenter	...
2	27	second	44	Baker	...
2	27	second	83	Hope	...
2	27	second	2	Everett	...
2	27	second	27	Collins	...
2	27	second	104	Moorman	...
2	27	second	7	Wise	...
2	27	second	57	Brown	...
2	27	second	39	Bishop	...
2	27	second	112	Bailey	...
2	27	second	8	Newcastle	...
2	27	second	100	Parmenter	...
2	27	second	28	Collins	...
2	27	second	95	Miller	...

The WHERE clause:

TEAMNO	PLAYERNO	DIVISION	PLAYERNO	NAME	...
1	6	first	6	Parmenter	...
2	27	second	27	Collins	...

The SELECT clause and end result:

```
NAME
---------
Parmenter
Collins
```

7.3   SELECT   PAYMENTNO, AMOUNT, P.PLAYERNO, NAME
      FROM   PENLTIES PN, PLAYERS P
      WHERE   PN.PLAYERNO = P.PLAYERNO

7.4   SELECT   PAYMENTNO, NAME
      FROM   PENLTIES PN, PLAYERS S, TEAMS T
      WHERE   PN.PLAYERNO = T.PLAYERNO
      AND   T.PLAYERNO = S.PLAYERNO

7.5   SELECT   S.PLAYERNO, NAME
      FROM   PLAYERS S, PLAYERS S27
      WHERE   S.TOWN = S27.TOWN
      AND   S27.PLAYERNO = 27
      AND   S.PLAYERNO <> 27

7.6   SELECT   DISTINCT P.PLAYERNO, P.NAME, CAP.PLAYERNO,
               CAP.NAME
      FROM   PLAYERS P, PLAYERS.CAP, GAMES GAM, TEAMS T
      WHERE   GAM.PLAYERNO = P.PLAYERNO
      AND   T.TEAMNO = GAM.TEAMNO
      AND   GAM.PLAYERNO <> T.PLAYERNO
      AND   CAP.PLAYERNO = T.PLAYERNO

Chapter 8

8.1   SELECT   PLAYERNO
      FROM   PLAYERS
      WHERE   BIRTH > 1960
      or

      SELECT   PLAYERNO
      FROM   PLAYERS
      WHERE   BIRTH >= 1961

      or

      SELECT   PLAYERNO
      FROM   PLAYERS
      WHERE   1960 < BIRTH

      or

```
         SELECT   PLAYERNO
         FROM     PLAYERS
         WHERE    BIRTH - 1960 > 0

8.2      SELECT   TEAMNO
         FROM     TEAMS
         WHERE    PLAYERNO <> 27

8.3      SELECT   PLAYERNO
         FROM     GAMES
         WHERE    WON > LOST

8.4      SELECT   PLAYERNO
         FROM     GAMES
         WHERE    WON + LOST = 10

8.5      SELECT   PLAYERNO, NAME, TOWN
         FROM     PLAYERS
         WHERE    SEX = 'F'
         AND      TOWN <> 'Stratford'
         or

         SELECT   PLAYERNO, NAME, TOWN
         FROM     PLAYERS
         WHERE    SEX = 'F'
         AND      NOT (TOWN = 'Stratford')
```

In the second example the brackets may be left out!

```
8.6      SELECT   PLAYERNO
         FROM     PLAYERS
         WHERE    JOINED >= 1970
         AND      JOINED <= 1980
         or

         SELECT   PLAYERNO
         FROM     PLAYERS
         WHERE    NOT (JOINED < 1970 OR JOINED > 1980)

8.7      SELECT   PLAYERNO, NAME, BIRTH
         FROM     PLAYERS
         WHERE    MOD(BIRTH,400) = 0
         OR       (MOD(BIRTH,4) = 0 AND NOT(MOD(BIRTH,100) = 0))

8.8      SELECT   NAME, INITIALS, DIVISION
         FROM     GAMES GAM, PLAYERS P, TEAMS T
         WHERE    GAM.PLAYERNO = P.PLAYERNO
         AND      GAM.TEAMNO = T.TEAMNO
         AND      BIRTH > 1965
         AND      WON > 0
```

```
8.9    SELECT   PAYMENTNO
       FROM     PENLTIES
       WHERE    AMOUNT BETWEEN 50 AND 100

8.10   SELECT   PAYMENTNO
       FROM     PENLTIES
       WHERE    NOT (AMOUNT BETWEEN 50 AND 100)
       or

       SELECT   PAYMENTNO
       FROM     PENLTIES
       WHERE    AMOUNT NOT BETWEEN 50 AND 100

       or

       SELECT   PAYMENTNO
       FROM     PENLTIES
       WHERE    AMOUNT < 50
       OR       AMOUNT > 100

8.11   SELECT   PAYMENTNO
       FROM     PENLTIES
       WHERE    AMOUNT IN (50, 75, 100)

8.12   SELECT   PLAYERNO
       FROM     PLAYERS
       WHERE    TOWN NOT IN ('Stratford', 'Douglas')
       or

       SELECT   PLAYERNO
       FROM     PLAYERS
       WHERE    NOT PLACE IN ('Stratford', 'Douglas')

       or

       SELECT   PLAYERNO
       FROM     PLAYERS
       WHERE    TOWN <> 'Stratford'
       AND      TOWN <> 'Douglas'

8.13   SELECT   PLAYERNO, NAME
       FROM     PLAYERS
       WHERE    NAME LIKE '%is%'

8.14   SELECT   PLAYERNO, NAME
       FROM     PLAYERS
       WHERE    NAME LIKE '_____'
```

```
8.15  SELECT    PLAYERNO, NAME
      FROM      PLAYERS
      WHERE     NAME LIKE '_____%'
      or

      SELECT    PLAYERNO, NAME
      FROM      PLAYERS
      WHERE     NAME LIKE '%_____'

      or

      SELECT    PLAYERNO, NAME
      FROM      PLAYERS
      WHERE     NAME LIKE '%_____%'

8.16  SELECT    PLAYERNO, NAME
      FROM      PLAYERS
      WHERE     NAME LIKE '__l%l_'

8.17  SELECT    PLAYERNO, NAME
      FROM      PLAYERS
      WHERE     PLAYERNO IN
                (SELECT    PLAYERNO
                 FROM      PENLTIES)

8.18  SELECT    PLAYERNO, NAME
      FROM      PLAYERS
      WHERE     PLAYERNO IN
                (SELECT    PLAYERNO
                 FROM      PENLTIES
                 WHERE     AMOUNT > 50)

8.19  SELECT    TEAMNO, PLAYERNO
      FROM      TEAMS
      WHERE     DIVISION = 'first'
      AND       PLAYERNO IN
                (SELECT    PLAYERNO
                 FROM      PLAYERS
                 WHERE     TOWN = 'Stratford')

8.20  SELECT    PLAYERNO, NAME
      FROM      PLAYERS
      WHERE     PLAYERNO IN
                (SELECT    PLAYERNO
                 FROM      PENLTIES)
      AND       PLAYERNO NOT IN
                (SELECT    PLAYERNO
                 FROM      TEAMS
                 WHERE     DIVISION = 'first')
```

or

```
SELECT    PLAYERNO, NAME
FROM      PLAYERS
WHERE     PLAYERNO IN
          (SELECT  PLAYERNO
          FROM     PENLTIES
          WHERE    PLAYERNO NOT IN
                   (SELECT  PLAYERNO
                   FROM     TEAMS
                   WHERE    DIVISION = 'first'))
```

8.21
```
SELECT    PLAYERNO, NAME
FROM      PLAYERS
WHERE     BIRTH =
          (SELECT  BIRTH
          FROM     PLAYERS
          WHERE    NAME = 'Parmenter'
          AND      INITIALS = 'R')
AND       NOT (NAME = 'Parmenter'
              AND INITIALS = 'R')
```

8.22
```
SELECT    PLAYERNO
FROM      GAMES
WHERE     WON =
          (SELECT  WON
          FROM     GAMES
          WHERE    PLAYERNO = 8
          AND      TEAMNO = 2)
AND       TEAMNO = 2 AND PLAYERNO <> 8
```

8.23
```
SELECT    PLAYERNO
FROM      PLAYERS
WHERE     BIRTH <= ALL
          (SELECT  BIRTH
          FROM     PLAYERS
          WHERE    TOWN = 'Stratford')
AND       TOWN = 'Stratford'
```

8.24
```
SELECT    PLAYERNO
FROM      PLAYERS
WHERE     PLAYERNO = ANY
          (SELECT  PLAYERNO
          FROM     PENLTIES)
```

```
8.25  SELECT   NAME, INITIALS
      FROM     PLAYERS
      WHERE    EXISTS
               (SELECT   *
               FROM      TEAMS
               WHERE     PLAYERNO = PLAYERS.PLAYERNO)

8.26  SELECT   NAME, INITIALS
      FROM     PLAYERS
      WHERE    NOT EXISTS
               (SELECT   *
               FROM      TEAMS
               WHERE     PLAYERNO = PLAYERS.PLAYERNO
               AND       TEAMNO IN
                         (SELECT   TEAMNO
                         FROM      GAMES
                         WHERE     PLAYERNO = 112))
```

8.27 1. Correct.

2. Incorrect, because the UNION operator cannot be used in a sub-query.

8.28 1. A.C1 : Q1, Q2, Q3, Q4, Q5

2. B.C1 : Q2, Q3, Q4

3. C.C1 : Q3

4. D.C1 : Q4

5. E.C1 : Q5

```
8.29  SELECT   NAME, INITIALS
      FROM     PLAYERS
      WHERE    PLAYERNO IN
               (SELECT   PLAYERNO
               FROM      GAMES
               WHERE     TEAMNO IN
                         (SELECT   TEAMNO
                         FROM      TEAMS
                         WHERE     DIVISION = 'first'))
      AND      PLAYERNO IN
               (SELECT   PLAYERNO
               FROM      GAMES
               WHERE     WON > LOST)
      AND      PLAYERNO NOT IN
               (SELECT   PLAYERNO
               FROM      PENLTIES)
```

```
8.30  SELECT    PLAYERNO, NAME
      FROM      PLAYERS
      WHERE     PLAYERNO IN
                (SELECT   PLAYERNO
                 FROM     GAMES
                 WHERE    TEAMNO = 1)
      AND       PLAYERNO IN
                (SELECT   PLAYERNO
                 FROM     GAMES
                 WHERE    TEAMNO = 2)
```

Chapter 9

9.1
1. 8
2. 8
3. 1
4. 5
5. 24
6. 3
7. 5
8. 1
9. 5
10. 15
11. $15 / 5 = 3$

```
9.2   SELECT    AVG(AMOUNT)
      FROM      PENLTIES
```

```
9.3   SELECT    AVG(AMOUNT)
      FROM      PENLTIES
      WHERE     PLAYERNO IN
                (SELECT   PLAYERNO
                 FROM     GAMES
                 WHERE    TEAMNO = 1)
```

```
9.4   SELECT    NAME, INITIALS
      FROM      PLAYERS
      WHERE     PLAYERNO IN
                (SELECT   PLAYERNO
                 FROM     GAMES
                 WHERE    WON >
                          (SELECT   SUM(WON)
                           FROM     GAMES
                           WHERE    PLAYERNO = 27))
```

```
9.5   SELECT    SUM(WON), SUM(LOST),
                SUM(WON) - SUM(LOST)
      FROM      GAMES

9.6   SELECT    PLAYERNO, BIRTH
      FROM      PLAYERS
      WHERE     BIRTH =
                (SELECT   MIN(BIRTH)
                 FROM     PLAYERS
                 WHERE    PLAYERNO IN
                          (SELECT   PLAYERNO
                           FROM     GAMES
                           WHERE    TEAMNO = 1))

9.7   SELECT    PLAYERNO, NAME
      FROM      PLAYERS
      WHERE     LENGTH(RTRIM(NAME)) >
                (SELECT   AVG(LENGTH(RTRIM(NAME)))
                 FROM     PLAYERS)
```

Chapter 10

```
10.1  SELECT    BIRTH
      FROM      PLAYERS
      GROUP BY  BIRTH

10.2  SELECT    BIRTH, COUNT(*)
      FROM      PLAYERS
      GROUP BY  BIRTH

10.3  SELECT    PLAYERNO, AVG(AMOUNT), COUNT(*)
      FROM      PENLTIES
      GROUP BY  PLAYERNO

10.4  SELECT    TEAMNO, COUNT(*), SUM(WON)
      FROM      GAMES
      WHERE     TEAMNO IN
                (SELECT   TEAMNO
                 FROM     TEAMS
                 WHERE    DIVISION = 'first')
      GROUP BY  TEAMNO

10.5  SELECT    NAME, INITIALS, COUNT(*)
      FROM      PLAYERS P, PENLTIES PEN
      WHERE     P.PLAYERNO = PEN.PLAYERNO
      AND       P.TOWN = 'Douglas'
      GROUP BY  P.PLAYERNO
```

```
10.6   SELECT   T.TEAMNO, DIVISION, SUM(WON)
       FROM     TEAMS T, GAMES GAM
       WHERE    T.TEAMNO = GAM.TEAMNO
       GROUP BY T.TEAMNO, DIVISION

10.7   SELECT   TOWN
       FROM     PLAYERS
       GROUP BY TOWN
       HAVING   COUNT(*) > 4

10.8   SELECT   PLAYERNO
       FROM     PENLTIES
       GROUP BY PLAYERNO
       HAVING   SUM(AMOUNT) > 150

10.9   SELECT   NAME, INITIALS, COUNT(*)
       FROM     PLAYERS, PENLTIES
       WHERE    PLAYERS.PLAYERNO = PENLTIES.PLAYERNO
       GROUP BY PLAYERS.PLAYERNO, NAME, INITIALS
       HAVING   COUNT(*) > 1

10.10  SELECT   TEAMNO, COUNT(*)
       FROM     GAMES
       GROUP BY TEAMNO
       HAVING   COUNT(*) >= ALL
                (SELECT   COUNT(*)
                 FROM     GAMES
                 GROUP BY TEAMNO)

10.11  SELECT   TEAMNO, DIVISION
       FROM     TEAMS
       WHERE    TEAMNO IN
                (SELECT   TEAMNO
                 FROM     GAMES
                 GROUP BY TEAMNO
                 HAVING   COUNT(*) > 4)

10.12  SELECT   NAME, INITIALS
       FROM     PLAYERS
       WHERE    PLAYERNO IN
                (SELECT   PLAYERNO
                 FROM     PENLTIES
                 WHERE    AMOUNT > 40
                 GROUP BY PLAYERNO
                 HAVING   COUNT(*) > 2)
```

```
10.13 SELECT    NAME, INITIALS
      FROM      PLAYERS
      WHERE     PLAYERNO IN
                (SELECT    PLAYERNO
                 FROM      PENLTIES
                 GROUP BY PLAYERNO
                 HAVING    SUM(AMOUNT) >= ALL
                           (SELECT    SUM(AMOUNT)
                            FROM       PENLTIES
                            GROUP BY PLAYERNO))

10.14 SELECT    PLAYERNO
      FROM      GAMES
      WHERE     PLAYERNO <> 6
      GROUP BY PLAYERNO
      HAVING    SUM(AMOUNT) =
                (SELECT    SUM(AMOUNT)
                 FROM      GAMES
                 WHERE     PLAYERNO = 6)

10.15 SELECT    PLAYERNO
      FROM      GAMES
      WHERE     PLAYERNO <> 6
      GROUP BY PLAYERNO
      HAVING    COUNT(*) =
                (SELECT    COUNT(*)
                 FROM      GAMES
                 WHERE     PLAYERNO = 6)

10.16 SELECT    TEAMNO, COUNT(*)
      FROM      GAMES
      WHERE     PLAYERNO IN
                (SELECT    PLAYERNO
                 FROM      PLAYERS
                 WHERE     TOWN = 'Stratford')
      AND       WON > LOST
      GROUP BY TEAMNO
```

Chapter 11

11.1 1.   ORDER BY 1
         2.   ORDER BY PLAYERNO
         3.   ORDER BY 1 ASC
         4.   ORDER BY PLAYERNO ASC

11.2 1.   Correct.

2.   Incorrect, because there is no twentieth column in the PLAYERS table.

3.   Incorrect, because sorting is specified twice on the INITIALS column.

4.   Incorrect, because a column in an ORDER BY clause may not be specified twice.

11.3
```
SELECT    PLAYERNO, TEAMNO, WON - LOST
FROM      GAMES
ORDER BY 3 ASC
```

Chapter 13

13.1 1.   Correct.

2.   Incorrect, because NAME and POSTCODE do not have the same data type.

3.   Correct.

4.   Incorrect, because a SELECT clause used with a UNION operator may not contain DISTINCT.

5.   Incorrect, because when a UNION operator is used, only the last SELECT statement can include an ORDER BY clause.

13.2 1.   6

2.   14

3.   18

Chapter 14

14.1
```
SELECT    1 / (AVG (1 / AMOUNT))
FROM      SALARIES
```

14.2
```
SELECT    O1.ORDERNO, O1.ROWNO, O1.COSTS, SUM(O2.COSTS)
FROM      ORDERROW O1, ORDERROW O2
WHERE     O1.ORDERNO = O2.ORDERNO
AND       O1.ROWNO >= O2.ROWNO
GROUP BY  O1.ORDERNO, O1.ROWNO, O1.COSTS
ORDER BY 1, 2
```

14.3
```
SELECT    O1.ORDERNO, O1.ROWNO, O1.COSTS,
          (O1.COSTS * 100) / SUM(O2.COSTS)
FROM      ORDERROW O1, ORDERROW O2
WHERE     O1.ORDERNO = O2.ORDERNO
GROUP BY  O1.ORDERNO, O1.ROWNO, O1.COSTS
ORDER BY 1, 2
```

```
14.4  SELECT   SUM(AMOUNT)
      FROM     ORDERROW
      SAVE TO  TEMP TOT (COSTS) KEEP

      SELECT   O1.ORDERNO, SUM(O2.COSTS)
               (SUM(O2.COSTS) * 100) / TOT.COSTS
      FROM     ORDERROW O1, ORDERROW O2, TOT
      WHERE    O1.ORDERNO = O2.ORDERNO
      GROUP BY O1.ORDERNO, O1.ROWNO, O1.COSTS
      ORDER BY 1, 2

14.5  SELECT   COUNT(*), O1.ORDERNO, O1.ROWNO, O1.COSTS
      FROM     ORDERROW O1, ORDERROW O2
      WHERE    O1.ORDERNO >= O2.ORDERNO
      AND      (O1.ROWNO >= O2.ROWNO OR
               (O1.ROWNO < O2.ROWNO
               AND O1.ORDERNO > O2.ORDERNO))
      GROUP BY O1.ORDERNO, O1.ROWNO, O1.COSTS
      ORDER BY 1

14.6  SELECT   ORDERNO, ROWNO
      FROM     ORDERROW O1
      WHERE    COSTS >= ALL
               (SELECT   COSTS
                FROM     ORDERROW O2
                WHERE    O1.ORDERNO = O2.ORDERNO)

14.7  SELECT   ORDERNO
      FROM     ORDERROW
      GROUP BY ORDERNO
      HAVING   SUM(COSTS) >= ALL
               (SELECT   SUM(COSTS)
                FROM     ORDERROW
                GROUP BY ORDERNO)

14.8  SELECT   PLAYERNO, SUM(WON)
      FROM     GAMES
      GROUP BY PLAYERNO
      UNION
      SELECT   PLAYERNO, 0
      FROM     PLAYERS
      WHERE    PLAYERNO NOT IN
               (SELECT   PLAYERNO
                FROM     GAMES)
```

```
14.9  SELECT    PLAYERNO, SUM(AMOUNT)
      FROM      PENLTIES
      GROUP BY PLAYERNO
      UNION
      SELECT    PLAYERNO, 0
      FROM      PLAYERS
      WHERE     PLAYERNO NOT IN
                (SELECT  PLAYERNO
                 FROM    PENLTIES)

14.10 SELECT    PLAYERNO, TEAMNO
      FROM      GAMES
      UNION
      SELECT    PLAYERNO, 0
      FROM      PLAYERS
      WHERE     PLAYERNO NOT IN
                (SELECT  PLAYERNO
                 FROM    GAMES)
      ORDER BY 1, 2

14.11 SELECT    PLAYERNO
      FROM      PLAYERS
      WHERE     PLAYERNO NOT IN
                (SELECT  PLAYERNO
                 FROM    GAMES
                 WHERE   WON IN (5, 6))

14.12 SELECT    TEAMNO, DIVISION
      FROM      TEAMS
      WHERE     TEAMNO NOT IN
                (SELECT  TEAMNO
                 FROM    GAMES
                 WHERE   PLAYERNO = 6)

14.13 SELECT    PLAYERNO
      FROM      PLAYERS
      WHERE     PLAYERNO NOT IN
                (SELECT  PLAYERNO
                 FROM    GAMES
                 WHERE   TEAMNO IN
                         (SELECT  TEAMNO
                          FROM    GAMES
                          WHERE   PLAYERNO = 57))
```

```
14.14 SELECT    PLAYERNO, NAME
      FROM      PLAYERS
      WHERE     EXISTS
                (SELECT    *
                FROM       PENLTIES
                WHERE      PLAYERNO = PLAYERS.PLAYERNO)

14.15 SELECT    PLAYERNO, NAME
      FROM      PLAYERS
      WHERE     PLAYERNO IN
                (SELECT    PLAYERNO
                FROM       GAMES G1
                WHERE      WON > LOST
                AND        EXISTS
                           (SELECT    *
                           FROM       GAMES G2
                           WHERE      G1.PLAYERNO = G2.PLAYERNO
                           AND        WON > LOST
                           AND        G1.TEAMNO = G2.TEAMNO))
      or

      SELECT    PLAYERNO, NAME
      FROM      PLAYERS
      WHERE     1 <
                (SELECT    COUNT(*)
                FROM       GAMES
                WHERE      WON > LOST
                AND        PLAYERS.PLAYERNO = PLAYERNO)

14.16 SELECT    NAME, INITIALS
      FROM      PLAYERS
      WHERE     NOT EXISTS
                (SELECT    *
                FROM       PENLTIES
                WHERE      PLAYERS.PLAYERNO = PLAYERNO
                AND        PEN_DATE BETWEEN {01/01/80}
                           AND {12/31/80})

14.17 SELECT    DISTINCT PLAYERNO
      FROM      PENLTIES P1
      WHERE     EXISTS
                (SELECT    PENLTIES P2
                WHERE      P1.AMOUNT = P2.AMOUNT
                AND        P1.PAYMENTNO <> P2.PAYMENTNO)
```

Chapter 15

15.1 UPDATE   PLAYERS
         SET   SEX = 'W'
         WHERE   SEX = 'F'

15.2 DROP   INDEX TEA_PRIM

         UPDATE   TEAMS
         SET   TEAMNO = TEAMNO + 1

         CREATE   UNIQUE INDEX TEA_PRIM ON
                    TEAMS (TEAMNO)

         UPDATE   GAMES
         SET   TEAMNO = TEAMNO + 1

15.3 SELECT   AVG(AMOUNT)
         FROM   PENLTIES
         SAVE TO   TEMP HOLD (AMOUNT)

              UPDATE   PENLTIES
              SET   AMOUNT = AMOUNT * 1.2
              WHERE   AMOUNT >
                         (SELECT   AMOUNT
                          FROM   HOLD)

15.4 DELETE
         FROM   PENLTIES
         WHERE   PLAYERNO = 44
         AND   YEAR(DATE) = 1980

15.5 DELETE
         FROM   PENLTIES
         WHERE   PLAYERNO IN
                    (SELECT   PLAYERNO
                     FROM   GAMES
                     WHERE   TEAMNO IN
                               (SELECT   TEAMNO
                                FROM   TEAMS
                                WHERE   DIVISION = 'second'))

15.6 SELECT   TOWN
         FROM   PLAYERS
         WHERE   PLAYERNO = 44
         SAVE TO   TEMP TOWN44(TOWN)

```
DELETE
FROM      PLAYERS
WHERE     TOWN =
          (SELECT    TOWN
          FROM       TOWN44)
AND       PLAYERNO <> 44
```

Chapter 16

16.1 1.   Basic strategy:

```
RESULT := [];
FOR EACH T IN TEAMS DO
   IF (T.TEAMNO > 1)
   AND (T.DIVISION = 'second') THEN
      RESULT :+ T;
OD;
```

Optimized strategy:

```
RESULT := [];
FOR EACH T IN TEAMS
WHERE DIVISION = 'second' DO
   IF T.TEAMNO > 1 THEN
      RESULT :+ T;
OD;
```

2.   Basic strategy:

```
RESULT := [];
FOR EACH P IN PLAYERS DO
   FOR EACH G1 IN GAMES DO
      IF P.PLAYERNO = G1.PLAYERNO AND
         P.BIRTH > 1963 THEN
         RESULT :+ P;
   OD;
OD;
```

Optimized strategy:

```
RESULT := [];
FOR EACH P IN PLAYERS
WHERE BIRTH > 1963 DO
   FOR EACH G1 IN GAMES DO
      IF P.PLAYERNO = G1.PLAYERNO THEN
         RESULT :+ P;
   OD;
OD;
```

Chapter 17

17.1 CREATE   VIEW NUMBPLAY
                   (TEAMNO, NUMBER) AS
        SELECT   TEAMNO, COUNT(*)
        FROM   GAMES
        GROUP BY TEAMNO

17.2 CREATE   VIEW WINNERS AS
        SELECT   PLAYERNO, NAME
        FROM   PLAYERS
        WHERE   PLAYERNO IN
                  (SELECT   PLAYERNO
                   FROM   GAMES
                   WHERE   WON > LOST)

17.3 CREATE   VIEW TOTALS
                   (PLAYERNO, TOT_PEN) AS
        SELECT   PLAYERNO, SUM(AMOUNT)
        FROM   PENLTIES
        GROUP BY PLAYERNO

17.4

view	UPDATE	INSERT	DELETE
TOWNS	no	no	no
COMPPLAY	yes	no	yes
SEVERAL	yes	no	yes
SFD_FOLK	yes	no	yes
RESIDENT	no	no	no
YOUTH	no	no	no
VETERAN	yes	yes	yes
TOTALS	no	no	no
AGES	yes	no	yes

17.5 1. No, because the original PLAYERS table can only be reconstructed
            with the UNION operator, and UNION is not permitted in views.

       2. Yes

       3. Yes

Chapter 18

18.1

GRANTOR	TNAME	USERID	TYPE	S	I	D	A	X	UPDATE	GRANT
SQLDBA	PLAYERS	PUBLIC	T	1	0	0	0	0	NONE	Y
SQLDBA	PLAYERS	OLGA	T	0	2	0	0	0	NONE	G
OLGA	PLAYERS	REGINA	T	0	3	0	0	0	NONE	Y
OLGA	PLAYERS	SUSAN	T	0	4	0	0	0	NONE	G
SUSAN	PLAYERS	REGINA	T	0	5	0	0	0	NONE	Y

18.2 The SYSAUTH table looks like this:

GRANTOR	TNAME	USERID	TYPE	S	I	D	A	X	UPDATE	GRANT
SQLDBA	PLAYERS	PUBLIC	T	1	0	0	0	0	NONE	Y

18.3

GRANTOR	TNAME	USERID	S	I	D	A	X	UPDATE	GRANT
SQLDBA	TEAMS	DIANE	1	1	1	1	1	NONE	Y
DIANE	TEAMS	KAREN	2	0	0	0	0	ALL	Y

Chapter 19

19.1
```
SELECT    COLNAME, COLTYPE
FROM      SYSCOLS COL
WHERE     EXISTS
          (SELECT    *
          FROM      SYSVDEPS
          WHERE     TBNAME = 'PLAYERS'
          AND       VIEWNAME = COL.TBNAME)
```

19.2
```
SELECT    COUNT(*)
FROM      SYSIDXS
WHERE     CREATOR = 'JAKE'
AND       TBNAME = 'PLAYERS'
```

19.3
```
SELECT    SEQNO, SQLTEXT
FROM      SYSVIEWS VW, SYSVDEPS USG
WHERE     VW.VIEWNAME = USG.VIEWNAME
AND       USG.TBNAME = 'PLAYERS'
ORDER BY SEQNO
```

19.4
```
SELECT    ICREATOR, INAME
FROM      SYSTEM.SYSINDEXES
WHERE     ICREATOR = CREATOR
```

```
SELECT    IXNAME
FROM      SYSIDXS
WHERE     CREATOR = TBCREATOR
```

Appendix B
Syntax of SQL

In this appendix we explain the notation method we have used to describe the statements and give definitions of the SQL statements themselves. We also list the reserved words or keywords.

B.1　The BNF notation

In this appendix and throughout the book we have used a formal notation method to describe the syntax of all SQL statements and the common elements. This notation is a variant on the *Backus Naur Form* (BNF) which is named after John Backus and Peter Naur. The meaning of the metasymbols that we use is based on that of the metasymbols in the SQL standard.

BNF adopts a language of so-called *substitution rules* or *production rules* consisting of a series of symbols. A *symbol* is defined in each production rule. A symbol could be, for example, an SQL statement, a table name or a colon. A *terminal symbol* is a special sort of symbol. All symbols, apart from the terminal symbols, are defined in terms of other symbols in a production rule. Examples of terminal symbols are the word CLOSE and the semi-colon.

You could liken a production rule to the definition of an element, where the definition of that element uses elements that are defined somewhere else. In this case, an element equates with a symbol.

The following metasymbols do not form part of the SQL language, but belong to the notation.

- < >
- ::=
- |

- [ ]
- . . .
- { }
- "

We now explain each of these symbols.

The symbols < and >

Non-terminal symbols are presented in < >. A production rule exists for every non-terminal symbol. We will show the non-terminal symbols in lower case letters. Two examples of non-terminal symbols are <select statement> and <table name>.

The ::= symbol

The ::= symbol is used in a production rule to separate the non-terminal symbol that is defined (left) from the definition (right). The ::= symbol should be read 'is defined as'. See the example below of the production rule for the CLOSE statement:

        <close statement> ::= CLOSE <cursor name>

Explanation: The CLOSE statement, then, consists of the terminal symbol CLOSE followed by the non-terminal symbol, cursor name. There should also be a production rule for <cursor name>.

The | symbol

Alternatives are represented by the | symbol. Below we give an example of the production rule for the element <character>:

        <character> ::= <digit> | <letter> | <special character>

Explanation: We should take from this that a character is a digit, a letter or a special character: one of the three.

The symbols [and]

Whatever is placed between square brackets [and] *may* be used. Here is the production rule for the ROLLBACK statement:

        <rollback statement> ::= ROLLBACK [WORK]

Explanation: A ROLLBACK statement always consists of the word ROLLBACK and can optionally be followed by the word WORK.

The ... symbol

The ellipsis shows what may be repeated one or more times. Here our example is the production rule for an integer:

```
<integer> ::= <digit>...
```

Explanation: An integer consists of a series of digits (with a minimum of one).

The symbols { and }

All symbols between braces form a group. For example, braces used with the |
symbol show precisely what the alternatives are. The next example is the production rule for the FROM clause:

```
<from clause> ::=
    FROM <table reference> [ { , <table reference> }... ]
```

Explanation: A FROM clause begins with the terminal symbol FROM and is followed by at least one table reference. It is possible to follow this table reference with a list of elements, whereby each element consists of a comma followed by a table reference. Don't forget that the comma is part of SQL and not of the notation.

The " symbol

A small number of metasymbols, such as the " symbol, are part of particular SQL statements themselves. In order to avoid misunderstanding, these symbols are enclosed by double quotation marks. Among other things, this means that the symbol " that is used within SQL, is represented in the production rules as """".

Additional remarks

- Whatever is presented in upper case letters, as well as the symbols which are not part of the notation, must be adopted unaltered.

- The sequence of the symbols in the right hand part of the production rule is fixed.

- Blanks in production rules have no significance. Generally, they have been added to make the production rules more readable. The two following production rules are equal:

```
<alphanumeric literal> ::= ' [ <character>... ] '
```

and

```
<alphanumeric literal> ::= '[<character>...]'
```

B.2 Reserved words in SQL

A, ADD, ALL, ALTER, AND, ANY, AS, ASC, AVG,
B, BEGIN, BETWEEN, BLANK, BY,
C, CHAR, CHECK, CLOSE, COUNT, CREATE, CURRENT, CURSOR,
D, DATA, DATABASE, DATE, DBASEII, DBCHECK, DBDEFINE, DECIMAL,
DECLARE, DELETE, DELIMITED, DESC, DIF, DISTINCT, DROP,
E, END, EXISTS,
F, FETCH, FLOAT, FOR, FROM, FW2,
G, GRANT, GROUP,
H, HAVING,
I, IN, INDEX, INSERT, INTEGER, INTO,
J,
KEEP,
LIKE, LOAD, LOGICAL,
MAX, MIN,
NOT, NUMERIC,
OF, ON, OPEN, OPTION, OR, ORDER,
PRIVILEGES, PROTECT, PUBLIC,
REVOKE, ROLLBACK, RPD, RUNSTATS,
SAVE, SDF, SELECT, SET, SHOW, SMALLINT, SOME, START,
STOP, SUM, SYLK, SYNONYM,
TABLE, TEMP, TO, TRANSACTION, TYPE,
UNION, UNIQUE, UNLOAD, UPDATE, USER, USING,
VALUES, VIEW,
WHERE, WITH, WKS, WORK

B.3 Definitions of SQL statements

```
<alter table statement> ::=
   ALTER TABLE <table identifier>
      ADD ( <table element> [ {,<table element>}... ] )

<begin transaction statement> ::= BEGIN TRANSACTION

<close statement> ::= CLOSE <cursor name>

<create database statement> ::=
   CREATE DATABASE [ <directory path> ] <database name>

<create index statement> ::=
   CREATE [ UNIQUE ] INDEX <index name>
   ON      <table identifier>
   ( <column in index> [ {,<column in index>}... ] )

<create synonym statement> ::=
   CREATE SYNONYM <table name> FOR <table identifier>
```

```
<create table statement> ::=
   CREATE TABLE <table name>
      ( <table element> [ {,<table element>}... ] )

<create view statement> ::=
   CREATE VIEW <view name>
      [ <column list> ] AS
      <select statement>
      [ WITH CHECK OPTION ]

<dbcheck statement> ::= DBCHECK [ <table identifier> ]

<dbdefine statement> ::= DBDEFINE [ <file name> ]

<declare statement> ::=
   DECLARE <cursor name> CURSOR FOR
   <select block>
   [ { UNION <select block> }... ]
   [ <order by clause> | <for update clause> ]

<delete statement> ::=
   DELETE
   FROM    <table identifier>
   [ WHERE { <condition> | CURRENT OF <cursor name> } ]

<drop database statement> ::= DROP DATABASE <database name>

<drop index statement> ::= DROP INDEX <index name>

<drop synonym statement> ::= DROP SYNONYM <table identifier>

<drop table statement> ::= DROP TABLE <table identifier>

<drop view statement> ::= DROP VIEW <table identifier>

<end transaction statement> ::= END TRANSACTION

<fetch statement> ::=
   FETCH <cursor name> INTO  <variable list>

<grant statement> ::=
   GRANT         <privileges>
   ON [ TABLE ] <table identifier>
   TO            <grantees>
   [ WITH  GRANT OPTION ]

<insert statement> ::=
   INSERT INTO <table identifier>
         [ <column list> ]
   { <select statement> | VALUES ( <expression> [ {,<expression>}... ] ) }

<load statement> ::=
   LOAD DATA FROM [ <directory path> ] <file>
   INTO TABLE <table identifier>
   [ [ TYPE ] <format identifier> ]

<open statement> ::= OPEN <cursor name>
```

```
<revoke statement> ::=
   REVOKE        <privileges>
   ON [ TABLE ] <table identifier>
   FROM          <grantees>

<rollback statement> ::= ROLLBACK [ WORK ]

<runstats statement> ::= RUNSTATS [ <table identifier> ]

<select statement> ::=
   <select block>
   [ { UNION <select block> }... ]
   [ <order by clause> |
     <save clause> ]

<select into statement> ::=
   <select clause>
   <into clause>
   <from clause>
   [ <where clause> ]

<show database statement> ::= SHOW DATABASE

<start database statement> ::= START DATABASE <database name>

<stop database statement> ::= STOP DATABASE

<unload statement> ::=
   UNLOAD DATA TO [ <directory path> ] <file>
   FROM TABLE <table identifier>
   [ [ TYPE ] <format identifier> ]

<update statement> ::=
   UPDATE <table identifier>
   SET    <object column> [ {,<object column>}... ]
   [ WHERE { <condition> | CURRENT OF <cursor name> } ]
```

B.4   Common elements

```
<alphanumeric literal> ::=
   ' [ <character>... ] ' | """ [ <character>... ] """

<alphanumeric data type> ::= CHAR ( <length> )

<alphanumeric expression> ::=
   <alphanumeric literal> |
   <column identifier> |
   USER |
   <memory variable> |
   <scalar function> |
   <statistical function> |
   <alphanumeric expression> + <alphanumeric expression> |
   ( <alphanumeric expression> )
```

```
<array element> ::=
   <array name> "[" <numeric expression> [ , <numeric expression> ] "]"

<avg function> ::= AVG ( <function object> )

<boolean factor> ::= <predicate> | ( <condition> )

<boolean term> ::=
   <boolean factor> |
   <boolean term> AND <boolean factor>

<character> ::= <digit> | <letter> | <special character>

<column identifier> ::= [ <table identifier> . ] <column name>

<column in index> ::= <column name> [ ASC | DESC ]

<column list> ::=
   ( <column name> [ {,<column name>}... ] )

<comparison operator> ::=
   = | < | > | <= | >= | <> | !< | !> | != | #

<condition> ::=
   <boolean term> |
   <condition> OR <boolean term>

<count function> ::= COUNT ( { * | [ DISTINCT ] <column name> } )

<data type> ::=
   <numeric data type> |
   <alphanumeric data type> |
   <date data type> |
   <logical data type>

<date literal> ::= "{" <year> . <month> . <day> "}"

<date data type> ::= DATE

<date expression> ::=
   <date literal> |
   <column identifier> |
   <memory variable> |
   <scalar function> |
   <statistical function> |
   <date expression> { + | - } <numeric expression> |
   <numeric expression> + <date expression>

<day> ::= <integer>

<decimal literal> ::=
   [ + | - ] <integer> [ .<integer> ] |
   [ + | - ] <integer>. |
   [ + | - ] .<integer>

<directory path> ::= \ { <file> \ }...

<exponent> ::= <integer literal>
```

```
<expression> ::=
   <numeric expression> |
   <alphanumeric expression> |
   <logical expression> |
   <date expression>

<file> ::= <file name> [ .<file type> ]

<floating point literal> ::= <mantissa> [ E<exponent> ]

<format identifier> ::=
   SDF | DIF | WKS |
   SYLK | FW2 | dBASEII | RPD |
   DELIMITED { WITH BLANK | WITH <separator> }

<for update clause> ::=
   FOR UPDATE OF <column name> [ {,<column name>}... ]

<from clause> ::=
   FROM <table reference> [ {.<table reference> }... ]

<function object> ::=
   [ ALL ] <column expression> |
   [ ALL | DISTINCT ] <column name>

<grantees> ::=
   PUBLIC |
   <userid> [ {,<userid>}... ]

<group by clause> ::=
   GROUP BY <column identifier> [ {,<column identifier>}... ]

<having clause> ::= HAVING <condition>

<integer> ::= <digit>...

<integer literal> ::= [ + | - ] <integer>

<into clause> ::=
   INTO <memory variable> [ {,<memory variable>}... ]

<length> ::= <integer>

<literal> ::=
   <numeric literal> |
   <alphanumeric literal> |
   <date literal> |
   <logical literal>

<logical literal> ::=
   .T. | .t. | .Y. | .y. | .F. | .f. | .N. | .n.

<logical data type> ::= LOGICAL

<logical expression> ::=
   <logical literal> |
   <column identifier> |
   <memory variable>
```

```
<mantissa> ::= <decimal literal>

<max function> ::= MAX ( <function object> )

<memory variable> ::=
   <simple variable> |
   <array element>

<min function> ::= MIN ( <function object> )

<month> ::= <integer>

<non quote character> ::= <character> | ''

<numeric literal> ::=
   <integer literal> |
   <decimal literal> |
   <floating point literal>

<numeric data type> ::=
   NUMERIC ( <precision> , <scale> ) |
   SMALLINT |
   INTEGER |
   DECIMAL ( <precision> , <scale> ) |
   FLOAT ( <precision> , <scale> )

<numeric expression> ::=
   <numeric literal> |
   <column identifier> |
   <memory variable> |
   <scalar function> |
   <statistical function> |
   <date expression> - <date expression> |
   <numeric expression> <numeric operator> <numeric expression> |
   ( <numeric expression> )

<numeric operator> ::=
   * | / | + | - | ** | ^

<object column> ::= <column name> = <expression>

<order by clause> ::=
   ORDER BY <sort specification> [ {,<sort specification>}... ]

<parameter> ::= <expression>

<precision> ::= <integer>

<predicate> ::=
   NOT <predicate> |
   <expression> <comparison operator> <expression> |
   <expression> <comparison operator> <subquery> |
   <logical expression> |
   <expression> [ NOT ] BETWEEN <expression> AND <expression> |
   <expression> [ NOT ] IN ( <expression> [ {,<expression>}...] ) |
   <expression> [ NOT ] IN <subquery> |
   <column identifier> [ NOT ] LIKE { <mask> | <memory variable> } |
   <expression> <comparison operator> ALL <subquery> |
   <expression> <comparison operator> ANY <subquery> |
   <expression> <comparison operator> SOME <subquery> |
   EXISTS <subquery>
```

```
<privileges> ::=
   ALL [ PRIVILEGES ] |
   <table privileges>

<save clause> ::=
   SAVE TO TEMP <table identifier>
      [ <column list> ] [ KEEP ]

<scalar function> ::=
   <function name> ( [ <parameter> {,<parameter>}... ] )

<scale> ::= <integer>

<separator> ::= <character>

<select block> ::=
     <select clause>
     <from clause>
   [ <where clause> ]
   [ <group by clause>
   [ <having clause> ] ]

<select clause> ::=
   SELECT [ DISTINCT | ALL ] <select list>

<select list> ::=
   [ <table identifier>. ] * |
   <expression> [ {,<expression>}... ]

<simple variable> ::= <variable name>

<sort specification> ::=
   <column identifier> [ ASC | DESC ] |
   <sequence number> [ ASC | DESC ]

<statistical function> ::=
   <count function> |
   <min function> |
   <max function> |
   <sum function> |
   <avg function>

<subquery> ::=
   SELECT { <expression> | * }
   <from clause>
   [ <where clause> ]
   [ <group by clause>
   [ <having clause> ] ]

<sum function> ::= SUM ( <function object> )

<table element> ::= <column name> <data type>

<table identifier> ::= <table name>
```

```
<table privilege> ::=
   SELECT |
   INSERT |
   DELETE |
   UPDATE [ <column list> ] |
   INDEX  |
   ALTER

<table reference> ::= <table identifier> [ <pseudonym> ]

<variable list> ::=
   <memory variable> [ {,<memory variable>}... ]

<year> ::= <integer>
```

Appendix C
Scalar functions

Description: dBASE IV recognizes a large number of scalar functions, though not all of these are available to SQL statements. In the following pages we present the name, a description, the data type of the result of the description and a few examples of functions which *can* be used in SQL statements.

Note: We assume that the following SET commands are in force for all the examples:

```
SET DATE TO DMY
SET CENTURY OFF
SET HOURS TO 24
SET DECIMALS TO 2
SET PRECISION TO 16
```

ABS

Description: Gives the absolute value of a numeric expression.
Data type: numeric

```
ABS(-25) --> 25
ABS(-25.89) --> 25.89
```

ACOS

Description: Gives, in radians, the angle size for any given cosine value. The value of the parameter must lie between -1 and 1 inclusive. The precision of the result is determined by the commands SET DECIMALS and SET PRECISION.
Data type: numeric

```
ACOS(0) --> 1.57
```

```
ACOS(-1) - PI() --> 0
ACOS(1) --> 0
```

ASC

Description: Gives the ASCII decimal code of the first character of an alphanumeric expression (see Appendix E). The value of the result is always a whole number between 0 and 255 inclusive.
Data type: numeric

```
ASC('Pete') --> 80
ASC('pete') --> 112
```

ASIN

Description: Gives, in radians, the angle size for any given sine value. The value of the parameter must lie between -1 and 1 inclusive. The precision of the result is determined by the commands SET DECIMALS and SET PRECISION.
Data type: numeric

```
ASIN(1) --> 1.57
```

AT

Description: Gives a number which shows the starting position of an alphanumeric expression within a second expression. The AT function has a value of zero if the first alphanumeric expression does not appear within the second.
Data type: numeric

```
AT('bas','database') --> 5
AT('bas','system') --> 0
```

ATAN

Description: Gives, in radians, the angle size for any given tangent value. The precision of the result is determined by the commands SET DECIMALS and SET PRECISION.
Data type: numeric

```
ATAN(0) --> 0
ATAN(100) --> 3.14
```

ATN2

Description: Gives, in radians, the angle size when the cosine and sine are specified. The precision of the result is determined by the commands SET DECIMALS and SET PRECISION.
Data type: numeric

```
ATN2(30,30) --> 0.79
ATAN(1) --> 0.79
ATN2(8,4) - ATAN(2) --> 0
```

CDOW

Description: Gives the name of the weekday from a date expression.
Data type: alphanumeric

```
CDOW({07/29/88}) --> 'Friday'
```

CEILING

Description: Gives the smallest whole number that is greater than or equal to the value of the parameter.
Data type: numeric

```
CEILING(13.43) --> 14
CEILING(-13.43) --> -13
CEILING(13) --> 13
```

CHR

Description: Gives the ASCII character of a numeric expression. The value of the parameter must be a whole number between 0 and 255 inclusive.
Data type: alphanumeric

```
CHR(80) --> 'P'
CHR(82) + CHR(105) + CHR(99) + CHR(107) --> 'Rick'
```

CMONTH

Description: Gives the name of the month from a date expression.
Data type: alphanumeric

```
CMONTH({05/20/88}) --> 'May'
CMONTH({05/20/88}+80) --> 'August'
```

COS

Description: Gives, in radians, the cosine value for any angle size. The precision of the result is determined by the commands SET DECIMALS and SET PRECISION.
Data type: numeric

```
COS(0) --> 1
COS(PI()/2) --> 0
COS(PI()) --> -1
```

CTOD

Description: Converts an alphanumeric expression to a date. The alphanumeric expression must be in a specific format; this is dependent on the commands SET DATE and SET CENTURY. In fact, CTOD acts the same as a date literal with {}.
Data type: date

```
CTOD('05/20/88') - {05/20/88} --> 0
```

DATE

Description: Gives the system date.
Data type: date

```
DATE() --> '05/20/88'
{12/31/88} - DATE() --> 32
```

DAY

Description: Gives the number of the day of the month. The value of the result is always a whole number between 1 and 31 inclusive.
Data type: numeric

```
DAY({05/20/88}) --> 20
DAY(DATE()) --> 20
```

DIFFERENCE

Description: Gives the difference between two literal strings (see the SOUNDEX function).
Data type: numeric

```
DIFFERENCE('J500','J400') --> 4
```

DMY

Description: Presents a date according to the format 'day month year'. The century is shown or not depending on the SET CENTURY command.
Data type: alphanumeric

```
DMY({07/29/88}) --> '29 july 88'
```

DOW

Description: Gives the number of the weekday from a date expression. The value of the result is always a whole number between 1 and 7 inclusive.
Data type: numeric

```
DAY({07/29/88}) --> 6
```

DTOC

Description: Converts a date to an alphanumeric value. The result is dependent on the commands SET DATE and SET CENTURY.
Data type: alphanumeric

```
DTOC({07/29/88}) --> '07/29/88'
DTOC(DATE()) --> '12/02/88'
```

DTOR

Description: Converts degrees to radians. The precision of the result is determined by the commands SET DECIMALS and SET PRECISION.
Data type: numeric

```
DTOR(45) --> 0.79
DTOR(0) --> 0
DTOR(180) --> 3.14
```

EXP

Description: Gives the result of the number e to the power of x, where x is the value of the parameter.
Data type: numeric

```
EXP(1) --> 2.72
EXP(2) --> 7.39
```

FIXED

Description: Converts floating-point values to decimal values.
Data type: numeric

```
FIXED(1.2E3) --> 0.0012
```

FLOAT

Description: Converts decimal values to floating-point values.
Data type: numeric

```
FLOAT(0.0012) --> .12000000E-2
```

FLOOR

Description: Gives the largest whole number that is less than or equal to the value of the parameter.
Data type: numeric

```
FLOOR(13.9) --> 13
FLOOR(-13.9) --> -14
```

INT

Description: Truncates any numeric expression to an integer.
Data type: numeric

```
INT(5.45) --> 5
INT(5.72) --> 5
```

LEFT

Description: Gives the left hand part of the alphanumeric value of the parameter.
The second parameter indicates the number of characters to extract.
Data type: alphanumeric

```
LEFT('database system', 8) --> 'database'
LEFT('database system', 0) --> ''
LEFT('database system', 50) --> 'database system'
```

LEN

Description: Gives the length of an alphanumeric value.
Data type: numeric

```
LEN('database') --> 8
LEN(RTRIM('abcd    ')) --> 4
LEN('') --> 0
```

LOG

Description: Gives the logarithm to the base value e of the parameter.
Data type: numeric

```
LOG(50) --> 3.91
LOG(EXP(3)) --> 3
```

LOG10

Description: Gives the logarithm to the base 10 of the parameter.
Data type: numeric

```
LOG10(1000) --> 3
LOG10(10**5) --> 5
```

LOWER

Description: Converts all upper case letters to lower case.
Data type: alphanumeric

```
LOWER('RICK') --> 'rick'
```

LTRIM

Description: Removes leading blanks from a character string.
Data type: alphanumeric

```
LTRIM('    start') --> 'start'
```

MDY

Description: Converts the date format to 'Month, Day, Year'. The result is dependent on the commands SET DATE and SET CENTURY.
Data type: alphanumeric

```
MDY({07/29/88}) --> 'July 29, 88'
MDY(DATE()) --> 'November 22, 88'
```

MOD

Description: Gives the remainder from the division of two parameters.
Data type: numeric

```
MOD(15, 4) --> 3
```

MONTH

Description: Gives the number of the month from a date expression. The value of the result is always a whole number between 1 and 12 inclusive.
Data type: numeric

```
MONTH({07/29/88}) --> 7
```

PI

Description: Calculates *pi*. The SET DECIMALS command determines the accuracy of the displayed number (the number of places after the decimal point).
Data type: numeric

```
PI() --> 3.14
PI()*100000 --> 314159.27
```

RAND

Description: Generates a random number. The default seed number is 100001.
Data type: numeric

```
RAND() --> 0.47
RAND() --> 0.95
RAND(23) --> 0.23
RAND(100001) --> 0.47
```

REPLICATE

Description: Repeats an alphanumeric value a specified number of times.
Data type: alphanumeric

```
REPLICATE('bla',4) --> 'blablablabla'
```

RIGHT

Description: Gives the right hand part of the alphanumeric value of the parameter. The second parameter indicates the number of characters to extract.
Data type: alphanumeric

```
RIGHT('database system', 7) --> 'system'
RIGHT('database system', 0) --> ''
RIGHT('database system', 50) --> 'database system'
```

ROUND

Description: Rounds numbers to a specified number of decimal places.
Data type: numeric

```
ROUND(123.456,2) --> 123.46
ROUND(123.456,1) --> 123.50
ROUND(123.456,0) --> 123
ROUND(123.456,-1) --> 120
ROUND(123.456,-2) --> 100
```

RTOD

Description: Converts radians to degrees. The precision of the result is determined by the commands SET DECIMALS and SET PRECISION.
Data type: numeric

```
RTOD(0) --> 0
RTOD(1) --> 57.30
RTOD(DTOR(45)) --> 45
RTOD(PI()) --> 180
```

RTRIM

Description: Removes trailing blanks from a character string.
Data type: alphanumeric

```
RTRIM('cap      ') --> 'cap'
RTRIM('data     ') + 'base' --> 'database'
```

SIGN

Description: Gives a number representing the mathematical sign of a numeric expression.
Data type: numeric

```
SIGN(50) --> 1
SIGN(-50) --> -1
```

SIN

Description: Gives, in radians, the sine value for any angle. The precision of the result is determined by the commands SET DECIMALS and SET PRECISION.
Data type: numeric

```
SIN(0) --> 0
SIN(1) --> 0.84
SIN(PI()/2) --> 1
```

SOUNDEX

Description: Gives the four character SOUNDEX code of the parameter. Alphanumeric expressions which sound similar are converted to identical SOUNDEX codes.

The SOUNDEX code is defined in the following way:

1. All blanks at the beginning of the parameter are removed.
2. The following letters are removed from the parameter: *a e h i o u w y*, except if they are in the first position.
3. A number is assigned to the remaining letters:

```
b f p v        = 1
c g j k q s x z = 2
d t            = 3
l              = 4
m n            = 5
r              = 6
```

4. If two adjacent letters have the same code, the second is removed.
5. The code stops after the fourth character.
6. If the remaining code consists of fewer than four characters, trailing zeros are added.
7. Characters after a blank are skipped.
8. If the value of the parameter does not begin with a letter, the code given is '0000'.

Data type: alphanumeric

```
SOUNDEX('John') --> 'J500'
SOUNDEX('Jan') --> 'J500'
SOUNDEX('coop') --> 'C100'
SOUNDEX(' coop') --> 'C100'
SOUNDEX('coop Carol') --> 'C100'
```

SPACE

Description: Generates a row with a specified number of blanks.
Data type: alphanumeric

```
SPACE(1) --> ' '
SPACE(5) --> '     '
```

SQRT

Description: Gives the square root of the value of the parameter. The precision of the result is determined by the commands SET DECIMALS and SET PRECISION.
Data type: numeric

```
SQRT(225) --> 15
SQRT(200) --> 14.14
```

STR

Description: Converts a numeric expression to an alphanumeric expression. Data type: alphanumeric

```
STR(45) --> '45'
STR(-12.98) --> '-13'
STR(-12.13) --> '-12'
STR(123456789012) --> 1234567890
STR(123456789012, 15) --> 123456789012
STR(123456789012, 4) --> ****
```

STUFF

Description: Replaces part of a character string with a new character string.
Data type: alphanumeric

```
STUFF('gyrate',2,1,'ene') --> 'generate'
```

SUBSTR

Description: Extracts part of the value of the parameter.
Data type: alphanumeric

```
SUBSTR('database', 5, 3) --> 'bas'
SUBSTR('database', 5) --> 'base'
```

TAN

Description: Gives, in radians, the tangent value of any angle size. The precision of the result is determined by the commands SET DECIMALS and SET PRECISION.
Data type: numeric

```
TAN(0) --> 0
TAN(PI()) --> 0
TAN(1) --> 1.56
```

TIME

Description: Gives the system time in the following format: HH:MM:SS. The HH stands for hours, MM for minutes and SS for seconds.
Data type: alphanumeric

```
TIME() --> 16:42:24
```

TRIM

Description: Removes trailing blanks from an alphanumeric value.
Data type: alphanumeric

```
TRIM('cap    ') --> 'cap'
TRIM('data    ') + 'base' --> 'database'
```

UPPER

Description: Converts lower case letters to upper case in an alphanumeric expression.
Data type: alphanumeric

```
UPPER('Rick') --> 'RICK'
```

VAL

Description: Converts a character string to a number. The precision of the result is determined by the commands SET DECIMALS and SET PRECISION.
Data type: numeric

```
VAL('123') --> 123
VAL('123.4') --> 123.4
VAL('abcd') --> 0
```

YEAR

Description: Gives the year from a date expression. The result is always a number greater than 1.
Data type: numeric

```
YEAR({07/29/88}) --> 1988
YEAR(DATE()) --> 1990
```

Appendix D
dBASE IV limits

The following important limits are relevant in dBASE IV's SQL environment. We use the ∞ symbol to represent the absence of a specific dBASE IV limit. In these cases the storage capacity of the physical environment often imposes a limit instead.

Limits for rows

- Maximum number of characters per row in a table: 4000

Limits for columns

- Maximum mumber of characters per alphanumeric column: 254
- Maximum number of characters per numeric column: 20

Limits for tables

- Maximum number of columns per table: 255
- Maximum number of characters per table: 2 billion
- Maximum number of rows per table: 1 billion
- Maximum number of indexes per table: 47

Limits for indexes

- Maximum number of characters in the value of an index: 100

Limits for databases

- Maximum number of characters per database: ∞

- Maximum number of columns per database: ∞
- Maximum number of rows per database: ∞
- Maximum number of indexes per database: ∞
- Maximum number of tables per database: ∞

dBASE IV system limits

- Maximum number of databases per system: ∞

SQL statement limits

- Maximum number of characters per SQL statement: 1024
- Maximum number of tables per SELECT statement: dependent on the amount of available internal memory

General limits

- Maximum number of databases open at any one time: 1
- Maximum number of cursors open at any one time: 10

Appendix E
ASCII character set

The following two tables show the ASCII values and the characters they represent. The ASCII values 174 to 223 inclusive have been omitted. These values represent graphical characters like ⊣ and ⊨.

ASCII value	character	ASCII value	character	ASCII value	character	ASCII value	character
0	NUL	32	blank	64	@	96	`
1	SOH	33	!	65	A	97	a
2	STX	34	"	66	B	98	b
3	ETX	35	#	67	C	99	c
4	EOT	36	$	68	D	100	d
5	ENQ	37	%	69	E	101	e
6	ACK	38	&	70	F	102	f
7	BEL	39	'	71	G	103	g
8	BS	40	(	72	H	104	h
9	HT	41	)	73	I	105	i
10	LF	42	*	74	J	106	j
11	VT	43	+	75	K	107	k
12	FF	44	,	76	L	108	l
13	CR	45	-	77	M	109	m
14	SO	46	.	78	N	110	n
15	SI	47	/	79	O	111	o
16	DLE	48	0	80	P	112	p
17	DC1	49	1	81	Q	113	q
18	DC2	50	2	82	R	114	r
19	DC3	51	3	83	S	115	s
20	DC4	52	4	84	T	116	t
21	NAK	53	5	85	U	117	u
22	SYN	54	6	86	V	118	v
23	ETB	55	7	87	W	119	w
24	CAN	56	8	88	X	120	x
25	EM	57	9	89	Y	121	y
26	SUB	58	:	90	Z	122	z
27	ESC	59	;	91	[	123	{
28	FS	60	<	92	\	124		
29	GS	61	=	93	]	125	}
30	RS	62	>	94	^	126	~
31	US	63	?	95	__	127	⌂

ASCII value	char-acter	ASCII value	char-acter	ASCII value	char-acter	ASCII value	char-acter
128	Ç	148	ö	168	¿	238	∈
129	ü	149	ò	169	⌐	239	∩
130	é	150	û	170	¬	240	≡
131	â	151	ù	171	$1/2$	241	±
132	ä	152	ÿ	172	$1/4$	242	≥
133	à	153	Ö	173	¡	243	≤
134	å	154	Ü	224	α	244	⌠
135	ç	155	c	225	β	245	⌡
136	ê	156	£	226	§	246	÷
137	ë	157	¥	227	π	247	≈
138	è	158	Pt	228	—	248	°
139	ï	159	ƒ	229	σ	249	•
140	î	160	á	230	μ	250	·
141	ì	161	í	231	τ	251	√
142	Ä	162	ó	232	'	252	ⁿ
143	Å	163	ú	233	θ	253	2
144	É	164	ñ	234	Ł	254	■
145	æ	165	Ñ	235	δ	255	FF
146	Æ	166	a	236	∞		
147	ô	167	o	237	φ		

Appendix F
Bibliography

Literature consulted

American National Standards Institute Inc., (1985). *Draft proposed American National Standard Database Language SQL*, February 1985, 1430 Broadway, New York

Astrahan, M.M. *et al*, (1980). A history and evaluation of System R, *IBM RJ 2843*, June

Boyce, R.F., and Chamberlin, D.D., (1973). Using a structured english query language as a data definition facility, *IBM RJ 1318*, December

Chamberlin, D.D., (1980). A summary of user experience with the SQL data sub language, *IBM RJ 2767*, March

Codd, E.F., (1971). A relational model of data for large shared banks In *Communications of the ACM*, Vol 13, number 6, June

Codd, E.F., (1971). Relational completeness of database sublanguages In *Database Systems*, May

Codd, E.F., (1979). Extending the database relational model to capture more meaning In *ACM Transactions on Database Systems*, Vol 4, number 4, December

Date, C.J., (1983). *Database: a Primer*, Reading MA: Addison-Wesley

Date, C.J., (1986). *An Introduction to Database Systems Volume I* 4 edn., Reading MA: Addison-Wesley

Elmasri, R. and Navathe, S.B., (1989). *Fundamentals of Database Systems*, Menlo Park CA: Benjamin/Cummings

ISO TC97/SC21/WG3 en ANSI X3H2, (1987). *ISO 9075 Database Language SQL*

ISO/IEC JTC1/SC21/WG3 en ANSI X3H2, (1989). *ISO-ANSI Database Language SQL2*, working draft, December

Kim, W., Reiner, D.S. and Batory, D.S. eds, (1985). *Query Processing in Database Systems*, Berlin: Springer-Verlag

van der Lans, R.F., (1989). *Introduction to SQL*, Wokingham: Addison-Wesley

van der Lans, R.F., (1989). *The SQL Standard, A Complete Reference*, Prentice-Hall/Academic Service,

Manuals consulted

Ashton-Tate, (1988). *Advanced Topics*

Ashton-Tate, (1988). *Learning dBASE IV*

Ashton-Tate, (1988). *Quick Reference*

Ashton-Tate, (1988). *Using the Menu System*

Ashton-Tate, (1988). *Introduction to the Dot Prompt*

Ashton-Tate, (1988). *Guide to dBASE IV*

Ashton-Tate, (1990). *Getting Started with dBASE IV*

Ashton-Tate, (1990). *dBASE IV Change Summary*

Ashton-Tate, (1990). *Language Reference*

Index